MW01631963

STAN LEE

For Joseph

STAN LEE

HOW MARVEL CHANGED THE WORLD

ADRIAN MACKINDER

WHITE OWL
AN IMPRINT OF PEN & SWORD BOOKS LTD.
YORKSHIRE – PHILADELPHIA

First published in Great Britain in 2021 by
PEN AND SWORD WHITE OWL
An imprint of
Pen & Sword Books Ltd
Yorkshire - Philadelphia

ISBN 978 1 52677 134 6

A CIP catalogue record for this book is available from the British Library.

Typeset in Times New Roman 11.5/14 by
SJmagic DESIGN SERVICES, India.
Printed and bound in the UK by TJ Books Limited.

Pen & Sword Books Ltd incorporates the Imprints of Pen & Sword Books Archaeology, Atlas, Aviation, Battleground, Discovery, Family History, History, Maritime, Military, Naval, Politics, Railways, Select, Transport, True Crime, Fiction, Frontline Books, Leo Cooper, Praetorian Press, Seaforth Publishing, Wharncliffe and White Owl.

For a complete list of Pen & Sword titles please contact
PEN & SWORD BOOKS LIMITED
47 Church Street, Barnsley, South Yorkshire, S70 2AS, England
E-mail: enquiries@pen-and-sword.co.uk
Website: www.pen-and-sword.co.uk

Or

PEN AND SWORD BOOKS
1950 Lawrence Rd, Havertown, PA 19083, USA
E-mail: Uspen-and-sword@casematepublishers.com
Website: www.penandswordbooks.com

Contents

Acknowledgements

One of the toughest aspects of writing this book is that a large number of major players in the story of Stan Lee are dead. This doesn't look like a situation that will change any time soon, so I wish them well in the next realm, wherever that may be. Fortunately, Stan was able to assist me from beyond the veil, thanks to the size of his ego. Practically all of his life, works, interviews and appearances are on record, which proved helpful to say the least. He wasn't exactly the shy, retiring type. Along the way, Stan amassed an army of fans and also detractors, all of whom were more than happy to let the record show where they stood. For good or ill, their words have proved invaluable.

I was fortunate enough to assemble a veritable rogues' gallery of former writers, artists and editors from Marvel UK, kind enough to spare me the time to share their thoughts. Thanks, then, to Alan Cowsill, Simon Furman, Tim Quinn, Kev Hopgood, John Tomlinson, Ned Hartley and Glenn Dakin. I would also like to extend my thanks to Matt McAllister and Dave Jackson for helping me track down this elusive band of Merry Marvel Marching Men.

Others who have contributed to this adventure, no matter how big or small, deserve mention here. Thanks to school friends William Hughes, Jack Love and Tom Lackey for being as much into comics as I was, and for coming to my birthday trip to Forbidden Planet in the early 1990s. I cannot think of nicer people to help play a part in the downfall of an empire. Thanks also to fellow geeks Alex Reid and James Devonshire, the former for being my 'Marvel date' to many of the earlier films from the Marvel Cinematic Universe; the latter for getting me back into comics as an adult by generously lending me his stack of *Ultimates* graphic novels. More recently, Nick de Semlyen and Marc Burrows kindly shared their thoughts and advice on their own creative writing process. Special thanks go to Hannah George and Kate Bohdanowicz, as without their facilitating, this journey would never have happened at all. I would also like to thank the many coffee houses of Copenhagen and also my improv performing partner Sarah McGillion, partly for her encouragement and helping me stay sane, but mainly because she didn't believe me when I said I would thank her in this book.

Writing a book is not exactly an overnight project and since I began I have endured several illnesses, family bereavement and becoming a father for the second time. The circle of life rolls ever onwards and rarely smoothly. Thanks to all the folk at Pen and Sword Books for their patience, guidance and support, and Jordon Collver for his truly superb cover design and artwork. The final stages of this book were written during the Covid-19 virus outbreak. Strange times. Arguably perfect conditions for a writer, self-isolation being an occupational hazard. That said, with everyone stuck at home, getting anything done has proved tricky to say the least. So, I'd like to thank my wonderful and beloved family, my impossibly precious wife Tessa and my two satanic children Joseph and Carla for their patience, support and cooperation, as well as putting up with me on days when I was grumpy, confused, quiet and sometimes downright absent. I love you all and I am eternally blessed to even have you in my life.

Finally, I'd like to thank not only Stan Lee for his towering legacy, but also Jack Kirby, Steve Ditko and the thousands of men and women who helped make Marvel such a powerhouse of creativity and inspiration for so many across the decades. The sheer number of talented souls who continually and consistently found new ways to vividly show and tell timeless stories, entertaining billions around the globe, is staggering. That's the true Marvel. To all those folk, celebrated and forgotten, this is for you.

Adrian Mackinder
March 2020

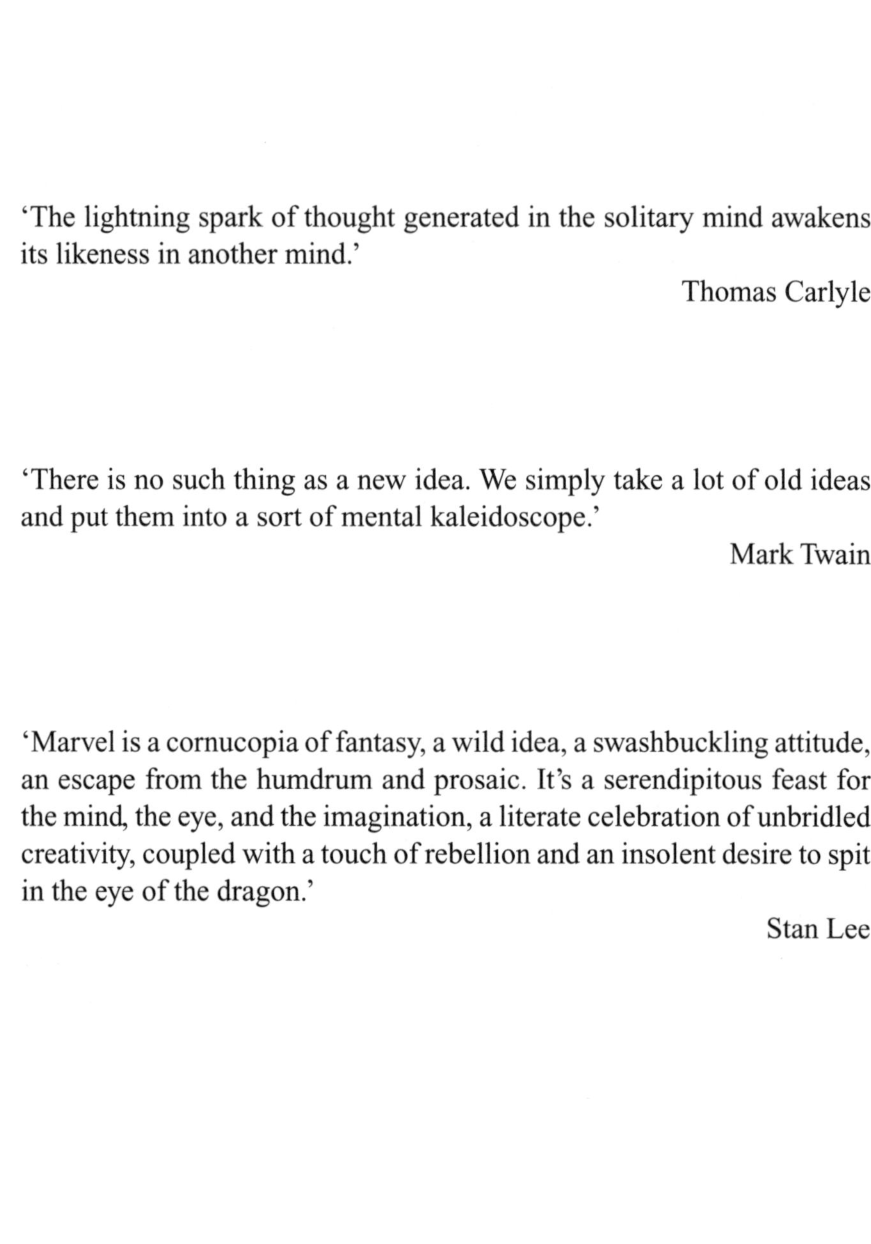

'The lightning spark of thought generated in the solitary mind awakens its likeness in another mind.'

Thomas Carlyle

'There is no such thing as a new idea. We simply take a lot of old ideas and put them into a sort of mental kaleidoscope.'

Mark Twain

'Marvel is a cornucopia of fantasy, a wild idea, a swashbuckling attitude, an escape from the humdrum and prosaic. It's a serendipitous feast for the mind, the eye, and the imagination, a literate celebration of unbridled creativity, coupled with a touch of rebellion and an insolent desire to spit in the eye of the dragon.'

Stan Lee

Prologue

Face Front, True Believer!

Of all Stan Lee's many catchphrases, this one is perhaps the most revealing. During his time as editor-in-chief of Marvel Comics, back in the 1960s, he used it wherever he could. Be it in a caption within the pages of a comic book story itself, or as part of regular editorial feature 'Stan's Soapbox'; 'face front, true believer' was a rallying cry for the ages. This was Stan positioning himself as a pseudo-military leader of the growing legion of loyal Marvel fans. As their glorious commander-in-chief, Stan had called them to attention for inspection and they had to look sharp. Because they were part of something special. They didn't just read. They believed.

This fascinating story that's about to unfold before your very eyes also requires a certain amount of belief on your part. Don't worry, I've not made it all up. There will be no claims in this book that Stan invented Velcro or represented Lithuania in the Winter Olympics as a champion skier. You just need to know that when it comes to facts, Stan's memory can get a little hazy. This proves, on occasion, to be very convenient for him, but less so when you're trying to write a book about the guy.

There is general consensus on the significant events of Stan's long life, but there are also moments where the truth becomes elusive. As the old adage goes, history is written by the winners. And Stan was very much a winner. The creative world is one of egos, at once massive and yet gossamer thin, and the creative ego is driven to varying degrees by recognition and approbation. Some will go further than others to obtain this. A few will push things beyond what might be considered ethically acceptable. History shows that whenever something becomes a phenomenal success, everyone involved suddenly clambers over each other to claim credit. It has been argued that Stan Lee's status and reputation as 'the man behind Marvel' came at the expense of others who never received the recognition they deserved, their humbler voices drowned out by Stan's larger-than-life personality and overtly ambitious tendencies. While this is ultimately an uplifting tale of how one man truly did help revolutionise mainstream entertainment, together we shall probe beneath the surface. Did he stand on the shoulders of giants, make them do the hard work and seize all the glory? Stan Lee is considered one of the most important creative forces in recent history. But does he deserve it?

To know this, we must expose the man behind the mask. Stan presented himself to the world as the smiling face of Marvel; his cheesy grin a permanent fixture beneath the iconic thick-rimmed glasses and bristling moustache. To the public he was forever quick-witted and blessed with boundless enthusiasm. Yet his private life was blighted by personal tragedy, financial hardship, ugly legal disputes and public scandal. It's possible that Stan Lee was himself a superhuman creation. A breezy persona he developed to protect his true identity, that of Stanley Lieber, a complicated, ruthless and ambitious soul who embellished aspects of his life to spin yarns as fantastic and memorable as the characters he helped create. This book will prove that, just like the vibrant panels of the comics he wrote, Stan's life was never black and white.

It is, of course, impossible to tell the story of Stan's life without telling the story of Marvel. The two are synonymous and equally remarkable. It is beyond a doubt that Marvel have singularly changed the face of global entertainment. Their cavalcade of flawed, multidimensional and ultimately grounded superheroes resonates across the globe. The Marvel Cinematic Universe is the most successful feature-film franchise of all time. Since 2008, these films have collectively grossed over $20 billion – and counting. But as we all know, getting there is half the fun, so this book will trace every step of the eventful journey Marvel have taken to reach such levels of unprecedented, game-changing success. This book recounts the unique story of a company that suffered the slings and arrows of outrageous fortune like no other. More than eighty years since their foundation by Martin Goodman as Timely Comics back in 1939, Marvel have veered wildly from success to failure and back again, many times over. They have assumed the roles of plucky underdog, lumbering dinosaur, all-conquering leviathan, cultural milestone, financial millstone, meandering irrelevance and endangered species. This is a tale of burgeoning creativity, fiscal smarts, preening arrogance and catastrophic mistakes. Along the way, you will meet the various colourful personalities who each made their distinct contribution to Marvel's tumultuous rise to global domination. Some quietly drift in and out of the story. Others deserve a separate book of their own.

And yet we will always return to the one constant in Marvel – Stan Lee. He is the hero at the heart of this adventure. From humble immigrant origins in 1920s New York, Stan Lee is the embodiment of the American Dream: an aspirational success story, but not without its dark side. It is through Stan's long life, which staggeringly covered almost a century, that we shall also explore the history of modern popular culture. From the dying embers of American vaudeville and the birth of radio and television, to the evolution of mainstream Hollywood and the early days of the internet, we shall lose ourselves in the fascinating world of twentieth-century entertainment, as seen through the eyes of one of the few who helped shape it.

As you might have already guessed by now, Stan Lee was a complicated figure. As his story unfolds, you shall be the judge of his character, with this book simply serving as your humble guide on this voyage of discovery. At the end, you may not like him very much. Conversely, your admiration for him may actually grow. That, brave reader, is up to you. This book has been created from Stan's own words, his many interviews and detailed examination of conversations with those who worked alongside him over the decades. It also includes brand new and exclusive interviews with Marvel comic book writers, creators and illustrators for whom Stan's work proved an invaluable inspiration. So, without further ado, prepare yourself for a roller-coaster ride so thrilling, so amazingly spectacular, you will stay up all night, you will call in sick from school or work and you will definitely miss your stop due to being so utterly engrossed in every word of every sentence of every page. Are you sitting comfortably? Well, face front, True Believer. It's time to begin.

Chapter One

Once Upon a Time in Romania

To understand what makes a person tick, you need to wind back the clock. Our past informs our present, and what came before illuminates who we really are. Ask any storyteller. To relate to a character, you need to understand where they've been. There's a reason we talk about life's 'defining moments'. There's a reason we think the struggles and challenges we've endured in life 'build character'. One of the reasons the recent Marvel Cinematic Universe franchise has proved so successful is because the filmmakers took their time introducing their central characters *before* they became who they were destined to be. From an arrogant billionaire arms dealer with a change of heart to a wartime science experiment put on ice, we spent time with Tony Stark and Steve Rogers before they became superheroes. We followed them to that fork in the road that transformed their lives, and so when they ultimately became Iron Man and Captain America, we cared about what happened next.

Outside the Marvel universe, Christopher Nolan's excellent 2005 reboot *Batman Begins* revitalised the character by being arguably the first live-action adaptation to place Bruce Wayne at the heart of the story. Prior to this, all we'd had was Batman portrayed as a rather two-dimensional supporting player in his own story, second fiddle to whichever actor *du jour* was chewing up the scenery as one of Batman's more flamboyant villains. *Batman Begins* works so well because Nolan and co-scriptwriter David S. Goyer extensively explored Bruce Wayne's formative years, from traumatised and guilt-ridden orphan, to lost teen with a mind for revenge, to angry soul seeking guidance to conquer his fears and find his true purpose as the saviour of Gotham City. It's an hour into the film before Wayne first dons the iconic cape and cowl, but by this point we truly cared about the man under the mask. *Batman Begins* is a hugely compelling and satisfying character study that at once deconstructs and reaffirms the enduring appeal of the Dark Knight.

More than this, you cared about Batman because you'd seen what Bruce Wayne had been through.

An origin story not only grounds us in a sense of time and place, but also helps us invest in everything that happens to the character. It adds layers and depth. If we know a hero's background, we obtain a fuller insight into what motivates them, the decisions they make, as well as how and why they interact with others. A hero's origin enriches every stage of their journey and rewards us for tagging along for the ride.

So, we come to the hero of this particular adventure: Stan Lee. Now. We could jump straight in at the fun stuff. We could swing straight into the hip and happening 1960s when Marvel Comics created a wealth of iconic characters that not only redefined the comic book industry, but raised the bar for popular mainstream entertainment across the globe. Tall tales of clobberin' crooks through bank walls, destroying swathes of foes with a mighty hammer or dazzling feats of astral projection through inter-dimensional portals. We *could* start there. But that would be short-changing all of us. Especially Stan. After all, he was almost 40 years old when that happened. A lot of water had flowed under the bridge before then. Not all of it clean. These groundbreaking characters were not created out of thin air. You can't build worlds on a whim. To do justice to Stan's remarkable life and many achievements, we need to see the whole picture. The fact you picked up this book in the first place suggests you're interested in uncovering how he got there. What made Stan the man he became. So, settle in. We're going on an adventure.

Stanley Martin Lieber was born in New York City on 28 December 1922. But that's not where his story begins. Stan proudly considered himself a quintessential New Yorker, but we need to look beyond the gleaming monoliths and brownstone rooftops of the Big Apple. We must voyage across the sea to Romania at the end of the nineteenth century, where prejudice and violence forced much of its Jewish population to join the millions across Europe heading overseas to escape persecution. It was a tumultuous time for Romania's Jews, even though the 1800s had begun favourably. During the early to mid part of the century, the country was a haven for Jewish immigrants. Those fleeing pogroms from neighbouring countries had found sanctuary in its relatively tolerant climate.[1] Scores of new arrivals intermingled with Romania's existing Jewish community to build a considerable social, economic and even political presence within the country. This changed in 1866, when Romania established a new constitution that barred non-Christians from becoming citizens. This naturally affected its now-burgeoning Jewish population. Twelve years later, the pendulum swung back in favour of a more tolerant climate when Romania won independence from Ottoman rule. Now a constitutional monarchy under the cold, detached gaze of King Carol I, its fledgling Romanian government revoked this discriminatory law, promising fair and equal rights for all its citizens. It didn't last.

More laws were soon introduced that prohibited Jews from taking certain kinds of trades and professions. Many Jewish men were forced into unemployment. In 1893, Jewish children were barred from the Romanian public education system unless they paid additional fees, which, of course, many families couldn't afford. This legislation was extended in 1898 to include senior schools and universities. Then the Romanian economy took a downturn, and that's when things turned nasty. In times of economic hardship, people often seek out a scapegoat for their country's ills. Those considered different or 'alien' are usually first against the wall. History has tragically shown that blame is often laid at the doors of the local synagogue. Sure enough, aggressive strains of anti-Semitism re-infected Romanian society, sometimes erupting into brazen acts of violence. With grim inevitability, many in Romania had mistakenly concluded that there was a 'Jewish problem'.

With such bleak and dangerous prospects on the horizon, many Romanian Jews inevitably looked beyond their borders for a chance of a life free from threat. So began the Romanian Jewish exodus. Between 1899 and 1904, approximately a third of all Romanian Jewry emigrated. Most set sail for the United States of America. Many wound up on the East Coast, in that paradigm of multicultural freedom, New York City. Among those tired, poor, huddled masses landing on Ellis Island was a teenager named Hyman Lieber.[2] Hyman docked in the shadow of Lady Liberty in 1905, along with his teenage relative Abraham. The two Lieber boys entered into the throng of immigrants starting a new life in Manhattan. They lived in cramped conditions and often on servile wages. In this melting pot, the Romanian Jewish immigrants understandably stuck together. A ghetto was formed in an area previously dominated by German and Irish immigrants: New York's Lower East Side.[3]

While no concrete evidence exists that Hyman Lieber started his American life in the heart of the ghetto, it's highly likely he would have been very familiar with the First Roumanian American Synagogue on Rivington Street and the bustling and vibrant Orchard Street with its many Yiddish storefront signs, kosher butchers and horse-drawn carts clattering across crowded cobbled streets. This was the centre of the universe for New York's Jewish community during the early 1900s; a new home in the new world where they could be safe. Not that immigrant life in New York was a walk in Central Park. Most relocated without even a basic understanding of English, so had to learn the language as best they could as fast as they could, simply to expand employment options. The alternative route for Jewish immigrants was to remain in the trades and professions offered within the community, who spoke more German than Yiddish. Tensions between different ethnic communities in that area did, on occasion, spiral into violence, notably in 1902 when an almighty scuffle broke out on Grand Street between workers at R. Hoe & Company's printing press factory and Jews marching past in a funeral procession for Chief Orthodox Rabbi Jacob Joseph. While only eleven Jews and four factory workers were arrested by police, the Jacob Joseph Funeral Riot gained notoriety for alleged Irish Catholic anti-Semitism as large numbers of police officers were said to side with the factory workers.[4]

Despite tensions and hardships, life for Hyman and Abraham Lieber progressed. Census details reveal that by 1910 both were boarding with a family called Moshkowitz on Avenue A[5], where Manhattan borders the Lower East Side. By this time, Hyman had changed his name to Jacob, and had begun working in the garment industry. It was a trade that would no doubt serve him well for years. The records then jump forward a decade to reveal that, in 1920, Jacob was lodging with a fellow rag-trade worker in the heart of Manhattan on 114th Street, just north of Central Park. Within two years, Jacob had married Celia Solomon, a girl also of Romanian Jewish origin. Her large family had moved to the US at the turn of the century, but Celia had been born in New York.[6] The newlyweds quickly moved into an Upper West Side apartment, on the corner of Manhattan's West 98th Street and West End Avenue,[7] between Broadway and the Hudson River. As 1922 drew to a close, Jacob and Celia welcomed a new addition to the Lieber family, a bouncing baby boy they named Stanley. The timing wasn't great. In October 1929, two months before Stan's seventh birthday, Wall Street crashed. Following a recent similar financial collapse in London, share prices at the New York Stock Exchange tumbled catastrophically. Billions of dollars were wiped out in a matter of days, ushering in a twelve-year stretch of economic darkness later branded The Great Depression.

During this time, mass employment affected just about everyone, not least those trying to earn an honest wage in New York, such as Jacob Lieber. Work dried up, even in garment manufacturing. People just weren't buying new clothes. Stan's earliest recollections of family life were not always the fondest. His abiding memories were of his parents frequently arguing as they struggled to make ends meet. Financial pressures on the family grew in 1931 with the arrival of Stan's younger brother Larry, forcing the Liebers to move north from their West End apartment to a meagre one-bedroom apartment on Fort Washington Avenue in Washington Heights.

The highest point of Manhattan, Washington Heights was bordered to the south by Harlem, Inwood to the north, the Hudson River to the west, and to the east the Harlem River and Coogan's Bluff. The area was a lively mix of ethnicities, largely Irish and Greek. Some financial pressure was alleviated, however, and although Stan had some nearby green space for play, things were still far from rosy.

Stan would later vividly recall his father's seemingly endless job hunting. The young boy would watch the weight of the Depression slowly compress his father into a crumpled heap. A normal routine involved Jacob either returning home from a day trudging the streets for work or scouring the 'want ads' for any opportunity. Some glimmer of hope. This fruitless endeavour chipped away at both his father's confidence and the family unit. Jacob and Celia rowed incessantly about money. By Stan's account, and to their eternal credit, they never took it out on the children. This was their burden to bear and bear it alone they must – at all costs. As with many self-made immigrants, Jacob was a product of his time, a proud man who wanted to be the *pater familias,* chief breadwinner and main provider. This was just how things were done. To feel his dignity and inherent value seemingly being stripped from him would have cut deep. It didn't help that Celia contributed by borrowing from her considerably wealthier family. While not unusual today, back then this would have further needled Jacob's fragile male pride.

Those early years left a profound mark on Stan, who said: 'I realized at an early age how the spectre of poverty, the never-ending worry about not having enough money to buy groceries or to pay the rent, can cast a cloud over a marriage.'[8] If there is a silver lining, it was that observing his father's increasing despondence sowed the seeds of a strong work ethic in Stan that informed him for the rest of his life. 'Seeing the demoralizing effect that his unemployment had on his spirit, making him feel that he just wasn't needed, gave me a feeling I've never been able to shake,' he later said. 'It's a feeling that the most important thing for a man is to have work to do, to be busy, to be needed.'[9] Stan would attribute this as the reason why he spent his entire life juggling multiple projects at once and, while this armchair psychology may be a tad simplistic, it certainly goes some way to explain his astonishingly prolific career. 'I'll always regret the fact,' he would reminisce, 'that by the time I was earning enough money to make things easier for them, it was too late.'

Stan was the favourite son, but he felt guilty about such preferential treatment. He always wished his parents had lavished as much praise on young Larry as they did on him, but his mother worshipped the ground he walked on. 'I used to come home from school … and she'd grab me and fuss over me and say "you're home already? I was sure today was the day a movie scout would discover you and take you away from me!"'[10] Larry also idolised Stan, but the two boys initially shared no relationship with each other, largely due to the nine-year age difference. Stan subsequently regretted this distance, but made up for it later when he actively brought Larry into the comic book industry as artist and writer, an act which no doubt assuaged the guilt he felt about his mother's blatant favouritism. Larry went on to establish himself as a major creative force in his own right, best known as co-creator of Iron Man and illustrator of the newspaper comic strip *The Amazing Spider-Man* for over thirty years.

At school, Stan was a bright boy who worked hard. Driven by the need to finish his education so he could go out into the real world and contribute to the family coffers, his diligence was rewarded by skipping grades. Being the youngest boy in class led Stan to see himself as an outsider. He did not form lasting friendships at school, and in the summer months the kids he did befriend were spirited away to summer camps or driven off for family adventures. Too young for camp and in a family that could not afford a car, Stan had to find other ways to amuse himself. His rear-facing apartment didn't even have a street view. Every time Stan looked out from his tiny home, he was literally staring at a brick wall. It is no coincidence then, that Stan found comfort, joy and inspiration in activities that he could do by himself and that cost nothing. Because when there's no one to interact with, kids inevitably rely on their imagination. And that's exactly what Stan did. He lost himself inside worlds that would, in time, help him transform from lonely little Stanley Lieber into the mighty Stan Lee. And what worlds there were to discover.

Chapter Two

Worlds of Pure Imagination

For Stan's twelfth birthday, Jacob and Celia scraped enough cash together to buy him a bicycle. Their son cherished this as if it was his best friend – because it was. There's nothing quite like the thrill of freedom your first bike gives you, and the joy of racing around the neighbourhood fuelled his burgeoning imagination. Stan wasn't just a boy on a bike. Oh no. That would be far too dull. He was a courageous astronaut, boldly going where no kid had gone before on 'a two-wheeled spaceship'. He was a brave knight in armour, atop a mighty steed, riding into countless battles – from which he no doubt always emerged triumphant.

This escapism offered Stan respite from a home filled with argument, stress and worry. And it wasn't getting any better. By the 1930s, the Lieber family had to move again. Heading out of Manhattan altogether, they relocated to a one-bedroom apartment in the Bronx, on 1720 University Avenue. Tucked between Brandt Place and West 176th Street, this once-rural area had, after the First World War, undergone major urban growth. Then a huge influx of immigrants, notably French, German, Poles and Jews, transformed the borough into an effervescent melting pot. In 1937, it was recorded that nearly 600,000 Jews lived in the Bronx, just under half the borough's entire population.[1]

Even by their own modest standards, the Bronx was much less affluent than the Liebers were accustomed to. The area had started to suffer rapid economic decline as middle-class residents began relocating elsewhere. It would not see urban renewal and regeneration until the late 1980s. Despite this second money-saving move, living conditions were no less restrictive than before. 'My brother and I slept in the bedroom,' Stan recalled, 'my parents on a foldout couch.'[2] This third-floor apartment was also rear facing. Yet again, Stan was denied a view. So, when he found himself such stifling circumstances, he lost himself in books.

It's no surprise that a future writer found sanctuary in reading. But what may raise an eyebrow is that Stan had no real interest in comic books. Back then they were more primitive, far from the sophisticated established formats we have today. What truly sparked young Stan's imagination were the novels of Edgar Rice Burroughs, Mark Twain and Jules Verne.

It's easy to see why such escapist fiction appealed to Stan. These novels would transport him to times and places far away, joining adventures with heroes who personified freedom and exploration. Burroughs' Tarzan stories allowed Stan to soar among the African jungle treetops alongside the iconic elegant wild man, and his Barsoom books enabled him to explore the Martian world with brave and handsome Civil War veteran John Carter. Mark Twain's adventures of Tom Sawyer and Huckleberry Finn gave Stan safe passage to roam the antebellum South with two boys who were best friends and as thick as thieves – something missing in Stan's solitary world. The two heroes of Twain's defining stories are both bright and cunning lads, always pushing their luck. Their discovery of hidden treasure in McDougal's Cave may also have been pure wish fulfilment for Stan; Tom and Huck stumbling upon a level of financial security so absent from his real life.

Then there were Jules Verne's genre-defining novels, *Journey to the Center of the Earth* (1864), *Twenty Thousand Leagues Under the Sea* (1870), and *Around the World in Eighty Days* (1873).[3] This trio of seminal tales explores the wondrous that lies all around us. Verne was fascinated by science, geography, cartography and technology, pouring meticulous research into each work. From Professor Lidenbrock's subterranean journey of discovery to Captain Nemo's underwater odyssey or Phileas Fogg's globetrotting wager, these stories explore all that is possible through human endeavour, toil and genius. The juxtaposition of the fantastical and the familiar would be a rich vein running through pretty much all of Stan's notable creations, but let's not rush things, because Stan's early literary heroes don't stop here.

As he grew older, Stan gravitated towards the paranoid prophecies of H. G. Wells, the dark dread of Edgar Allan Poe, the detective page-turners of Arthur Conan Doyle and then older still, the complex and richly detailed character studies of Charles Dickens and Victor Hugo. Even the Bible and Shakespeare get a nod from Stan as influencing his own comics, which he filled with tall tales 'about Norse gods, incantation-spouting magicians, and long-winded philosophers from outer space'. The Bard's powerful command of narrative in particular left an impression on young Stan. Such boyhood reminiscences show that he was keen to present himself as a highly literate and literary child. In his autobiographical writings, Stan always saw himself as a frustrated author who longed to write the Great American Novel, but never delivered on that lofty aspiration. Given his lasting legacy to popular culture, however, he needn't have beaten himself up too much.

Beyond the pages of classic novels, young Stan also found escapism through sound and screen. Prior to these interwar years, especially during the nineteenth century, mainstream entertainment had been dominated by the song, dance and variety shenanigans of vaudeville. With French origins via saloon entertainment, circus clowning and freak shows, this so-called 'heart of American show business' held audiences in rapture while a harlequin tumbled on stage, a male singer squawked parody in an oversized frock or a chap with a colossal moustache behaved appallingly to a bear in a tutu. It was a different time.

The main limitation of vaudeville came from its inherent live and costly nature; to be part of the audience, you had to physically attend a theatre. The invention of radio, however, allowed families to enjoy a shared entertainment experience like never before. Radio placed those talented performers and artists right in the audience's living room for free. This new technological marvel foreshadowed the ultimate demise of vaudeville. It's no coincidence that throughout America, at the same time as families huddled round their increasingly available and relatively inexpensive radio sets, traditional vaudeville was on its last legs. It didn't help that the most successful vaudevillians were also being coaxed away to radio and more traditional theatre. The final nail in the red velvet-lined coffin[4] was hammered in by the widespread rise of talking pictures. Vaudeville's dwindling appeal saw many once-popular entertainers fade into obscurity, while others survived the transition and went on to become household names in the exciting new forms of media taking over the world. Vaudeville's brightest star was Russian immigrant Asa Yoelson, who changed his name to Al Jolson and then made his name with his unique singing voice and 'blacking up' by smearing burnt cork all over his face. It really was a different time.

Jolson revolutionised the entertainment world with the first 'talkie'. *The Jazz Singer* was released on 6 October 1927. With just four musical numbers and minimal dialogue, astonished audiences gasped and leapt to their feet in thunderous applause. They had seen the future, only as celluloid can deliver. Within two years of the film's release, the number of theatres wired for sound had expanded from around 200 to more than 4,000. By 1930, any remaining live theatres which hadn't been forced by the Depression to close their doors, converted their auditoria into cinemas as a cheaper alternative to paying live performers and musicians. While there was no single historical event that destroyed vaudeville, a hugely significant moment came on 16 November 1932, when its epicentre, New York's Palace Theatre on Broadway and 47th Street, shifted to only showing movies.

Stan remembers fondly how cinema quickly became another route of escape for him as a youth. When living in Washington Heights, he would walk to the Loews Theater on 175th Street and Broadway to catch a Saturday matinee, marvelling at a man called Lou playing the organ before the film. Stan would also frequent one of the five theatres within three blocks around 181st Street, an experience he later described as 'heaven'. Between this handful of motion picturehouses, he would revel in silver-screen escapades starring Errol Flynn, Roy Rogers and Charlie Chaplin, or gasp with pleasure as literary favourites such as *Frankenstein*, *The Hound of the Baskervilles* or *Moby Dick* were adapted into magisterial studio productions.

During these early days of public broadcasting, there were three major networks keeping Americans happy: the National Broadcasting Company (NBC, founded 1926), Columbia Broadcasting System (CBS, founded 1927) and the Mutual Broadcasting System (Mutual, founded 1934). While these three corporations aggressively competed for nationwide coverage, millions of Americans were spoiled by the variety of entertainment on offer. Radio sales continued to soar and the medium fast became the country's favourite evening pastime. By 1932, thirty million radio sets had been sold in America alone, with over 500 stations to choose from.[5] The Liebers loved radio as much as the next family. Sunday night was a special night where all woes were put aside as they crowded round their set, quite possibly a snazzy five-tube Silvertone receiver with mahogany finish.

The main agents of invention for Stan were comedian Jack Benny and ventriloquist Edgar Bergen. And yes, the idea of having a ventriloquist on the radio is preposterous, but he was a massive hit, so there you go. It's no surprise that Stan most fondly remembers two comedians. After all, the Depression was still choking the life out of millions of people like Jacob Lieber every single day. Everyone really needed a laugh.

Benny and Bergen provided a much-needed antidote to the sadness that had seeped into the Lieber home during Stan's formative years.

Jack Benny made his radio debut on an Ed Sullivan broadcast on NBC in March 1932 and was an instant hit. Months later, he landed his own show, *The Canada Dry Ginger Ale Program*. Bergen became a breakout star after his 1936 radio debut; the following year he was a regular on *The Chase and Sanborn Hour*, a series of variety shows sponsored by Standard Brands' Chase & Sanborn Coffee. Back then, broadcasters were clearly not so subtle about who was sponsoring their programming. Over the years, Benny's radio show was rebranded several times to *The Chevrolet Program*, *The General Tire Revue*, *The Jell-O Program*, *The Grape Nuts Flakes Program* and *The Lucky Strike Program*[6]. But people didn't tune in to hear about what wonderful product they might want to consume, it was always about the stars.

Jack Benny was born Benjamin Kubelsky to Polish and Lithuanian Jews. Benny had played violin in vaudeville as a youth, often working in theatres alongside the Marx Brothers. After signing a five-motion picture deal with MGM which led to not much, Benny returned to live performance only to be scooped up by radio. He was a unique comic voice at a time when many performers were loud and brash, still clinging to the vestiges of vaudeville. Benny's comedic mastery came from downbeat, dry sarcasm and long pauses. The very first thing he uttered on that Sullivan showcase was the now-famous line, 'This is Jack Benny talking. There will be a slight pause while you say, "Who cares?"' Over the course of his radio show, he developed a heightened version of himself, evolving into a character that was financially tight to a fault, arrogant, vain and deluded about his musical ability. Benny's show featured a host of richly defined characters filled out by superb comic actors. These included Phil Harris, better known as the voice of Baloo the bear in Disney's 1967 version of *Jungle Book*, and the genius that was Mel Blanc, familiar to generations as the original voice of pretty much all the *Looney Tunes* cartoon characters, including Bugs Bunny, Daffy Duck, Porky Pig and Yosemite Sam. *The Jack Benny Program* was enjoyed by millions, making the transition to television in 1950 and running until 1965. The show is still regarded as a high point in broadcast comedy history and sowed the seeds for many future sitcoms. If you're a comedy fan, hunt down any episode from that original radio show that is floating around online. They're out there. You won't regret it.

Edgar Bergen was also from an immigrant family, born Edgar John Berggren to Swedish parents. Also like Benny, Bergen was born in Chicago, Illinois and cut his teeth during the final years of vaudeville. He taught himself ventriloquism aged 11, from a pamphlet. He had his wooden ventriloquist dummy made while still at school and called him Charlie McCarthy. Edgar and Charlie swiftly became a much-loved double act. As he was on the radio, audiences couldn't see how proficient a ventriloquist he was, so he honed his craft through the material and the strongly defined characters he created. Bergen devised several other wooden sidekicks over the years, but motor-mouth Charlie was always the most popular. Really, Charlie was another side to Bergen's personality. While he presented himself as gentle and mild-mannered, he used Charlie as a conduit for more aggressive, snarky and innuendo-laden material that was pretty racy for the time. Together, the pair would carve out a career that also lasted decades. Indeed, Edgar and Charlie made their final screen appearance in 1979's *The Muppet Movie*, and there was a touching dedication to both in its closing credits.

While Stan never explicitly cited either Benny or Bergen as a direct influence, you can see their comedy stylings all over his work. Stan instinctively knew the value of strong characterisation to reflect views and attitudes he might not have felt comfortable sharing as himself. He also injected wisecracking, street-smart humour into his writing. There's no doubt all of this owes a debt of thanks not just to the novels in which he frequently lost himself, but also the whip-smart alter egos both Benny and Bergen created to delight millions of listeners every Sunday night.

One more radio creation sparked particular interest in young Stan, but this was definitely a direct influence on his later work. *Chandu the Magician* was a long-running radio drama series that first launched in 1931 on local Los Angeles radio network station KHJ ('Kindness, Happiness, and Joy'), before making its nationwide debut on Mutual on 8 October 1932. Sponsored by the far from mystical White King Soap and Beech Nut Gum, the show starred Gayne Whitman as Frank Chandler, an American who travelled to India to master ancient occult arts such as astral projection and teleportation, as well as hypnosis and escapology. Adopting the alter ego of Chandu the Magician, Chandler vowed to battle evil in all its forms, aided by his sister Dorothy and various exotic love interests. Each week, young Stanley Lieber sat gripped by Chandu's adventures, neatly packed into fifteen-minute romps that were pure pulp adventure, transporting the listener to many far-flung locations.

So popular was this radio show right from the get go, a feature-film adaptation was released, also in 1932, starring NBC regular Edmund Lowe in the title role. *Chandu the Magician* saw our eponymous hero travel to Egypt to defeat a wicked foe named Roxor, played by a certain Hungarian actor by the name of Bela Lugosi. Of course, Lugosi is forever etched in film history for playing Dracula, and as Roxor he was perfectly cast, biting great chunks out of the scenery with the same hypnotic stare and wicked grin that made his Transylvanian count so transfixing and memorable. Two years later, audiences would see the return of Chandu in 1934's aptly named film *The Return of Chandu*, but this time Lugosi played the magician. This serialised sequel, spliced into twelve parts, marks one of the exceedingly rare occasions that Lugosi played the hero. Again, cineastes might want to seek this one out, just to see an actor synonymous with unconscionable on-screen villainy playing against type.

In 1935, radio production of *Chandu the Magician* moved to Chicago, with Whitman replaced by Howard Hoffman in the lead role. This version lasted only for one year, but the show was revived after the Second World War, with Tom Collins as Chandu, squaring off against Mexican-born actor Luis van Rooten as the villainous Roxor. This revival fared slightly better than the 1935 version, and the show finally ground to a halt in 1950.

Today, *Chandu the Magician* is largely forgotten and is very much a product of its time, with casual racism and sexism dropped into its many fantastical plotlines. Its significance in this story, however, is great as, thirty years later, Stan took Chandu as the inspiration for one of his more out there co-creations, Doctor Strange. Like Chandu, Strange is an American who learns to harness mystical powers from the East. Both are dressed in ornate garments, including an impressive cloak, and both feature stylised facial hair. Chandu and Strange share a fondness for occult spells and incantations, not to mention teleportation and astral projection. Doctor Strange may reflect the 1960s' resurgent fascination with Eastern mysticism, the occult and even hallucinogenic experiences, but there's no doubt that when Stan and co-creator Steve Ditko came up with the character, the Master of the Mystic Arts was also the psychedelic lovechild of Chandu the Magician.

Despite the respite from reality all these literary and broadcast stories offered the American people, the Depression continued to grind them down. Stan diligently continued his studies, anxious to get out there and earn an honest wage. He delivered lunches to office workers in the Rockefeller Center and dabbled briefly and unsuccessfully in the garment industry making trousers (turns out he was not a chip off the old block). He also worked as an usher at the Rivoli Theater on Broadway, just north of Times Square which, predictably, he enjoyed immensely. He was finally in the movies! He even got to meet the First Lady at the time, Eleanor Roosevelt, who visited the movie house and required being shown to her seat, accompanied by a small army of secret service men. Stan leapt to it, only to take a tumble while ushering FLOTUS and her armed entourage to her seat. It was not his proudest moment.

He juggled study with these part-time jobs, but it was only a matter of time before his education would give way to a regular income. Still, school did provide Stan with opportunities to develop skills and interests that would serve him well. He attended DeWitt Clinton High School at 100 West Mosholu Parkway South and East 205th Street in the Bronx. An all-boys school that favoured immigrants and sons of immigrants, it was one of the largest high schools in the world, sprawling across twenty-one acres. Several alumni from DeWitt Clinton went on to fame and fortune, including writer James Baldwin, Nobel Prize-winning physician Robert Hofstadter, designer Ralph Lauren, boxer Sugar Ray Robinson, play and screen writer Neil Simon, Hollywood icon Burt Lancaster and cartoonist Will Eisner. Two more alumni, especially significant to Stan's story, were Robert Kahn and Milton 'Bill' Finger. Soon after graduation, Robert changed his surname to Bob Kane and, together with Finger, went on to create Batman. But we'll get to those guys soon.

A few years younger than this dynamic duo, Stan got stuck into life at Clinton. He joined the public-speaking club and the law society. He actually considered training as a lawyer, but that didn't last when he realised it involved much hard graft at law school and not just the courtroom theatrics he had seen in a 1932 movie called *The Mouthpiece*. At Clinton, there was one teacher in particular who inspired him, a young man called Leon B. Ginsberg Jr. His amusing stories told at the start of each class showed young Stan how humour could make learning fun. 'It was a lesson I never forgot,' he reflected, 'a lesson I've tried to apply to everything I do.'[7] His other high school role model was a fellow student called John J. McKenna Jr. A grade or two above Stan, John also had a job selling subscriptions to *The New York Times*. He would stand up in front of the class and persuade everyone in the room that they should subscribe. Stan was so wowed by John's gift of the gab that he vowed he would follow in his footsteps. Already Stan saw the benefit of being able to hold an audience's attention through charisma and confidence. The seeds were being sown in Stan's mind that showmanship was incredibly important, and this would come to be one of his signature personal and professional traits. But deep down he knew his calling in life. He would become a writer. Fortunately, that path became open to him, sooner than he expected.

Chapter Three

The Golden Years

Stan began writing on a professional level when still a teenager. But it wasn't much fun. He landed a grim part-time job typing out obituaries for famous people … before they'd actually passed away. He then took a scintillating gig covering publicity for the National Tuberculosis Hospital in Denver. It was all rather depressing, but it was a start. It gave Stan confidence and even kick-started his lifelong fascination with advertising. Back at school, Stanley signed up to work as 'publicity director' on Clinton's literary magazine, *Magpie.*

This was not Stan's first foray into journalism. That happened when he was 10 and became obsessed with the larger-than-life *Chicago Tribune* war correspondent Floyd Gibbons. He sent him fan mail and never forgot the day that he actually received a reply. Fast forward to age 15, when Stan entered a high school writing competition sponsored by one of New York's biggest newspapers, the *Herald Tribune*. Entrants were invited to submit a 500-word article on that week's most important news story. Stan claimed to have won this competition three times in a row, even receiving a letter from the editor asking him to stop submitting so someone else could have a chance[1]. This may have been a total fib,[2] but we *do* know that Stan did indeed win a prize in this competition. More importantly, this prize had a profound effect on him, setting him on his course towards a writing career.

Shortly before leaving high school, Stan finally followed in the footsteps of John J. McKenna Jr, when he got a chance to test his own budding oratory skills to flog the *Herald Tribune* in the classroom. By now, Stan had grown in confidence and popularity. He was tall, handsome and outspoken, with a rising interest in the opposite sex. In no time, Stan was deploying his own gift of the gab to win over subscribers to the *Tribune* and any girls he had an eye on. His particular wooing tactic involved self-taught parlour tricks with thimbles. Stan never revealed what they were, and they're probably best left to the imagination. Surprisingly, this technique worked, not least on the daughter of the local confectionery store owner, to whom Stan claimed to have lost his virginity.

While Stan was sowing his wild oats in New York, America was enjoying gradual economic recovery from the Depression, largely thanks to President Franklin D. Roosevelt's New Deal. Initiated in 1933, the New Deal was essentially a large-scale, country-wide overhaul of EVERYTHING, including the establishment of the social security system. Through a series of programmes and public work projects, the New Deal benefitted and protected the unemployed and vulnerable members of society. It also provided much-needed financial reforms and restrictions to ensure the country didn't slump back into another black hole. These programmes included the hiring of unemployed teachers to provide free adult education, schemes to allow people to keep their homes, and other lifelines that enabled millions to get back on their feet. One such programme, the 1935 Works Progress Administration (WPA), included arts projects for unemployed artists, musicians and writers. Shortly after graduation from high school, Stan himself benefitted directly from the WPA as it enabled him to join a youth theatre (at the same time as a young Orson Welles). Stan claims he trod the boards primarily to get a particular girl, and while the pair did enjoy a short-lived time together both on and off stage, the WPA also sated Stan's appetite for the theatrical.

The Great Depression was far from over, but Roosevelt's New Deal did boost people's confidence. Millions felt empowered to claw back their self-respect and began to feel hopeful. Change was coming. Stan was 17 when he left DeWitt Clinton, with a spring in his step and a desire to trade in his part-time jobbing experience for something more permanent. It was 1939, but war in Europe was yet to break out. To many across America, the sun seemed to be finally shining through the clouds, casting gilded rays of opportunity. At the same time, the comic book industry was exploding. The American Dream was being reaffirmed to a mass audience through the two most iconic superheroes of all time. It was the dawn of the Golden Age of Comics. But who were the movers and shakers that helped make this happen? To answer this question, True Believer, we must briefly travel back to the roaring '20s, when the publishing industry in New York owed as much to organised crime as creative genius.

During the inter-war period, America developed an insatiable thirst for sensational magazines. Publishing companies sprang up from nowhere, often dying a death almost as quickly. Multiple players with huge egos, formidable reputations and dubious backgrounds emerged in the publishing industry during the 1920s, all competing for financial success in a burgeoning and lucrative medium. Men such as privileged, ruthless media tycoon William Randolph Hearst, the inspiration for Welles' seminal *Citizen Kane.* Men such as Bernarr MacFadden, a charismatic bodybuilder with a leonine mane and a nose for business. Macfadden tapped into popular interest of the time and published hugely successful special-interest magazines including *Physical Culture* and *True Story.* Men such as Hugo Gernsback, an aristocratic European Jewish immigrant and founder of Experimenter Publishing. In 1926, Experimenter launched *Amazing Stories*,[3] a science fiction magazine that inspired many a young boy to look to the stars. A lot of the publications produced during the 1920s reflected the sumptuous and hedonistic nature of the times. Producing titles such as *Strange Suicides*, *Medical Horrors*, *Paris Nights*, *Spicy Stories* and *Juicy Tales*, these publishing entrepreneurs tapped into the more lascivious side of human interest, and made a killing.

One key figure in the industry was Harry Donenfeld, another Romanian Jewish immigrant, only a few years younger than Stan's father. Harry was a bullish and self-aggrandising printing salesman with ties to the New York mob. Having spent his youth on the Lower East Side running with street gangs, Harry enjoyed a brief dalliance with the rag trade before seeing the huge financial potential offered by the printing industry. With his brothers, he set up his own company and started small. They began by printing subscription leaflets for the likes of *Cosmopolitan* and *Good Housekeeping,* as well as publishing cheap tittle-tattle titles. Harry was not afraid to push against the law, and it was rumoured that he was involved in smuggling hooch across the Canadian border during Prohibition. At the end of the 1920s, Harry formed a partnership with accountant Jacob 'Jack' Liebowitz, who possessed a savvy understanding of the stock exchange. With Harry, the ever-confident, charming salesman, and Jack in charge of the bookkeeping behind the scenes, the pair made a robust professional team. In 1932, they set up Independent News Company, a publishing house with its own distribution system. This was a smart move, as being responsible for distributing titles meant no longer being reliant on any third party. With greater control, Harry and Jack expanded their new company into gangster and detective fiction.

Across town, another young man of Jewish immigrant stock was also carving out a solid reputation as a magazine publisher. Moe Goodman was born in Brooklyn in 1908, but spent his formative years living on the fringes of society. He dropped out of school and travelled around the States by train, often living in collectives of similarly transient people, which were known as 'hobo camps'. In the early 1930s, Moe returned to New York and cleaned up his act. He changed his name to Martin and landed a job at a magazine distributing company before co-founding his own firm, Newsstand Publications. Newsstand produced disposable cowboy and detective hokum printed on rough-edged paper. Titles of this so-called 'shudder pulp' fiction included *All Star Adventure Fiction*, *Complete Western Book*, *Mystery Tales*, *Real Sports*, *Star Detective* and a lurid sci-fi magazine *Marvel Science Stories.*

Martin Goodman was notoriously dismissive of both his products and his readership, once remarking that 'fans are not interested in quality'.[4] Originality was not his thing; he just copied what was already popular. And he was damn good at it too. Stan later described Goodman as 'sharp as a tack', a man who 'knew the publication business inside and out'. Goodman summed up his business strategy quite simply, saying that 'if you get a title that catches on, then add a few more, you're in for a nice profit'.[5] Newsstand went under in 1934, but Goodman continued publishing a multitude of magazines. From his offices in the iconic McGraw-Hill Building at 330 West 42nd Street in Hell's Kitchen, he traded under different company names to stay one step ahead of the tax office, until one finally stuck: Timely Publications.

While Harry Donenfeld and Martin Goodman were making a name for themselves with magazines, strips previously printed in daily newspapers were now being published as collected works. Despite a few immediate precursors[6], the first true American modern comic book is generally considered to be *Famous Funnies: A Carnival of Comics.* Published in 1933, this thirty-six-page landmark publication can be credited to Charlie Gaines, a salesman who had been searching for a way to keep printing presses going during the Depression. *Famous Funnies* was produced with Dell Publishing and distributed nationwide through the Woolworth's department store chain. This was the comic book young Stan would have thumbed through. As we have seen, it didn't set his world alight, but he has said that as a boy he enjoyed the adventures of anvil-jawed law enforcer *Dick Tracy* and Sidney Smith's comedic middle-class family creation, *The Gumps*.

Charlie Gaines' *Famous Funnies* is important in this story because it essentially launched a new mass medium. Cheap and disposable amusement was welcome during these hard times and soon *Famous Funnies* became an ongoing monthly comic book series, readily available at newsstands throughout the country. *Famous Funnies* was also a vibrant showcase of how hard many writers and illustrators were working in the newspapers on daily strips to entertain millions of Americans. Many featured in *Famous Funnies* struck a balance between comedy and kitchen-sink drama, but there were a few more high-concept fantastical strips that foreshadowed what was on the horizon. Notable examples include *Buck Rogers*, a First World War veteran who falls into suspended animation only to reawaken in the year 2419. Then there was The Phantom Magician, a mysterious supporting character in fantasy strip *The Adventures of Patsy,* considered by many cultural historians to be the very first comic book superhero. For the most part, however, *Famous Funnies* was a light-hearted collection of short stories that parodied American life.

The final player instrumental in ushering in the Golden Age of Comics was ex-Army major turned writer and entrepreneur Malcolm Wheeler-Nicholson. In 1934, he founded National Allied Publications, and the following February he launched *New Fun*, the first ever comic book to contain completely original stories. *New Fun* is also historically significant because it bucked the trend of corporate sponsorship, instead being funded through featured advertising within its pages.

With so many creative forces at play within this new and exciting medium, it was only a matter of time before something amazing happened. That moment came when Malcolm Wheeler-Nicholson came knocking on the door of Harry Donenfeld and Jack Liebowitz. *New Fun* was struggling in sales, so the major had a business proposition. He wanted Harry and Jack's Independent News Company to distribute *New Fun,* and, together, they would publish more titles using the hot new talent Wheeler-Nicholson had already discovered for *New Fun*. For instance, new kids from Cleveland, Jerry Siegel and Joe Shuster, had apparently submitted other exciting characters that were yet to be used. Maybe they could bring something truly special to the table?

The timing was perfect. Vice and corruption were becoming increasingly scrutinised by the law during the Depression. A man like Harry Donenfeld, a purveyor of sleazy magazines with Mob connections, was keen to move his business affairs into a more wholesome arena. Taking on board *New Fun* would be just the ticket. And if they accepted, Malcolm Wheeler-Nicholson, who had recently made some unsound business decisions that left him strapped for cash, would be dug out of a potentially very deep hole. So it came to pass, a deal was struck. And the fruit of this union was Marvel's arch rival to this very day, DC Comics.

From this point onwards, things moved pretty fast. The trio registered their new company, Detective Comics, Inc., and in addition to *New Fun* they published *New Comics* in 1935, followed in early 1937 by *Detective Comics #1*. That year they got on board *Famous Funnies*' mastermind Charlie Gaines, which only strengthened the business and their resources. Malcolm Wheeler-Nicholson's personal financial strife was ongoing, however, and it soon became apparent that a fourth comic book title needed to be produced fast. Pooling their resources, the team rummaged through what was lying around the offices. One of the unused strips they dug up from the pile that caught the eye of the editorial team was indeed by Siegel and Shuster. It was a character so striking they all decided it should grace the front of this new title, which would be called *Action Comics*. The first issue was launched in June 1938. On its cover was a single, full-page image of what looked like a champion weightlifter holding a green car above his head. He wore a blue leotard with red underpants on the outside. His broad chest was emblazoned with a yellow shield. On that shield was a single letter: S. They didn't know it, but those boys from Cleveland had given the world The Man of Tomorrow. Nothing would ever be the same.

Superman's debut was met with little fanfare at the time. In 1938, *Action Comics #1* was sold for ten cents. For their trouble, Jerry Siegel and Joe Shuster received a cheque for $130, handing over all rights to the character in the process. Flash forward to 2014, a 'pristine' copy of *Action Comics #1* was sold on an eBay for $3.2 million.[7]

Back then, of course, everyone just carried on regardless. Realising Wheeler-Nicholson's financial troubles could be a liability, Donenfeld paid off the major and Detective Comics, Inc. continued with Liebowitz running the show. Superman was an instant hit, so first point of order under the new regime was to create more costumed superheroes.

But what to do next? Who should they ask to build on this success and create another hero for the ages? They turned to a certain young Jewish New York native. An ambitious alumnus of DeWitt Clinton High School with imagination and drive. But it wasn't Stan. It was Bob. Bob Kane.

At the end of 1938, *Detective Comics* editor Vin Sullivan spoke with Kane, then a freelance artist and contributor, asking if he would come up with something fresh that could light up the cover of *Detective Comics*. Kane obliged and knuckled down with part-time shoe salesman and aspiring writer Bill Finger to create a superhero they hoped would prove as successful as Superman. Despite both being Clinton alumni a couple of years older than Stan, Bob Kane and Bill Finger didn't know each other at school, but had struck up a friendship after meeting at a party. Over a single weekend towards the end of 1938, Finger fine-tuned Kane's preliminary drawings, creating a truly memorable character for the ages. With its dark undertones and ruthless methods, Detective Comics was given the hero it deserved.

After a single image teaser in *Action Comics #12,* the 'Bat-Man' made his debut in *Detective Comics #27*, cover dated May 1939. Unlike Superman, this costumed-crime fighter boasted no super powers and no alien origin; instead merely peak physical and mental prowess, superlative detective skills, a taste for the theatrical and a thirst for violent retribution. In his very first adventure, the Bat-Man actually seems to commit murder, punching a criminal so hard he tumbles through a railing and falls into a vat of acid. After such a grisly demise, the Bat-Man shrugs, saying it's 'a fitting ending for his kind'. Throughout subsequent decades, the character develops a strict moral code that forbids the killing of another human being. This first incarnation, however, had no such qualms. Tough justice for tough times. With Batman, Donenfeld and Liebowitz had landed another breakout hit. It would be another two years before the groundbreaking and magnificent Wonder Woman would join the all-star line-up, but the one-two punch of Superman and Batman had started the ball rolling on what would become a global phenomenon.

Meanwhile, at Timely Publications HQ in Hell's Kitchen, Martin Goodman had sniffed something was in the air. Pulp magazines were out and costumed heroes were in. After a persuasive meeting with a salesman for Funnies Inc, a New York company that created and packaged comics on demand for publishers, Goodman jumped into comic books with both feet. Timely Comics was born. The first title, published one day before the outbreak of the Second World War, was the very first issue of *Marvel Comics*.

Quick lesson. The reason a comic book's cover date is not the same as the date it goes on sale is simple. The cover date is more of an expiration date. It represents when newsstands should remove any unsold copies of that issue to make way for the next one. So, in this case, *Marvel Comics #1* was released on 31 August 1939, but was cover dated 'October', so vendors knew when to take it off the shelves for the next issue. The official name for this is 'pull date', but 'cover date' stuck. This tradition would continue for decades. Lesson ends.

Marvel Comics #1 featured cover art by sci-fi pulp artist Frank Paul and was jam-packed with fantastical heroes and villains, created by a roster of Funnies Inc's finest freelance writers, pencillers, inkers and letterers. There was righteous vigilante The Angel, hired to take down a gang of racketeers and gangsters, and the hooded cowboy The Masked Raider, a wronged man who dons a disguise to wreak frontier vengeance. Other stories include 'Jungle Terror', a mystery romp about buried treasure in the Amazon; and 'Ka-Zar the Great', a Tarzan rip-off left over from earlier pulp magazines. However, two characters stood out from the rest to become an instant hit with readers. More than this, they would mutate, evolve and endure in the Marvel Universe for decades: the Human Torch and Namor the Sub-Mariner.

Essentially a reworking of *Frankenstein* by creator Carl Burgos, the Human Torch was an android that ignited upon contact with oxygen, only to break free from his laboratory confinement and spread havoc wherever he went. The Sub-Mariner was created by Bill Everett as an undersea ruler who, for some reason, could fly. These elemental tales of fire and water proved hugely popular, sparking kids' imaginations and helped *Marvel Comics #1* flood the market: the first print run of 80,000 copies was followed by a reprint of an additional 800,000.

With his own comic book hit on his hands, Martin Goodman began assembling an in-house team. He first poached writer/artist Joe Simon from Funnies Inc. and installed him as Timely Comics' head writer and editorial director. Despite only being in his mid-twenties, Simon understood the comic publishing industry, thanks to his time as editor-in-chief at Fox Publications. Fox was also a player during this Golden Age, with notable titles including *Blue Beetle*, *Fantastic Comics* and *Mystery Men Comics*. In turn, Simon brought with him frequent Fox collaborator, Jacob Kurtzberg. This latest recruit to Timely is, without doubt, the second most important character in the story of Stan Lee and Marvel. An irascible young New Yorker who liked to chomp cigars while sketching furiously at his desk, Kurtzberg is better known by the name he chose for himself, Jack Kirby.

Goodman was also in the habit of changing names. After just one issue, he injected a little mystery into *Marvel Comics*, quite literally, by rebranding it *Marvel Mystery Comics*. At the same time, he put his new team to work creating more titles. The first Simon-Kirby collaboration, released in 1940, was *Red Raven Comics*, with its eponymous main character a human raised by birds who could fly using artificial wings. It was a misfire. So too was *Daring Mystery Comics* and *Mystic Comics*. Playing it safe, Goodman gave proven hits the Human Torch and the Sub-Mariner their own titles, while Simon and Kirby burned the midnight oil devising a new hero that reflected these troubled times.

Timely wasn't afraid to use real-life events in their stories. One Sub-Mariner story saw the grumpy merman take down a Nazi U-boat off the coast of New York. Inspired by the ever-growing threat from Europe and the need for a true patriot who exemplified his country's virtues, Simon sketched out another defining superhero of the Golden Age: Captain America.

With Simon and Kirby sharing writing and art, *Captain America Comics #1* went on sale 20 December 1940 (cover date March 1941). Like Superman, Captain America also fought for truth, justice and the American way, but was much more grounded in reality than the Man of Steel. For starters, Cap was not bullet proof and could not fly. The first issue told the story of how plucky weakling Steve Rogers was infused with a special potion concocted by Professor Reinstein. This Super Soldier Serum caused his physical and mental attributes to grow exponentially, becoming a one-man army primed to neutralise the threat of the Third Reich. It's thrilling stuff.

To say Cap captured the zeitgeist is a massive understatement. The cover art featured our star-spangled man with a plan of socking old Adolf Hitler right in the jaw. Cap was a huge hit, and despite the ever-cynical Goodman being concerned that Hitler would be assassinated before he saw a return on his investment, *Captain America Comics* remained a smash for the duration of the war, selling close to a million copies a month. Timely – and Martin Goodman – were in the game.

Superman, Batman and Captain America are all crowning achievements and high-water marks in this new Golden Age. Detective Comics Inc. and Timely Comics truly hit it out of the park. It was a perfect storm. After years of bleak uncertainty during the Great Depression, followed swiftly but assuredly by the looming spectre of large-scale conflict, the need for pure, unbridled escapism and patriotic fervour was immense. The US had received a welcome shot in the arm from the *übermenschen* created by Siegel and Shuster then Simon and Kirby. Even Kane and Finger's brawling Bat-Man was pure wish fulfilment, a nocturnal avenger striking out at the many injustices and crimes that threatened innocent, decent folk just trying to go about their day.

Although war had broken out across Europe, the US had yet to enter the fray. It wouldn't be until the Japanese bombing of Pearl Harbor in December 1941 that America's hand was forced. But in 1940 it was business as usual. That was also the year, just as Captain America made his comic book debut, that a young lad nervously strolled into the Timely offices to start a job as office junior. He was wet behind the ears and no one really paid him any attention. Stanley Martin Lieber would have to earn his place in the comic book industry. Would he be up to the challenge?

Chapter Four

War and Piecemeal

Stanley Lieber was never expected to set the world alight. Only 17, he was hired as office junior and general dogsbody. It seems he got the job not through merit, but nepotism. Not only was his cousin, Jean, married to Martin Goodman, but also his uncle, Robbie Solomon, worked there as circulation manager. Stan didn't really know his cousin's husband who ran the show, but we do know that Martin Goodman liked to keep things in the family.[1] Stan may have not even interviewed for the role. Stan insisted that he was,[2] but several accounts suggest that Uncle Robbie simply brought his young relative into the Timely offices and said to Joe Simon, 'This is my nephew, can you find something for him to do?'[3] It has also been reported that Martin Goodman had nothing to do with Stan's hiring, and was surprised to see the young man in the office at all.[4] Regardless of how Stan got the job, he was now gainfully employed, to the princely sum of eight dollars a week.

Although he had joined just before the release of *Captain America Comics #1*, its runaway success made Joe Simon and Jack Kirby hot property, both to Timely and in the wider comic book industry. They were only a few years older, but the pair were much more mature and intense figures than Stan, who kept a bright and breezy air at all times. With their cramped office constantly shrouded in cigar smoke, Simon offered out work assignments and continued to contribute to Goodman's ongoing pulp titles, whereas Kirby would puff away at his desk, relentlessly generating more daring adventures for Cap behind enemy lines. While Simon and Kirby created modern art, Stan did whatever he was told: refill inkwells, sweep floors, fetch sandwiches, and any other menial tasks that sprang to mind. Most significantly, however, he had unprecedented access to the two most sought-after creative forces in the industry. 'I admired their talents and their professionalism,' Stan later recalled, 'so it was like working for two idols.' Stanley watched. He watched and he learned.

Back then, there were no royalty or residual payments for comic book artists and writers. They got paid per page. This was standard at the time and Timely was no different. The more pages you churned out, the more cash hit your bank balance. Not that there was ever much cash flying around for the creatives. Simon and Kirby's output was essentially keeping Timely afloat, and soon they were overworked, straining under constant pressure to deliver, week in week out. It wasn't long before Stan was given more specific proofreading tasks, where he applied what editorial experience he had gleaned during high school as well as he could.

Stan was way down the pecking order, but he was not a wallflower. When not running errands, he would play *Yankee Doodle Dandy* on his ocarina. In case you're unfamiliar, this is a small and incredibly irritating instrument you blow into like you're abusing a crustacean. Whether Stan brought this in to lighten the mood or remind everyone he was actually there, we'll never know. He brimmed with confidence and charisma that bordered on arrogance. Simon remembered how this cocky Lieber boy asked for a promotion only a week into the job. 'I thought he was a pesky but nice kid. I used to take him out all over. I didn't guess what he would become. Who could?'[5] Only two months after he started his job, fate threw him a bone he could chew on.

As one of his many money-saving exercises, it was common for Martin Goodman's comics to include short stories as fillers. By creating these extra pages, Timely could send out subscriptions in the cheaper, second-class post. These short stories were entirely text based and ran across two pages. They were good for business but hardly a draw for readers. One day, a typically overstretched Joe Simon asked Stanley to write one of these two-page stories for Captain America. This may well have been just to stop him from tooting on that damn ocarina, but unsurprisingly, Stan jumped at the chance. He would be writing his first ever superhero adventure!

Twenty-six paragraphs later, Stanley turned in 'Captain America Foils the Traitor's Revenge', to be published in *Captain America Comics #3* (cover date May 1941). To preserve his actual name for when he inevitably wrote the Great American Novel, he submitted his comic book debut under a simple pen name. And just like that, the world was introduced to Stan Lee.

As stories go, Stan's was not exactly a game changer. Bolstered by a typically dynamic header image from Team Simon/Kirby, it's a simple tale about how Captain America, aided by his youthful sidekick Bucky (here described as the 'camp mascot'[6]), thwarted a threefold tent-based assassination attempt on a colonel while he slept. The attack on his life is led by a dishonourably discharged and decidedly disgruntled knife-wielding rotter named Lou Haines. Fortunately Cap and Bucky get wind of this dastardly plan and leap into action. The first two assassins are swiftly dispatched by Cap swinging Bucky straight into them, a move best described as unnecessarily ostentatious and highly inefficient. The 'Red White and Blue Knight' (that nickname would never stick) then disarms Haines inside the tent of Colonel Stevens with a hurl of his mighty shield. After a brief tussle, Haines is finally floored by a super-soldier sock to the jaw 'with enough force to fell an ox'. In the morning, back in their military uniforms, Stevens furiously reprimands Private Rogers for failing to intervene in the event. Oh, Colonel Stevens, if only you knew!

It's an undeniably cheesy story, but told with confidence and expressive melodramatic language that would become Stan's stock in trade. He also threw in a bit of humour, specifically the banter between Cap and Bucky and the irony-soaked climax. The entire story is commendably energetic and simple. After all, he was only 17. Stan knew no one would even read it[7], but this did not deter him from giving it all he had. Besides, he was now a professionally published author.

After 'Traitor's Revenge', Stan was let loose on his first proper comic book strip. Stan's feature story debut, 'Headline Hunter, Foreign Correspondent', appeared in *Captain America Comics #5* (cover date August 1941), and lasted across eight issues. Despite the comic in which it appeared, 'Headline Hunter' is not some Spandex-clad superhero adventure, but a wartime mystery wrapped up in espionage and subterfuge. It wasn't common practice in comic books at the time to start a story with a writing credit, but this title page included the caption 'story by Stan Lee'. This was a bold move that showed Stanley's canny awareness of self-promotion, even at a young age. There is no mention of who drew this story, but there is no chance of missing who wrote it.

'Headline Hunter' is a simple love letter to investigative journalism. 'Wherever we find news, excitement, mystery and adventure,' the story begins, 'there, too, we find the newspaper reporter!' The hero is Jerry Hunter, a daring American war correspondent sent on an assignment in foggy old London town to track down missing food contracts between the US and 'England', and expose a traitor in the process. No doubt Hunter was inspired by his beloved *Chicago Tribune* war correspondent Floyd Gibbons. Like Gibbons, Hunter is prepared to do what's necessary to get the scoop, even if that means being strapped to a bomb destined for No 10 Downing Street. Naturally, Stan has fun with the dialogue, hamming up ze German accents, vividly describing the 'death-dealing English anti-aircraft guns' while depicting the Nazi villain as a monster, happy to slaughter his men for making an easy mistake. Hunter escapes his bomb-based binds, vanquishes the traitor aboard a plane, retrieves the food contracts and returns to his London HQ for a cup of tea. Splendid.

It's another fast-paced tale that shows off Stan's grasp for simple, immediate storytelling. While still tapping into the war effort to drive sales, 'Headline Hunter' is interestingly much more low-key than the rest of the comic. There are no superhero powers on display here, but a conventional boys' own adventure, the kind that would inspire James Bond or Indiana Jones. Rather than copying what was popular in the comic books at the time, Stan was clearly more directly inspired by the kind of stories he grew up reading.

Stanley rapidly racked up more writing experience for Timely, but it was some time before he settled on Stan Lee as his professional pen name. He tried out a few others, such as S. T. Anley, Stan Martin and Neel Nats (see what he did there?), but ultimately, Stan Lee was the one that stuck.

Quickly finding his feet, he created more new characters. Jack Frost *(U.S.A. Comics #1*, cover date August 1941) was a weird reimagining of the traditional personification of winter weather. Stan turned him into a misunderstood lone crusader who fights crime and injustice while sporting a natty pair of blue shorts. Then there was Destroyer, (*Mystic Comics #6*, cover date October 1941), the tale of American newspaperman (again) Kevin Marlow. While undercover in Germany, Marlow is caught by the Nazis and forced to take a serum that enhances his natural strength and abilities. He then uses his new powers to become Destroyer and thwart the evil machinations of Hitler's Gestapo. Despite essentially being a Captain America rip-off, Destroyer proved quite popular; who doesn't love a bit of Nazi bashing? Stan was now making waves at Timely, albeit in a workmanlike fashion. What really boosted his career, however, was a seismic moment in the company. At the end of 1941, Martin Goodman fired Joe Simon and Jack Kirby.

Here's how it went down. At the time, the comic industry was on fire. There were over 100 titles on the stands. Millions were being bought, sold, read and made. Business was booming. Other publishing houses came out fighting. Quality Comics, Lev Gleason Publications, Fawcett Publications and Dell Publishing all waded in as healthy competition to DC and Timely. Naturally, talented writers and artists were highly sought after and fiercely protected. All that was expected in return was loyalty. Simon and Kirby were now seen as THE comic book creative force to be reckoned with. They were ripe for poaching, were it not for the vibranium-strong shield of security offered by Martin Goodman.

Simon and Kirby had quietly dabbled in freelancing here and there, but nothing that would rock the boat. Then one day, Timely's accountant Maurice Coyne informed Simon that Goodman had been short-changing them on royalties. Simon was told that his boss had allegedly been using deserved profits made from *Captain America* to cover Timely's overheads. Suitably miffed, Simon and Kirby's loyalty started to wane. Before long, they were reeled in by DC Comics' co-owner Jack Liebowitz, who offered them $500 a month for twenty-five pages of comics, plus extra for any additional development work. It was a very generous offer. Joe Simon and Jack Kirby accepted. They rented a hotel room around the corner from Timely and, after hours, they set to work for the enemy. It wasn't long before they were vanishing to their secret DC office during lunch hours.

One lunch break, young Stan pestered them to tag along and see what they were up to. Simon agreed on the condition that Stan swore he would tell no one. Days later, Martin got wind of the situation and confronted Simon and Kirby about what he saw as a major betrayal. His vengeance was swift and brutal. As soon as they finished work on *Captain America Comics #10* (cover date January 1942), they were marched out the door. Having lost both his editor and art director in one fell swoop, Goodman immediately installed Stanley as interim editor-in-chief of Timely's entire comic book line. He wasn't yet 20 years old.

Now. Here is where it gets messy. And we have to ask ourselves, did Stan rat out his mentors to further his own career?

Because all parties directly involved are no longer with us, the absolute truth is lost. What remains are tit-for-tat remarks and idle speculation. In his later memoirs, Joe Simon remained stoic and diplomatic, doubting that it was young Stanley who informed Goodman: 'It had to be an open secret that we had signed a deal with DC, because the guys at DC knew all about it, and it was all around the industry all the time.'[8] For Simon, it could have been any disgruntled or jealous employee wanting to bring down the golden boys of Timely. It's certainly plausible that their increasingly slapdash approach to moonlighting – vanishing at lunch no less – could have been taken as pure arrogance. Jack Kirby, on the other hand, was convinced Stan had got them fired, swearing to Simon at the time that 'if I ever see that little son of a bitch, I'm going to kill him.'[9] Some say Kirby believed until the day he died that Stan had betrayed them. Given that Stan and Jack would later reunite and collaborate to change the comic book landscape forever, this raises more questions about their working relationship than it answers. But that, True Believer, is for a later chapter.

Stan spent the rest of his own life denying that he ratted out Simon and Kirby. In one autobiographical account, Stan simply wrote that the pair 'unexpectedly left' Timely and the 'truth is, I never knew why they left'.[10] This is a wilfully naïve interpretation of what transpired. Of course Stan would have known they were fired, especially if their moonlighting for DC was the open secret Simon later claimed it to be. Stan more explicitly addressed this accusation of betrayal when he later wrote that 'they quit Timely a few months after I started working there. And no, it wasn't because of me!'[11]

Stan choosing to misremember Simon and Kirby being fired as *quitting* in this instance feels disingenuous. That throwaway last remark, no doubt with humorous intent, also feels like Stan now protesting his innocence to a charge he previously claimed to know nothing about. Bottom line, we'll never know what truly happened. Stan could indeed have ousted the power players at Timely to advance his career. He was perfectly positioned to take the role, and had already proven he was adept at self-promotion. Considering also that Goodman had a soft spot for keeping his business in the family, it's not hard to build a pretty strong case supporting Kirby's furious claim.

What is undeniable is that Martin Goodman had indeed been dishonest with Kirby and Simon over royalty pay, and in turn they did disrespect their boss by working directly for the competition. Goodwill had been destroyed on both sides, lines had been drawn and only bad blood remained.

It was, without a doubt, turning into a toxic working environment and it was probably only a matter of time before it all imploded.

With Joe Simon and Jack Kirby over at DC, Timely rattled on, now with the incredibly inexperienced but super-confident Stan Lee taking the creative reins as editor. His appointment was only ever intended to be a temporary one until Goodman found a suitable replacement, but Stan applied what he had learned from his erstwhile mentors and threw himself into his role feet first, grabbing everything with both hands along the way.

At first, Martin micromanaged Stan, reviewing practically every editorial decision his young relative made. More creatives were hired and installed in a cramped office that became nicknamed the 'bullpen', a popular baseball term that refers to the area where a team warms up together; it was also used in wartime to describe a holding pen for prisoners. Stan began outsourcing stories to freelancers, sometimes dictating plot devices over the phone. He collaborated with artists Al Avison and Syd Shores on *Captain America Comics,* while other notable bullpen artists included George Klein, Ed Winiarski and Dave Gantz. Much of the brilliant (and highly collectible) Timely Comics' cover art came courtesy of Alex Schomburg, who had made his name airbrushing erotic covers for pulp fiction.

With the bullpen ticking over nicely, Martin Goodman continued to jump on any trends that would edge Timely out from the competition. Aside from superheroes, he dabbled in westerns, horror, romance and humorous comic books. Stan was happy to try his hand at anything, reflecting later that, 'I was probably the ultimate, quintessential hack.'[12] He proved to be a valuable asset because he could write fast and he thrived on being thrown in at the deep end. Whether or not he ousted Simon and Kirby, Stan proved he was up to the challenge. He had the talent and the stomach for the job and quickly made the role his own.

Round about the same time things blew up with Simon and Kirby, the Japanese bombed Pearl Harbor. The inevitable escalation did wonders for the sales of *Captain America Comics* but, like many young Americans, Stan knew it was time to pause the comic book world and join the fight. On 9 November 1942, he handed over editor duties to new hire, Vince Fago, a former animator for Max Fleischer Studios who had worked on classic *Superman* and *Popeye* cartoons. Fago had moved back east to New York after the attack on Pearl Harbor, because he objected to Fleischer Studios deciding to produce war propaganda. For reasons known only to himself, Fago was not drafted to fight and instead sought freelance work in comics. Stan loved Fago's artwork and also his way of working. He had a lot of creative experience and Stan saw him as a safe pair of hands. He was also a fellow Clinton alumnus. With his replacement sorted, 19-year-old Stan enlisted in the US military.

His preliminary aptitude test results placed him more fit for technical operations than front-line duties and the US Army assigned him to the Signal Corps (USASC). Established in 1860, the Signal Corps first played a significant role in the American Civil War, managing lines of communication and information. It then supplied telephone and telegraph wiring and established telephony in combat situations. In 1908, aviation pioneers Orville and Wilbur Wright made their landmark test flights based on Signal Corps' specifications. During the First World War, the Corps' area of expertise – radio, telephone and telegraph – proved invaluable to the war effort. During the Second World War, the Signal Corps was once again a vital constituent of the US's colossal military juggernaut. Serving both the Army ground forces and the Army air forces, the Signal Corps operated the newly coined RADAR detection system, pioneering the first ever FM backpack radio.

Stan was sent to Fort Monmouth, New Jersey, for basic training, about five miles away from the Atlantic coast. At its peak during the Second World War, the training centre sprawled across nearly seven square kilometres, with up to 20,000 enlisted personnel. It was among this hive of military activity that Stan got his first taste of Army life. Not in the thundering death zones of the Pacific, but on the freezing Atlantic shoreline. Truth is, Stan felt conflicted about his assigned post. While he was glad not to be directly in harm's way, he knew that many brave young Americans, just like him, were risking it all on the front line in some far away land. Here was Stan, only a few miles from where he lived as a civilian, safe and sound on American soil. If things got tough, he could always pop home! He needed reassurance, therefore, that he was still playing a valued role in the theatre of conflict.

Stan's basic training involved sentry duty, keeping the night watch just in case any Nazi U-boats decided to dock in New Jersey, presumably for the wonderful food. Of course, none materialised and Stan experienced what he himself felt was simply a toughening-up exercise, standing out in the freezing night air without even so much as a comfy bed or cup of hot cocoa. 'When the next victim finally showed up to relieve me,' he later recalled, 'I raced back to the barracks so fast that I almost caused a sonic boom.' Mere months later, Stan would be transferred from Fort Monmouth and reassigned to an operation that he never knew existed; working on highly confidential operations alongside fellow recruits who would, in time, become as famous as he. Seriously, the calibre of talent in one room was astonishing.

Chapter Five

Back to the Front

As soon as Stan's superior officers got wind that he was a writer and an all-round creative type, they put him to work in the Signal Corps' Training Film Division, based in Queens. Before he knew it, Stan was back in New York. A mere skip over the Hudson River, hop across Manhattan and a final jump over the East River to a unit based in Astoria, on 35th Avenue and 25th Street.

Originally a settlement known as Hallett's Cove, during the early part of the nineteenth century the region was renamed after John Jacob Astor, a German immigrant who made a fortune as a fur trader, which he then ploughed into property. Astor was America's first ever multi-millionaire, and Astoria would be his lasting legacy. Aside from being the home of the legendary Steinway piano manufacturers, Astoria was also a major hub for filmmaking outside of Hollywood. Paramount had a base there, Eastern Studios, Inc., which boasted the largest sound stage on the East Coast. As Paramount's films were increasingly made in Hollywood, production was eventually phased out and in 1942, the same year Stan was transferred, Eastern Studios was converted by the military into the USASC Army Pictorial Service. This huge building was transformed into a base of operations for all film and photography production, exclusively designed to support the war effort. The main purpose of the facility was to make training films, posters and other written material for American troops of all shapes and sizes. While coming to terms with the fact he wouldn't be on the front line, there's no doubt this post played to Stan's strengths as a storyteller. He soon nestled in and, under the commanding eye of operations chief Colonel Melvin E. Gillette, busied himself on anything that required a flair for the written word in communicating exactly what every good GI needs to know. The work itself was perfunctory but essential. Regardless of intelligence and aptitude level, it was easier and more efficient to train soldiers through a punchy film than a dry, typed onboarding manual.

For some reason, Stan had been misclassified as a playwright – an error he did not discover until three months after leaving the Army at the end of the war – and soon found himself alongside recruits with similar creative backgrounds. 'There were only eight other men in the US Army with that particular military occupational speciality (MOS) classification beside me,' he said.[1] Chances are, you'll have heard of one or two.

The first honourable mention alongside Stan in the Signal Corps is Frank Capra who, by the time the US joined the war, was already a multi-Oscar-winning director. A nationalised Sicilian, Capra's family emigrated to the West Coast of the US in 1903 when he was just five years old. Soon after graduating from college, Capra became a second lieutenant in the Army and during the First World War he taught mathematics to artillery officers in San Francisco. After the war, Capra moved into filmmaking, first working on silent comedies. Like the rest of the world, he was blown away by Al Jolson's *The Jazz Singer*. Working steadily to hone his craft, he struck gold as co-producer and director of 1934's romantic screwball comedy *It Happened One Night.* Starring Clark Gable and Claudette Colbert, it is the first of only three films to land all five of the major Academy Awards.[2] Capra rode its wave of success with a series of films exploring the American Dream, now known as 'fantasies of goodwill'. *Mr. Deeds Goes to Town* (1936) landed Capra his second Best Director Oscar, then he nabbed a third for *You Can't Take It with You* (1938). Capra's hot streak continued with directing nominations for *Mr. Smith Goes to Washington* (1939) and then, after the war, he made arguably his most famous film, everyone's Christmas favourite, *It's a Wonderful Life* (1946).

Prior to this feel-good masterpiece, Capra was given a special assignment by the Signal Corps to make a series of seven documentaries called *Why We Fight.* These films were specifically designed to justify American military involvement in the war. This landmark work is now considered of huge cultural significance and has been preserved for posterity in the US National Film Registry, but all seven exist in the public domain so you can hunt them down and watch them online right now, if you wish.

Another huge figure in the Signal Corps at that time was the writer William Saroyan. Born in Fresno, California, to Armenian immigrant parents, Saroyan began a writing career at an early age, mining the immigrant life of Armenians in America for inspiration. Short stories, memoirs, essays and plays flowed from his pen, and he won a Pulitzer Prize in 1939 for his play *The Time of Your Life,* about the colourful characters who frequent a dive bar in San Francisco. Like Capra, Saroyan also received Hollywood accolades, winning an Academy Award in 1944 for an adaptation of his own screenplay, *The Human Comedy.*

Also assigned to the Army Pictorial Service in Astoria were Ivan Goff and Ben Roberts, screenwriters who would make their mark in Hollywood by collaborating on several screenplays. Goff was an Australian who left the tedium of his hometown of Perth to travel around the globe before settling in Los Angeles, taking work as a journalist. In 1937, he landed a staff writer contract with Warner Bros, which in turn led him to joining the Signal Corps to work on Army propaganda. It was in the studios in Astoria where he first met Ben Roberts, a graduate of New York University making a living writing Broadway musicals. After the war, Goff and Roberts wrote the screenplay for the iconic 1949 crime noir *White Heat*, frequently cited as one of the greatest gangster films ever made. Goff and Roberts collaborated on several more Hollywood productions, including receiving writing credits on *Man of a Thousand Faces* (directed by Joseph Pevney, 1957), a muddled biopic of pioneering horror actor Lon Chaney. The duo then turned more to television, and in 1976 created the hugely successful high-kicking, hair-flicking, crime-fighting romp *Charlie's Angels*.

Just to be in the company of these incredibly talented individuals would be enough for a man like Stan. But it doesn't end there. Also serving alongside him were Charles Addams and Theodor Geisel. The first name probably rings a bell on account of the celebrated and ghoulish family that bore his name. Addams was originally a cartoonist with a taste for the macabre. Growing up in Westfield, New Jersey, he was inspired by tales of family scandals that were hidden behind closed Victorian gothic doors. After attending New York's Grand Central School of Design, he enjoyed a short stint touching up crime scene photographs for pulp magazine *True Detective*. He ultimately achieved recognition for his amusing and warped cartoons in *The New Yorker* magazine. Among the many one-panel cartoons was a household of dark but close-knit characters created as a satire on American domestic life. Gomez, Morticia, Wednesday, Pugsley, Fester, Lurch, Thing and Cousin Itt became immortalised on television when, in 1964, ABC adapted these cartoons into the sitcom *The Addams Family*. With its memorable harpsichord and finger-snap theme tune, and devilishly black humour, the show was a hit. Despite only running for two seasons decades ago, Addams' characters are household names to American audiences. They have been resurrected several times on both the small and big screen, be it in traditional animation, CGI and live-action form, as well as on stage, record and in print. Charles Addams' gothic creations, who carry his legacy in more than just name, will never die.

Theodor 'Ted' Geisel, however, may not be a name that immediately rings any bells. That's because, like Stanley Lieber, he changed his name for professional purposes. And that name you *will* have heard of.

Massachusetts-born Geisel graduated from Dartmouth College in 1925 before aiming to earn a PhD in English literature at Lincoln College, Oxford. This plan was derailed when he met fellow American student Helen Palmer, who became his wife as well as a respected author in her own right. It was Palmer who noticed Geisel's flair for humorous wordplay and drawing, and she persuaded him not to become an English teacher, but to turn these gifts into a career. Dropping out of Oxford and now back in the US, Geisel accepted various writing and illustration jobs, as well as several opportunities in advertising. Like Stan, the name Geisel assigned to his cartoons was a bid to save his real name for when he wrote the Great American Novel. [3] His first illustrations were nationally published in 1927, and he took his middle name for a byline. It simply read 'Seuss'.

Geisel's first children's book, *And to Think I Saw It on Mulberry Street*, was published in 1937, after being rejected by twenty-seven publishers. When the war began, Geisel was assigned to drawing military posters and working on propaganda films. In 1945, he wrote the script for *Your Job in Germany*, directed by Frank Capra. Neither was credited, and it was remade later that year by Warner Bros into the short documentary film *Hitler Lives?*, which won an Academy Award for Best Documentary Short Subject.[4] After the war, Geisel returned to children's books. By this time, he had given his alter ego an honourable doctorate (maybe a nod to that English PhD he abandoned) and as Dr. Seuss, he wrote some of the most celebrated works of children's literature of all time. *Horton Hears a Who!* (1954); *The Cat in the Hat*; *How the Grinch Stole Christmas!* (both 1957); and *Green Eggs and Ham* (1960) cemented his reputation as a beloved author, world famous for his wonderful wordplay, simple yet distinctive illustrations and surreal, anarchic storylines. You just have to glance at a Dr. Seuss character to instantly know who drew it. That was his gift. Geisel died in 1991, but to this day his legacy endures.

When recalling his wartime experiences, Stan was happy to name drop, but we'll never know how much time he actually spent with these men. For instance, it's highly unlikely that Stan and Frank Capra hung out together. Capra was twice his age, a decorated First World War veteran and an award-winning Hollywood filmmaker. Stan was just another grunt, barely out of his teens, who had lucked into an editor position at a company that churned out kids' comics at a dime a pop. More than this, Capra had been given his filming assignments directly from the US Government, bypassing traditional military channels. Capra had his own mission, his own agenda and was probably rarely even in the Astoria studios. Similarly, Stan has described how he worked 'shoulder to shoulder' with William Saroyan, but research shows that Saroyan was also rarely in the Signal Corps offices. He chose instead to work out of a hotel room elsewhere in New York.[5]

It is more likely to assume that Stan had greater interactions with Addams and Geisel, as they worked in similar professions, but even then, we will never know. The reality of daily life in the Signal Corps is probably rather humdrum; each in their respective silos, churning out posters, instructions, scripts and guidelines in whatever format the US Government deemed the most appropriate to convince GI Joe to put his life on the line. Still, it's fun to imagine this raft of profoundly talented men, all of whom made a colossal impact on American popular culture, sitting around together over coffee or whisky, chewing the fat and sparking ideas off each other from beneath a fug of tobacco smoke.

So, what exactly did Stan do in the Signal Corps? He didn't actually write any plays, but he did type up film scripts, as well as write poster headlines and instruction manuals with thrilling titles such as *The Nomenclature and Operation of a M-10 Rifle Under Battle Condition* or *The G.I. Method of Organizing a Footlocker*. Stan played to his strengths. He took whatever complex instruction he was given and stripped it down to something a kid would understand, and something any recruit could grasp in a thrice.

Being a fast writer also helped. His role at Timely meant he had experience of bashing out stories, allegedly to the extent that his commanding officers told him to slow down as he made the others look bad.[6] Communicating training manuals was no light work, and in a short time it was acknowledged that a man of Stan's skills would be required across the country. Soon he was enjoying temporary station in places such as Fort Benjamin Harrison in Indiana. During his time there, Stan created a comic book character called Fiscal Freddie to help train officers in the Army Finance Department. Seems the payroll boys needed more than the usual level of morale boosting, so Stan went as far as to pen an inspiring marching song for them. He was also ordered to design an informative poster warning American soldiers of the dangers of catching syphilis while on overseas dalliances. Despite many prophylactic stations being set up where men could go for treatment, not many were actually going. So, Stan created something punchy to remind soldiers to visit these stations for help downstairs. Keeping it simple, the end result is a master class in economy of words: a smiling soldier marching out of one such station with a green light above the door, proudly declaring 'VD? Not Me!' The design was a hit with Stan's senior officers and the poster was reproduced and copies shipped overseas in their thousands.

Back in the real world, the comics trade was booming. Timely was shifting millions of comics each month and relocated to a brand-new HQ on the fourteenth floor of the Empire State Building. Martin Goodman's business was making enough money to plug the holes left by enlisted staff with new recruits, but also keep paying those still available on a freelance basis. Having not left American shores, Stan was firmly in the latter camp and continued working for Timely when Signal Corps' projects were light. For a dollar a page, Stan posted his scripts to Goodman and Fago, who, in turn, would send new assignments to him. Stan was never one to miss a deadline, even though on one occasion this conscientious attitude got him in hot water. He was awaiting news of his next job from Timely but the letter did not arrive until a Saturday. Even though he could see the damn thing in his cubby hole, weekend rules dictated that the mailroom was locked. Not to be deterred, Stan broke into his mailbox with a screwdriver and extracted the letter. After all, it was addressed to him, right? It was his property, right? Well, yes. But in the eyes of one particular base captain who didn't much care for Stan, breaking into your own mailbox was an offence worth pursuing. Our rebellious hero soon found himself facing charges of mail tampering and was even threatened with a spell in Leavenworth, a military correctional facility in Kansas. Things looked bleak for Stan, had it not been for the intervention of a colonel for whom he had worked in the Finance

Department. Not wanting to lose his one and only writer, the man who had boosted morale with his little ditty and Fiscal Freddie, the colonel stopped the process and saved young Stan from prison.

Aside from this incident, Stan enjoyed one of the least stressful wartime experiences a young man can have. Nevertheless, he continued to feel somewhat ashamed of his status as a desk jockey. This was particularly apparent when he was tasked with giving orientation lectures to soldiers returning from tours of duty. 'I felt like the world's biggest phony,' he said. 'But in an effort to seem credible to those great, battle-scarred guys, I wore dirty fatigues … and even tried to spit a lot, as if I was chewing tobacco, in a desperate attempt to look as rugged as I could.'[7]

His freelance work, combined with his own military salary, gave him the opportunity to purchase his first car. This was a big deal for him, even if it was a battered, third-hand '36 Plymouth, bought for the princely sum of twenty dollars. Stan soon upgraded to a black Buick convertible which he declared 'a symphony on four wheels'.

When the war finally came to an end, Stan literally hurtled back into civilian life as fast as his jet engine would take him. Receiving an honourable discharge on 29 September 1945, he was mustered out of the Army in Indianapolis. He skipped his own orientation class – his wartime life was not all that different from his civilian days – and drove himself back to New York to reclaim his old job at Timely.

He rented an apartment in the heart of the city's Upper West Side, at the Almanac Hotel on 160 West 71st Street. The Almanac was the first hotel in America to employ female bellhops, and would later be used by the CIA during the Cold War to house defecting German scientists. The huge nineteen-storey building still stands today, although now it's converted into private rental apartments known as South Pierre. Today a studio apartment in this building will set you back an eye-watering $2,500 a month, but after the war, Stan was able to rent a two-bedroom pad on a relatively modest salary. The war was over. He had served his time. Now to get back into the swing of things. How hard could it be?

Vince Fago happily stepped down to become a full-time freelancer, and Stan slipped back behind his editor's desk. But the Timely he returned to was very different from the one he left. Fago's experience was not superhero related and, as interim editor, he had steered the company more in the direction of humorous comics. While boys and young men still wanted their morale boosted by Captain America, many also just wanted a giggle. Always ready to cash in, Martin Goodman ensured Timely was now producing publications that spoke to a brand-new audience.

Stan quickly adjusted his scope to focus on writing teen humour and created stories involving young female protagonists, such as *Nellie the Nurse*. For someone used to churning out material, it wasn't so hard a transition to make. He was back doing what he loved. Despite the changing tide, Stan still tried to fly the superhero flag, uniting the A-list players of Captain America, Human Torch and Sub-Mariner in a single comic with *All Winners Comics #19* (cover date Fall 1946). It wasn't a hit. Public interest in costumed-crime fighters with fantastical powers, it seemed, was on the wane.

In 1947, *Writer's Digest* asked Stan to appear on the cover and feature in an interview about the comic book industry, plus divulge any advice he had for wannabe writers. This was a huge boost to his ego; his first-ever piece of national exposure. He may have been enthusing about the cultural significance of comic books more than he truly believed at the time, but he was happy to play the game. His profile was raised, there was cash in his pocket and there was still time to write that Great American Novel!

The end of the Second World War saw restrictions lifted on paper, which allowed the comic industry to swell and blossom even more. Basking in the post-war glow of peacetime prosperity, New York was Stan's playground and he made the most of being a tall, handsome, single gent about town. New York weather isn't much suited for a convertible, so Stan traded in his beloved Buick for a gleaming white Sedan, the first brand-new car he ever owned, which he used mainly as a means to get girls. By his own admission, Stan would enjoy walking to most places around the city – partly to stay in shape – even to and from work, despite the new Timely offices being forty blocks from the Almanac. On several occasions, he would rent a horse from stables on Central Park West and ostentatiously trot through the park before dismounting to resume his morning perambulation to work. Stan saw Central Park as his 'social arena', often taking dates on a rowing boat across the lake. He also enjoyed sitting with his date on the top deck of a city bus. He relished playing the field for a while but that all changed in 1947, when a specific woman rocked Stan's world. Perhaps most surprising of all for the walking epitome of the American Dream, the woman who floored Stan was a Brit.

Stan met the love of his life completely by chance. His cousin had arranged for him to go on a blind date with a model, but it wasn't the woman he had been set up with that stole Stan's heart. Instructed to meet his date at the modelling agency, Stan knocked on the office door and a different girl answered. A successful hat model and aspiring actress from Newcastle upon Tyne called Joan Clayton Boocock. Stan was infatuated immediately, convinced he had been drawing her face since he was a child. Joan had been a war bride to an American serviceman, but realised she had made a terrible mistake. When she and Stan met, she was in the process of getting a divorce and they soon became a couple. Shortly after, Joan sought a speedy divorce in Reno, where only a six-week wait is customary, provided she moved there for the required period. Back in New York, Stan grew nervous because, although they had been stepping out together, there had been other interested parties circling this beautiful woman – presumably all waiting out the divorce.

When Stan accidently received a letter from Joan addressed 'Dear Jack', he feared this one may well slip through his fingers unless he took decisive action. In a ridiculously romantic gesture, he flew straight to Reno. Twenty-eight hours later (Stan didn't fly direct), he made the biggest sales pitch of his young life. Armed with his gift of the gab and bolstered by his genuine feelings, Stan convinced Joan he loved her with all his heart. Despite having been approached by a wealthy, butch alpha male who worked in the oil business – the aforementioned 'Jack' – Stan's plan worked. Not wanting to waste any more time, straight after the judge in Reno granted the divorce, he rushed Joan into the room next door. Officiated by the exact same judge, on 5 December 1947, Stan married Joan. Told you he worked fast.

Shortly after their marriage, Stan's mother Celia passed away, aged just 54. Celia Lieber's death is clearly recorded to be 16 December 1947,[8] mere days after the record of Stan and Joan's marriage in Reno. In his own writing, however, Stan described how he and Joan lived for a couple of years as newlyweds *before* his mother passed away.[9] According to dates recorded on public documents, this simply does not add up. It is not clear how Celia died, but given how close they were, perhaps her early death proved too difficult for Stan to deal with and he preferred to omit details of the tragic event from his story. It's possible his mother's death didn't fit with the narrative he wanted to tell, but that feels like a disservice to a man who is frank and open about so much in his life.

So why the two-year time jump? An oversight? We'll never know. Still, the passing of his doting mother would have, without question, taken the shine out of Stan meeting the love of his life – and she really was. Stan and Joan stayed married until her death on 6 July 2017, aged 95. And until the day he died the following year, Stan always said Joan was the best birthday and Christmas present he ever received.

After the excitement of Reno, the couple moved into a small Manhattan apartment on 96th Street, between Lexington Avenue and Fifth Avenue. Taking up residence right by his beloved Central Park, Stan was ready to grab the next exciting chapter in his life with both hands. The 1940s were drawing to a close and, with his new wife by his side, he was excited to see what the next decade would bring. What Stan couldn't have known, however, was that the 1950s would almost cause him to quit comic books for good.

Chapter Six

The Rot Sets In

As the 1940s rolled into the 1950s, America was still adjusting after the devastation and upheaval of the Second World War. Those reunited after years apart had been afforded some perspective as to how fleeting life can be and promptly rushed to build families. Those born from 1946 onwards[1] became known as the baby boomers, a generation that would grow to represent wealth, privilege and opportunity. This was especially so in the US, thanks to post-war subsidies in housing and education. Following the war, the US emerged as a global influence in politics, technology, military might and mainstream culture. While some parts of society were still left out in the cold, especially the elderly and African Americans, the country saw unprecedented economic growth and the creation of millions of office and factory jobs. The middle classes were on the rise and gaining momentum. Suburbia grew exponentially, with sprawling middle-class homes across rural America, white picket fences and well-kept lawns. Everyone had a role to play as part of the perfect society and keeping up with the Joneses was a daily pastime.

Despite all this prosperity, things were far from settled. As white-collar jobs increased in number during the 1950s, greater discrimination spread through the southern states, forcing the early civil rights movement to take its first steps towards real change. It was a bloody battle and such a long walk ahead. On the home front, marriage and domesticity were seen as aspirational lifestyle choices for women, many being pushed or conditioned into finding contentment with roles as homemakers.

On a global scale, there were now only two superpowers: the Soviet Union and the US. After the war, the Soviet regime aggressively asserted control over neighbouring states while, across the Atlantic, the US moved away from its traditional isolationist stance to become more involved in world affairs. Both had something to prove. Each had very different social and political ideologies. Tensions between the two began to simmer. Distinct sides formed between East and West. The Cold War had begun, so called because there were never any direct military campaigns between the two superpowers. Instead, each indirectly reinforced their status as global leaders by supporting major regional conflicts around the world. Essentially, it was a massive competition of endless posturing and swagger over who had the biggest warheads. The space race was a direct product of the Cold War. What started as a nuclear arms race spilled over into a contest of macho technological grandstanding; dreams of interstellar domination built on the backs of cowed German rocket scientists. The Cold War infected American culture with fear, mistrust and paranoia. Many saw that the mighty Right of western capitalism, exemplified by the American Dream, was under attack from socialism, a sinister plot to undermine core American values. The red menace was foreign, treacherous and distinctly *other*. Suspicion and contempt were poured over anything deemed improper, morally ambiguous or potentially capable of corrupting the nation's youth on their path to becoming righteous American citizens. Behind those white picket fences, something wasn't quite right. And that something had to give.

The 1950s began promisingly for the Liebers. Steady job, decent income and increased responsibility. Stan was thriving in his hometown, one of the greatest cities on Earth. He was happily married to a smart, kind and beautiful woman who had given up her own professional aspirations to stand by her man. Very much a product of their time; when Stan told Joan no wife of his should be working, she agreed with surprising alacrity. Gladly retiring her own modelling and acting career, Joan became a full-time housewife. It was a standard deal back then. Joan supported Stan domestically and emotionally so he could support her financially. She was the domestic goddess, he the generous provider. He later joked that insisting Joan become a stay-at-home wife was 'the biggest mistake of my life', but having witnessed how financial insecurity almost destroyed his parents, Stan probably took pride in being the breadwinner. He was able to achieve what his father could not.

There was, however, a slight hiccup in their new life together, when Stan's teenage brother Larry moved in. Their mother's death meant that Larry needed somewhere to live until he was old enough to have a place of his own. Why their father Jack wasn't in the picture at this point is another mystery in Stan's story, but there you go. While young Larry's presence must have rumpled their honeymoon period, Stan and Joan were gracious and accommodating. They moved out of Manhattan and bought a large suburban house in Long Island. In April 1950, the couple expanded the Lieber family even more with the arrival of their daughter, Joan Celia, named after her mother and Stan's mother respectively and known as JC. It's not clear when Larry moved out, but he must have done so when he was legally old enough to embark on his own path. We *do* know, however, that in 1951, Stan, Joan and JC moved again, to a house in the village of Hewlett Harbor in Nassau County: 226 Richards Lane. Make a mental note of that address by the way. It'll prove significant later. By handy coincidence, they now lived near Martin Goodman. Despite being Stan's boss, he was still family, and this proximity meant that Stan's own family had more social interaction with Martin outside of office hours, which no doubt strengthened bonds at work.

Three years after JC came into the world, Stan and Joan endured the first tragedy in their life together. Joan had been warned that she had hormonal problems that might make it difficult for her to conceive, so when their daughter arrived, they were over the moon. They tried for another and sure enough, a second daughter, Jan, arrived, but she died three days later. The loss of their newborn crushed the young couple. As if this wasn't brutal enough, doctors informed Joan that she could never have another child. They tried to adopt but it was too soon and too traumatic, especially for Joan, who had not given herself time to grieve and heal. Eventually, they abandoned adoption plans. Stan thought that, in hindsight, this might not have been the right decision, but he remained stoic. Life, he simply observed, had to go on.

Life in Long Island certainly helped the family heal. It was an hour's commute to work in Manhattan, and so Martin allowed Stan to work a couple of days a week from home. Stan loved being close to his family: 'I guess I'm a creature of habit. I like being in my room, in my house, hearing Joanie moving about the place,' he said. It also took the pressure off the workload, since the time he saved commuting was spent typing up Dictaphone notes or reviewing artwork from freelancers. When the weather was warm enough, Stan would take his typewriter outside and enjoy scripting al fresco by the pool. He was even known to sit and type with parties taking place around him. This new lifestyle optimised his output no end, which was just as well. Goodman needed more and more comics to be created to meet demand. During this period, Timely was producing around eighty different comic books every month. As editor, Stan had to ensure this happened by any means necessary. He always lived up to the challenge, but there was also the chance of burn out. After all, there's only so much one person can do to keep an empire afloat.

This particular empire stayed above water thanks to being agile and shifting to reflect the ever-changing mood of the nation. Post-war, interest in superheroes had faltered. By the end of 1949, Timely had canned its trio of big hitters, cancelling the Human Torch's *Marvel Mystery Comics*, *Sub-Mariner Comics* and *Captain America Comics*. In 1951, Goodman set up his own distribution arm, Atlas News Co, and by year end had rebranded his comic book line Atlas Comics. When the Korean War kicked off, Goodman saw it as an opportunity to try and recreate the success of *Captain America Comics* by launching a range of military titles, such as *Battle*, *Battleground*, *Combat* and *War Action*. Atlas Comics was not prepared to turn its back on the superhero genre completely, however, and iconic characters were revived in a comic called *Young Men*. The Human Torch, the Sub-Mariner and Captain America were back, with Cap written by Stan and artwork by the talented young artist and key player in Stan's story, John Romita Sr. The revival was short-lived. By 1955, Atlas had ended their run. Superheroes had, once again, lost their power. Atlas Comics turned to every other genre under the sun, including the great American myth: the western. Titles were published such as *Kid Colt Outlaw*, *Black Rider* and *Two-Gun Kid*. Then there were the true crime titles *Justice*, *Crime Fighters* and *Lawbreakers Always Lose*.

Atlas' decisions to explore different genres was often influenced by the output of its competitor, Entertainment Comics (EC). EC was founded by *Famous Funnies*' mastermind, Charlie Gaines. When he died in 1947, his son Bill took over, signing some impressive talent that cemented EC's reputation as a creative powerhouse to rival Atlas. EC's in-house talent included Harvey Kurtzman, Johnny Craig, Wally Wood and Jack Davis, and you can bet your bottom dollar Stan would have loved to have any of these guys in the Atlas bullpen. Harvey Kurtzman had worked for Goodman before, as a freelancer, but had never been given this level of creative freedom. In 1952, Kurtzman launched EC's biggest hit, the hugely influential *Mad*. EC also launched two incredibly popular sci-fi titles, *Weird Science* and *Weird Fantasy,* as well as three in the horror genre, *Tales from The Crypt*, *The Vault of Horror* and *The Haunt of Fear*.

Seeing the success EC was enjoying, Atlas followed suit, publishing many similar titles, including a short-lived *Mad* rip-off called *Snafu*, and genre titles *Adventures into Terror*, *Venus* and *Spellbound*. While not all were breakout hits, Atlas continued to thrive in the comic book market not due to originality, but by having the resources and funds to churn out many titles – in no small debt to Stan's prolific talents. This did not come without a price.

Spitting out titles based purely on current trends turned Atlas into more of a production line than a creative hub. Without room for creative experimentation, people at Atlas grew bored and frustrated. They still produced original ideas – such is the curse of a creative mind – but they were not required, and were filed away in cupboards and store rooms. Stan knew their value and hoped this work would one day be in demand. After all, if this hadn't been done back in the 1930s, there would have been no Superman. When Goodman discovered that his creative team was being paid for producing material that was surplus to requirements, he decided the staff should be viewed in the same way. He dismantled the bullpen and shifted the business model to rely mainly on freelance contributors. The job of delivering this incredibly bad news fell on Stan's desk. He would later describe this period in his career as 'black days'. He understood the business reasons, but he loathed serving notices of redundancy to colleagues with whom he not only worked closely but also considered close friends. Once the deed was done, Atlas marched on with a significantly reduced bullpen of a minimum of five staff writers, while everything else was supplied by freelancers.

More trying times lay ahead. As 1950s conservatism progressed, the entertainment industry faced increased scrutiny from certain groups determined to destroy anything they saw as detrimental to traditional American family values. Comic books in particular were seen as dangerous new corruptors of the young. This misguided attitude spilled into the public forum when German-born psychologist Fredric Wertham launched a one-man crusade on comic books. While holding a senior post at New York's Bellevue Mental Hygiene Clinic, Wertham worked on juvenile delinquency and decided there was a connection between antisocial behaviour among minors and the violence, bloodshed and supposed sexual content in the comics they read. When studying these so-called delinquents, sure enough, a lot of them liked to read comic books. The fact that *all* kids of that age at the time read comic books did not deter Wertham from his mission to whip up moral panic.

In 1954, Wertham published *Seduction of the Innocent*, a polemic that declared comics to be a negative form of popular literature and a major cause of juvenile delinquency. He believed there were not-so-subliminal sexual themes on display. For instance, Wonder Woman's strength and intelligence made her a lesbian, while Batman and Robin were SO gay it was screaming out from the Batcave. Wertham even found fault in Superman, branding it a fascistic creation. *Seduction of the Innocent* struck a chord with several prominent figures on American society, including Senator Estes Kefauver, who sought to advance his political career by hunting down the New York mob, several of whom, as we saw earlier, had connections to the comic book industry. In 1954, Fredric Wertham found himself testifying before the Senate Subcommittee on Juvenile Delinquency. EC received particular focus. Gaines himself also testified, and it has to be said, he didn't do a great job of acquitting himself or his titles. One example of EC's output was *Crime SuspenStories #22,* the cover of which depicted a murdered woman on the floor while the killer held a bloody axe in one hand and her severed head with bulging eyes and open drooling mouth, in the other. Given this comic book was aimed at kids, it was a … bold choice. These hearings reached the national press and the negative publicity forced the comic book industry to change the way it did things.

There had been previous attempts by the industry to regulate itself. In 1948, the newly formed Association of Comics Magazine Publishers (ACMP) released a 'publisher's code' that laid down rules and guidelines forbidding certain themes or images. However, this code was often ignored in favour of scintillating adventure. Six years later, in 1954, the ACMP's successor, the Comics Magazine Association of America (CMAA) was founded. Influenced by the Hays Code that was enforced in the Hollywood film industry as a form of censorship, a more detailed set of rules came into effect from the CMAA's Comics Code Authority. Henceforth, a seal was designed to adorn every cover of every comic, which read, 'Approved by The Comics Code Authority'. It was a cast-iron guarantee that everything inside abided by that strict set of rules of conduct.

Stan attended one of the subcommittee hearings and found the concerns and attacks launched on comic books ridiculous. 'Wertham was a fanatic, pure and simple,'[2] he later declared. While it was true some of the titles pushed the envelope a little, not least the now-notorious 'severed head' cover, other examples of deviancy cited by Wertham were just ludicrous, such as trying to persuade the panel that an illustration of a caged giraffe within the pages of one Atlas comic was filled with sexual suggestion. Nevertheless, these hearings made their mark. Mud, as we know, sticks. Parents grew more sensitive to what their kids were reading. Certain genre comics began to disappear. The depiction of guns and gore was greatly restricted. The horror and western titles saw a rapid decline. EC in general got it in the neck, reducing their entire line down to just *Mad* magazine. Goodman regrouped and refocused his company's output into safer fare, from amusing animals and romance to Bible stories and sports. Looking back, Stan understood why the code was put in place, but remained sceptical as to whether it actually made an impact on his work at the time, as Stan just wrote the stories he wanted to tell. 'I was interested in creating stories that had *human* characters that could be *relatable* no matter *what* the reader's age,' he said.[3]

Despite these bumps in the road, he still enjoyed his work. While many of the new genres Atlas exploited were not to his liking – *Golfers Anonymous* anyone? – he continued to find satisfaction in the variety at his disposal. It kept things fresh. But there was one persistent niggle. He was frustrated that, despite the millions of comics flying off the newsstands each week, people he met did not take the medium seriously. When asked in social situations what he did for a living, he was uneasy revealing that he was a writer because he knew – as indeed any writer does – the follow-up question was always, 'Oh, what do you write?' When Stan admitted that he wrote comic books he would be met with derision or even hostility. This had been chipping away at Stan for some time, and he started to consider other professions. He wanted to be taken seriously as a writer, and as long as he stayed treading water in the splash pages of Atlas, his career wasn't going anywhere. Maybe he would never get to write the Great American Novel. Maybe this comic book malarkey wasn't for him. It was arguably only the support from Joan that kept him from quitting. Stan never forgot how, whenever he expressed doubts about his chosen path, his beloved wife would be the voice of reason, logic and common sense. Sure, he wasn't satisfied, but he made good money, his work was selling, his boss trusted him implicitly and he liked the people he worked with. Things really weren't so bad.

The rise of television during this time wasn't helping the comic book industry either. Sales declined and, for a second time, Goodman told

Stan that not only did he have to fire fellow employees, he also had to come up with fresh ideas that would blow away the competition, but which were too safe to offend anyone. This put Stan in a tight spot. That's a very narrow brief. After all, groundbreaking and original ideas will inevitably raise eyebrows from someone somewhere. To make matters worse, Goodman moved his company from the prestigious Empire State Building to a more modest address on Madison Avenue. Stan found himself back in a small office, feverishly working hard to run a much-diminished comic book arm of an ever-evolving company that was now thinking beyond the problematic genre pulp it had been producing. Goodman was growing the business in other areas, and comic books wasn't one of them. The triumphant sound of Captain America socking old Adolf in the jaw felt like a faint echo. Stan's work was now even being sneered at by people from within the company. Perhaps it had always been so, but now the negative press surrounding comic books on America's youth had legitimised a general disregard of the comic book as an art form.

Things didn't improve. In 1957 Goodman lost his distributing company, American News. Having recently shut down his own in-house distributing company, this was a huge blow. Desperate to continue trading, he signed a very poor deal with a distributing company owned by arch rivals DC. Jumping at the chance to neutralise the competition, DC made sure the deal crippled Atlas. DC forced Atlas to sign a ten-year contract on the condition that Goodman only publish eight comic book titles a month. With a heavily reduced range, Stan yet again had to personally sever contracts with more colleagues. Atlas crumbled under the weight of financial pressure. The name disappeared from the line. The last comic to bear the Atlas globe on the cover was the funny animal title *Dippy Duck #1* (cover date October 1957). And so it came to pass that the Atlas Age ended not with a bang, nor even a whimper, but a faintly embarrassed quack.

During this period, Stan was merely getting everything out of the door as quickly and efficiently as possible. History has not been kind to this era in Stan's career but that's with good reason. Most of his output was hugely forgettable. 'If Stan hadn't insisted on working against comic book tradition and signing his work wherever it might appear,' observed his biographer Jordan Raphael, 'it would be hard to discern from content alone exactly which scripts he contributed.'[4]

As if this wasn't bad enough, unexpected tragedy befell Atlas in June 1958 when one of its few-remaining bullpen creatives, talented leading artist Joe Maneely, was killed in a freak accident. Co-creator of popular Atlas titles such as *The Black Knight*, *Ringo Kid* and *Yellow Claw*, Maneely was a firm favourite of Stan's and the pair gelled creatively, with plans for numerous ambitious side projects. Maneely was heading home after a night out on the town, when he lost his footing while changing carriages on the train and fell to his death. He was 32. Stan was devastated. They had worked together since 1949 and he was the fastest artist in the bullpen, maybe even faster than Jack Kirby. Maneely was not only the lynchpin of the whole Atlas set-up, but a friend to the family. Stan later reflected that had Maneely lived, 'I would have eventually quit and gone off with Joe and done other stuff.'[5] Looking at the state of what was left of Atlas, you could easily see a host of other reasons why Stan should have walked away from the comic book industry.

The 1950s ended with a final burst of hope. Atlas company fortunes were on enough of a rise for Goodman to allow Stan once more to recruit in-house staff, rehire the core creatives and rebuild their line. In late 1958, science fiction was the order of the day, allowing for more creativity and originality, while also keeping things online with the Comics Code Authority. By now Stan's brother Larry was on board, and the pair shared writing duties on many of these titles, including *Strange Worlds*, *Tales to Astonish*, *Strange Tales*, and *Journey into Mystery*. However, Stan still needed to secure distinct talent that would fill the Maneely-shaped hole and reinvigorate what was left on the now-nameless comic book line. He reached out to two artists in particular who he knew would fit the bill. The first was a raw young talent who had previously impressed Stan as a freelancer; the second was a Timely veteran who had fallen out with his current employers and now really needed the money. Their names were Steve Ditko and Jack Kirby. Each had a style that would lend itself to the fantastical monsters in the science fiction titles. What Stan didn't know is that, together, the three of them would change the face of entertainment forever.

Chapter Seven

The Heroes We Need

With Steve Ditko on board and Jack Kirby back in the bullpen, Stan Lee saw this as a fresh start. It was the shot in the arm the company needed for sure, but more than that, Stan personally needed a lifeline. By this point he was done. Pushing 40, exhausted and jaded, he was fed up of writing repetitive, simplistic and juvenile stories. He needed to get his creative juices flowing, but it wasn't happening at work.

He felt comic books were dying a slow death, and that television would deliver the fatal hammer blow. Colour was added to broadcast programming in 1953 and by 1960, almost ninety per cent of American households had a television set. Even the radio networks had stopped producing entertainment shows; TV had won the battle of the airwaves, establishing itself as the new breeding ground for talent and the centrepiece in any home. Just as the Liebers had crowded round the radio receiver to listen to Jack Benny and *Chandu the Magician*, now families were glued to their big, chunky television sets. They devoured serials, variety shows and situation comedies, as well as event television, such as the first televised presidential debate on 26 September 1960 between Vice President Richard Nixon and Massachusetts senator John F. Kennedy. It is now widely considered that this debate made a star out of Kennedy and helped him win the election early the following year. This broadcast still stands as an early example of the power of television. People were no longer reading at home. They were watching the entire world unfold on the small screen in their living room.

Arguably the only person in comic books to truly cash in on this new medium had been DC's Jack Liebowitz.[1] He had already licensed Superman to the big screen in the late 1940s, resulting in animated shorts and movie serials starring Kirk Alyn. Then, in 1951, he sold the syndicated live-action series *Adventures of Superman* to television, now featuring doomed actor George Reeves in the red cape and boots.

The show had been a hit, making the all-important transition from black and white to colour and lasting until 1958. This kept the Man of Steel well in popular consciousness. During a decade that was turning its back on costumed heroes, there was Reeves, sticking out his chest, holding in his gut and proudly standing up for truth, justice and the American comic. Like Goodman, however, Liebowitz had also seen the writing on the wall. He invested in other areas, including Bill Gaines' *Mad* magazine and a certain gentlemen's publication by the name of *Playboy*. Intrigued by High Hefner's vision, Liebowitz saw its potential to be something more high end than your typical saucy magazine, thereby having a broader appeal. As history has shown, he was right on the money, literally.

Aside from a Captain America serial film in 1944, none of the Timely/Atlas superheroes had made any such giant leaps into film and television. They just didn't have the characters, whereas DC could always rely on the holy trinity. Superman, Batman and Wonder Woman are arguably the most iconic superheroes of all time, and DC had entered the new decade with a strong hand. In addition to this triumphant triumvirate, two more DC superheroes, the Flash and Green Lantern, had been reinvented, in 1956 and 1959 respectively. At the end of the decade, DC consolidated their creative assets and played their trump card. *The Brave and the Bold #28* (cover date March 1960) saw the debut of the brand-new Justice League of America: Superman, Batman, Wonder Woman, the Flash, Green Lantern, Aquaman and Martian Manhunter join forces to take on a huge, dangerous starfish-shaped foe called Starro. Despite this decidedly dodgy denizen of the deep, DC had assembled their A-list roster into a super team *über alles*. Naturally, a few months later, they had their very own comic. How could Stan and his team top that?

Well, to be honest they didn't have to. To stay in the running, they just had to not drop the ball. The recent installation of Steve Ditko and the return of Jack Kirby saw to that. It was evident straight off the bat that Kirby had not lost his touch when it came to creating unique art that really leapt off the page. He especially shone on the science fiction titles, where he vividly realised monsters so huge and intimidating, they would make H. P. Lovecraft hide under the table. Fantastical beasts with daft-yet-immense onomatopoeic names, such as Rommbu, Droom and Titano, would slather and sprawl across every inch of the covers, promising thrills, spills and smack downs impressive enough to destroy a small continent. Behind the eye-popping visuals, however, Stan was going through the motions. Since he was a teenager, Stan had loyally adhered to Martin Goodman's three rules about writing comics:

1. Never be the first to put out a comic book in a particular genre. But if you do, saturate the market with a host of imitators.
2. Keep all plots and characters simple enough for a child to understand. A stupid one.
3. The cover is everything. What's inside doesn't really matter.[2]

It's not hard to see how twenty years under this cynical regime had left Stan dried out and creatively bankrupt. By the 1960s, Goodman's resurgent comic book line didn't even have a name. Atlas had been shrugged into the trash and it felt wrong to continue without an overarching brand name for their new titles. After much debate, one eventually rose to the top.

The word Marvel had been bandied about in the past and even managed to grace the covers of one or two issues, but it never stuck. Stan was always a fan, as he enthused later:

> I loved the word 'Marvel' because it lent itself to so many slogans and catch phrases, such as 'Welcome to the Marvel Age of Comics', 'Make Mine Marvel', and 'Marvel Marches On'. I always loved dreaming up slogans and mottos, and Marvel was the perfect name around which to build a whole public relations campaign.[3]

The first modern comics published with the Marvel Comics logo were *Journey into Mystery #69* and *Patsy Walker #95* (both cover date June 1961). The word 'logo' is perhaps an overstatement. It was a simple box with the initials MC, so small you can barely see it among all the noise fighting for space on the busy covers. Not the most confident start for a name that would go on to dominate global entertainment. But big things truly have small beginnings. Then something happened. Something Fantastic.

Now. We're about to enter very muddy territory. Remember the part earlier about many people trying to claim sole credit for something successful? Well, we're going to wade right into the thick of it. Think the incident about Joe Simon and Jack Kirby being fired from Timely was a mess? You ain't seen nothing yet. What was cooked up in the Marvel bullpen during the early 1960s was undeniable magic. Diamond after diamond. How it came together is not so clear cut. So where to begin? As this is ultimately Stan's story, best start with his version of events. Of course, other accounts of what happened next will also be factored in. So, True Believer, hold fast in your designated title. We are about to venture into a brave new world. We are about to enter the Marvel Age of Comic Books.

According to Stan, it all begin with a round of power golf between Martin Goodman and DC head honcho Jack Liebowitz. In between swings, Jack had been boasting to Martin about the success of the all-star *Justice League* comic book and that superheroes were big business once more. This prompted Goodman to remember his number one rule: don't originate, replicate. Fresh from the links, Martin told Stan that Marvel should resurrect old Timely superheroes, Sub-Mariner, Human Torch and Captain America, then put them in a team to rival the Justice League. Problem was, aside from maybe Captain America, Marvel's superheroes were not a patch on DC's. Besides, Stan didn't want to recycle old characters for some cynical imitation, no matter how lucrative. It just didn't excite him. He went home to Joan and told her about Goodman's latest boring idea, how he had had enough of writing cheap rehashes of other people's ideas and that he was seriously thinking of throwing in the towel. Ever the voice of reason, Joan told Stan exactly what he needed to hear. She said that if he truly felt like quitting, she would support him. But. Why not come up with an original group of superheroes? Characters created from the heart, who have adventures of depth and detail, all written in the style that Stan always wanted to write. Stories that maybe Stan himself would want to read. Superheroes who are complicated and have flaws. Just like everyone else. What's the worst that can happen? Goodman would fire him, but he was going to quit anyway, so he had nothing to lose.

This clarion call from his wife ignited something inside Stan. He spent several days 'jotting down a million notes, crossing them out and jotting down a million more until I finally came up with four characters that I thought would work well together as a team.'[4] He knew exactly who to approach to visualise his vision. 'Nobody drew a strip like Jack Kirby,' Stan said later. 'He was not only a great artist, he was also a great visual storyteller.' Jack's superhero art had a distinctive, muscular visual style. Bold lines depicting heroes in highly macho, physical poses. Kinetic energy would crackle off the panels and spark thrills in the minds of their audience, mainly pre-pubescent boys. Stan knew Jack would realise his initial idea with stunning visuals. Enough time had surely passed for the pair to put aside what may or may not have happened back in 1941. Besides, Jack needed the money. When his daughter Lisa was born in 1960, he knew he had to make this new job work not just for him, but for the entire Kirby family. So, Stan and Jack hunkered down and collaborated on a bold new superhero team. The fruit of their toil changed the game.

The Fantastic Four was comprised of handsome scientist Reed Richards,[5] his loyal girlfriend Susan Storm, her hot-headed brother Johnny Storm and gruff pilot Ben Grimm. On a groundbreaking but dangerous experiment to beat 'the commies' into space, the four fly Richards' untested ship through a cosmic storm, its rays imbuing them with different superpowers. Reed becomes Mr Fantastic, with the ability to stretch his body. Susan is the Invisible Girl because she can, er, turn invisible. Her brother Johnny is transformed into the Human Torch, but this one can burst into flames at will and, significantly, can fly. Ben Grimm gains super strength but is horrifically disfigured and misshapen, hence becoming known as The Thing. Together they formed a crime-fighting superhero team the likes of which no one had ever seen before.

The Fantastic Four #1 hit the stands cover dated November 1961. It was a hit. This flashpoint is widely considered among comic book historians as marking the start of the Silver Age of Comics. Because it didn't stop there. Lee and Kirby were on a roll. Their creative collaboration over the next few years has now become the stuff of comic book legend. Science fiction writer Harlan Ellison once wrote that 'no matter how much the tots in us admired other artists, other writers, the highest massif of the Marvel pinnacle was tenanted solely by that two-headed monster.'[6]

Just to give you an indication of how fast Marvel found success, sales of their comic book titles in 1961 were seven million copies. In 1962, that had rocketed to thirteen million. That year, Stan and Jack smashed it with the first issue of *The Incredible Hulk*, brought the thunder with Thor in *Journey into Mystery #83*, then introduced the mighty Ant Man in *Tales to Astonish #27*. In 1963, Stan gave a new character and story outline to his brother Larry, who wrote a full script. With artwork created by Kirby and fellow staffer Don Heck, Iron Man made his debut in *Tales of Suspense #39*. Back as a duo, Lee and Kirby unleashed the *X-Men* and the *Avengers,* both debuting with a cover date of September 1963. That's the two most famous superhero teams launched in the same month! The latter even welcomed back Kirby's old pal Captain America to join the fun. And that, says Stan, is how it went down.

However, this was not the version of events that Jack Kirby remembered. Because whenever Stan and Jack are involved, there always follows a colossal clash of egos and competing claims of creative ownership. Interviewed for *Comics Feature #44* in May 1986, Kirby insisted he was the one who approached Stan with a bunch of ideas. 'I came in with presentations. I'm not gonna wait around for conferences. I said, "This is what you have to do."' Kirby clearly saw himself as responsible for the reversal of fortune that would precipitate the Silver Age. He reasserted this bold claim the following year in an interview for student newspaper *UCLA Daily Bruin*: 'Of course I didn't change things in one day; but I knew that in a couple of months I could do it. And that's where all your Fantastic Fours came from … I took anything powerful that could sell a magazine – and I did.'[7]

But it doesn't stop there. In February 1990, Kirby doubled down for an interview in *The Comics Journal #134*, claiming sole credit for pretty much all Marvel's first wave of iconic characters. 'When I went back to Marvel, I began to create the new stuff,' he said. 'I came up with The Fantastic Four, I came up with Thor (I knew the Thor legends very well), and the Hulk, the X-Men, and The Avengers.' According to Kirby, the Fantastic Four was essentially a reworking of an earlier quartet he wrote and illustrated for DC in 1957 called *Challengers of the Unknown.*

To pour more fuel on the fire, in the same interview he eviscerated Stan. Kirby dismissed him as 'a bother' and 'a pest', an irksome prankster and a simple 'office worker' who merely served as a go-between, facilitating meetings with Martin Goodman. 'It wasn't possible for Stan Lee to come up with new things – or old things for that matter,' said Kirby. Then the bombshell: 'Stan Lee and I never collaborated on anything! I've never seen Stan Lee write anything. I used to write the stories just like I always did.'[8] The entire interview makes for compelling reading but, in all honesty, Kirby doesn't paint himself in a great light. Curmudgeonly and bitter, he frequently says things that are simply untrue. For instance, he mentioned that Stan was only 'about 13' when he went to work for Goodman. That's several years off Stan's actual age at the time of 17, only five years Kirby's junior. We also know from many sources that Jack and Stan did indeed collaborate on projects and of course Stan was a writer. A highly prolific one. A lot of what Kirby said in this now notorious interview, conducted just four years before his death in 1994, must be taken with a dose of salt. The interview remains, more than anything, a fascinating insight into just how much resentment Jack carried for Stan until his dying day.

If you're interested in all the tit-for-tat arguing and conflicting accounts between the two, seek out *Jack Kirby Collector #75 – Kirby and Lee: Stuf' Said* by 'lifelong Kirby fan' John Morrow. This painstaking collation of all the key remarks made on the record by both parties is a fascinating read, if you can handle all the mudslinging. The way the two collaborated ultimately rests between them and them alone. Both Stan and Jack are no longer with us, nor for that matter is anyone else who would have been privy to any conversations during these first stages of creative collaboration.

One of Stan's skills was to present himself as simultaneously modest and self-deprecating, while at the same time an egotistical self-promoter. His account of how Joan encouraged him into action is a good early example. By crediting his wife with planting the seed of an idea in his head, he deflects any claims that he was solely responsible for kick-starting the Marvel winning streak, while keeping creative provenance firmly in the Lee camp. In other words, it wasn't his idea, but it was really. Who knows? Perhaps that is exactly what happened.

Certainly, Stan is more generous in his praise of Kirby:

> I only had to say, 'look, Jack, here's the story I want you to tell' and he'd bring back the concept I had given him, but with the addition of countless imaginative elements of his own … he never drew a character that didn't look interesting or a pose that wasn't dramatic.[9]

Stan also said he knew the press attention he received 'bothered Jack so much that I even drafted a letter that said "to whom it may concern" and stated that Jack Kirby was the co-creator of the many Marvel characters he drew for us.'[10] Interesting to note, however, the use of the word 'drafted', not 'published'.

Despite what Jack said over the years, the Fantastic Four was clearly Stan's brainchild, thanks to a 2007 reprint of the initial typed synopsis he gave to Jack back in 1961.[11] This document includes character outline, in terms of personality, how they are related and their special powers, the basic plot, and emphasis on the friction between the team that he hopes will be interesting to the reader. A few tweaks were made to this; in the finished comic Stan had thrown out Johnny's status as 'star athlete', Susan Storm's profession as 'actress' and Ben Grimm's crush on Susan. However, it's pretty much all there in this synopsis. The only thing missing in the description were the visuals which, of course, should never be underplayed. You can have the best story in the world but if the pencil work stinks then no one will want to read it. And that is where Kirby's genius shone bright and clear. He created simple but iconic costumes and a look for The Thing – described rather unhelpfully in Stan's memo as 'sort of shapeless' – that was striking and wholly original. It's also evident from this synopsis that Stan was more than open to creative input from Jack. When writing about Susan Storm's powers of invisibility, Stan wonders, 'I hope this won't seem too corny in art work. Better talk to me about it, Jack – maybe we'll change this gimmick somewhat.'

This collaborative process was dubbed 'the Marvel method'. John Tomlinson, former Marvel UK staffer and editor of iconic British comic book *2000 AD,* described this approach succinctly: 'The writer supplies a synopsis of a story, containing all characters, locations and relevant details. The artist breaks this down into pages of comic art, which are returned to the writer, who adds dialogue, captions and sound effects.'

The Marvel method was partly born out of necessity. Stan simply did not have enough time to write a full, detailed script. He was more than happy to farm out a basic idea to the bullpen, trusting that they would bring his ideas to life. It has also been suggested by Ned Hartley, comic book writer and author of *Marvel Museum: The Story of the Comics*, that the method also came to be partly because Stan wanted control over his personal brand. He didn't have the time to give each and every Marvel title the full attention it deserved, but he also didn't like to delegate writing duties to others. There were also times when Stan could only manage to supply a few notes, leaving it up to the artist to complete the idea. You can see why some Marvel artists may have felt they deserved more creative credit than they received.

British artist Kev Hopgood is a fan. He designed the character War Machine and Iron Man's Hulkbuster suit, both of which appeared in several Marvel Cinematic Universe blockbusters. He said:

> I've worked Marvel method and from tighter full scripts, and much prefer the Marvel method. It gives far more creative freedom to the artist. In fact, my character description from the writer for the design of War Machine was, 'it's Iron Man but cooler'. That seemed to work out well.

Given this huge amount of artistic freedom, it can easily be seen how the lines were blurred as to who should take credit, especially during Marvel's early years. Again, Tomlinson is right on the money:

> For an artist of Kirby's incredible imagination, little more than a short phone call would have been necessary to establish the direction of a forthcoming issue or storyline. Kirby would respond with twenty-two pages of breathtaking artwork, complete with pencilled captions and dialogue – which Stan no doubt used as a guide, but otherwise rewrote in his own wry, jokey style.

Working in this way, Stan and Jack changed the comic book landscape forever in just three years. But of course, we cannot pass through this period without mentioning another defining creation of the Silver Age. One that would become Marvel's most successful character ever, symbolising everything Stan helped build to this very day. But one that not even Kirby could crack. So, Stan turned to another artist, shy wunderkind Steve Ditko.

Spider-Man made his debut in *Amazing Fantasy #15* (cover date August 1962). Even though Stan Lee and Steve Ditko were credited, the dramatic image on the front cover was a typically bold illustration drawn by Jack Kirby, with colours by the ever-reliable Marvel man Stan Goldberg, while Ditko merely served as inker. As before, there is disagreement over who came up with Spider-Man. Of course there is. Here we go again.

Stan is on the record saying that he dreamed up the character. 'I'd always loved the Spider,' he later reflected, 'I also loved the name

Hawkman, but of course DC had a character by that name. But thinking about Hawkman led me to Spider-Man. The minute I said it out loud – "Spider-Man" – I knew we had to do it.'[12] Stan approached Martin Goodman for sign off on the idea. His boss hated it for three reasons. First, no one likes spiders; second, a teenager could never be the star but only ever the sidekick; and third, the world wouldn't be interested in a hero who was a dweeb. Not to be deterred, Stan continued developing the character.

He handed the idea to Jack Kirby to work on, and made the editorial decision to introduce the character in a way that would be of low risk to the company. This is why Spider-Man first appeared, not in his own title, but in *Amazing Fantasy*. This sci-fi/fantasy comic (previously called *Amazing Adult Fantasy*) was due to be put out to pasture.[13] If Goodman was right, Spider-Man would soon vanish with all the other forgettable monsters and aliens within its pages.

When Stan found Kirby's early pencil work too, well, Kirbyish – muscular, chisel-jawed and unashamedly heroic – he asked Ditko, already a regular contributor to *Amazing Fantasy*, to go back to the drawing board. Ditko obliged. His artistic sensibility for wiry, angular characters with pensive, angst-ridden facial expressions was the perfect fit. What truly set Spider-Man apart was that this was just as much a story of Spider-Man's secret identity, awkward high school misfit Peter Parker, 'with all the problems, hang-ups, and angst of any teenager'. With Steve's art and Stan's snappy, grounded dialogue, the character was a smash hit, refuting Martin Goodman's objections and vindicating Stan's unwavering conviction.

For years, Steve Ditko did not receive as much credit for Spider-Man as he should have. As with the other early Marvel heroes, Stan felt it was his initial idea. When asked about this, the typically mercurial Ditko would later offer the more diplomatic and vague reply that, 'I still don't know whose idea was Spider-Man.'[14] As with Kirby's artistic contribution, there is absolutely no doubt that Spider-Man's success would have been far from guaranteed without Ditko's fantastic costume design and overall artistic aesthetic. He did later say in a rare interview that when it came to Spider-Man:

> One of the first things I did was to work up a costume. A vital, visual part of the character. I had to know how he

> looked .... I wasn't sure Stan would like the idea of covering the character's face but I did it because it hid an obviously boyish face. It would also add mystery to the character.[15]

Kirby, however, claimed that he had a hand in Spider-Man's inception too, that he was an evolution of an unfinished character he came up with when working with Joe Simon called the Silver Spider, about an orphaned boy who finds a magic ring that gives him super powers. Again, whether Kirby was heavily involved in the birth of Spider-Man can never be conclusively proven one way or the other. He may have been referring to his initial conceptual drawings that were ultimately scrapped in favour of Ditko's take. That he was involved in preliminary development, however, means it would be fair to assume some of Jack's contribution filtered into the character.

The year after Spider-Man's amazing debut, Stan Lee and Steve Ditko would collaborate on just one other iconic Marvel character, Doctor Strange. A thinly veiled copy of Stan's beloved radio character Chandu the Magician, the Master of the Mystic Arts made his debut in *Strange Tales #110* (cover date July 1963), originally presented as 'Dr. Strange, Master of Black Magic'. While not in the same league as Spider-Man, the character proved popular, and this is in no small debt to Steve Ditko's magnificently psychedelic artwork. A million light years away from the rambunctious and disagreeable rants of Kirby, Ditko was essentially a recluse, refusing to have pictures taken of him after the 1960s. He withdrew from the limelight, largely declining to give interviews. He died in 2018 but remained in the shadows, which made it easier for history to forget a truly unique talent whose legacy should never be forgotten.

Now we have safely navigated through the murky waters of the Marvel bullpen during those early years, one question remains. Why have these characters endured? What is it about these fantastical, and at times ridiculous, creations that continues to entertain millions throughout the globe? Grab a shovel, True Believer. We're about to dig a little deeper…

Chapter Eight

More Human than Human

The problem with Superman is that he's just too super. It's hard to relate to the guy. Fighting for truth, justice and the American way is a noble ambition, especially for an illegal alien like the Last Son of Krypton, but it's probably not going to help your average kid get through a tough day in school. The power of flight is of little use to someone wrestling with acne, family or relationship problems. When you are a supreme being from another world who can do virtually anything, why care? That's the question Stan Lee asked at the start of the '60s, and his response led to the monumental ongoing success of the characters he helped create.

The superheroes created in the Marvel bullpen sixty years ago endure because they are profoundly human. Up until that point, the only wildly successful comic book superhero grounded in some semblance of reality was Batman. Unlike DC stablemates Superman and Wonder Woman, Batman has no superpowers and is very much from the mortal realm. But while the Dark Knight Detective is just a man in a suit, he's still not relatable. Under the cowl is dashing billionaire Bruce Wayne, a product of American high society. He has a butler. In Bob Kane's 1990 autobiography *Batman and Me*, Finger explained the inception of Batman's alter ego: 'Wayne, being a playboy, was a man of gentry. I searched for a name that would suggest colonialism.'[1] Over subsequent decades, as audiences craved more realism and introspection, Batman's origin story would focus on selling a tragic melodrama of a troubled orphan psychologically scarred by death and revenge, but you don't have to be a professional sociologist to know that if you've got your own butler, you're probably not going to be sharing the everyday problems of your average mortal.

With DC's otherworldly and remote heroes fixed firmly in his rear-view mirror, as well as the two-dimensional characters he had delivered for Goodman up until this point, Stan had a very different agenda for the newly christened Marvel Comics. 'What I wanted to do,' Stan explained in *The New York Times* in 2015, 'was take these characters who were obviously bigger than life and make them seem real. They've got these powers, they do wonderful things, but what are the things that worry them?'

This was Stan's mantra. It infused everything he wrote from this point forward. This is also the key to understanding exactly how important and groundbreaking these creations were, not just in terms of moving the comic book industry forward, but also in the wider sphere of popular mainstream entertainment. The gamble he took on doubling down with nothing to lose, empowered Stan with a freedom to create characters and stories that resonated beyond men of steel and Amazonian goddesses. Yes, there was still escapism on a grand scale, straight out of the finest science fiction and fantasy adventures that had permeated the previous 100 years. All those stories Stan devoured as a kid then studied as a teenager had been banked in his mind, percolating and distilling until they coalesced into fresh ideas infused with a decidedly modern flavour. Stan and his team told tales of courage, love and friendship in the face of overwhelming adversity, and injected a vital sense of modernity. As former Marvel UK editor Alan Cowsill acutely observes: 'He recreated a medium and made comics topical and relevant, with heroes readers could identify with.'

In hindsight, it seems so simple. Tell timeless stories, but make them current. Make them feel real. But the importance of the decade in which this fertile period grew roots shouldn't be underestimated. The 1960s was defined by creative counterculture, a time of complex socio-political changes, outrage and cultural backlash.

When the 1960s began, nearly half of America's population was under 18, the most affluent generation in the country's history. Its institutions were increasingly under fire by this young, entitled generation. Rejecting the old systems in favour of new ways and means to express yourself was a cornerstone of the decade's American counterculture. Government was seen as corrupt, filled with corporate and self-serving opportunists. Traditional religious orthodoxy was branded an increasingly irrelevant monolith, built on authoritarian self-righteousness. At the same time, the rise of evangelical conservative Christianity, with its threats of fire and brimstone unless you donated cash, only increased alienation from those craving something that would resonate with their brave new worldview. A 1966 cover of *Time* magazine even dared to ask, 'Is God Dead?' Traditional family values that had been so important during the 1950s were now dismissed by the younger generation. The institution of marriage was viewed with distain as a hypocritical prison that failed to reflect the wide and many-splendoured ways love and sexuality should be experienced. Even the hallowed halls of education came under scrutiny. Many saw these superstructures, created with the once-noble purpose of advancing knowledge, as little more than white-collar academic factories, churning out technicians and middle managers that were increasingly required by capitalism and consumer culture. The thinkers were being overrun by drones.

To echo the words of nineteenth-century American writer and poet Henry David Thoreau, whose philosophy proved an inspiration during this time,[2] many were being called to the beat of a different drum and stepped to the music they heard, however far away. And far it was. The British Invasion smashed through the mainstream music industry halfway through the decade. Led by the Beatles and the Rolling Stones, this bold new sound furthered the ideology of free thought, free love and free expression through mind-altering, psychedelic experiences. This new optimism was also fuelled by anger, exemplified by widespread opposition to the war in Vietnam. History has judged the Vietnam War as an act of staggering hubris and tragic error of judgment by the US. At the time, the conflict was vehemently reviled as entirely at odds with the spirit of the Love Generation. Millions would take to the streets protesting against a seemingly futile conflict which resulted in its fighters coming home in body bags. To many, the United States of America, a country which had so nobly stood up to bullies during the Second World War, had now become the exact thing it swore to defeat.

Of course, this doesn't mean that Stan and all those in the Marvel bullpen were at the forefront of the 1960s counterculture. The team was a combination of younger talent and veteran artists from the Timely days, such as Sub-Mariner creator Bill Everett. Quite a few were more comfortable in suits and slacks, smoking pipes and cigars than in beads and flares, smoking reefer. But, as creatives, they wouldn't have been blind to what was going on around them. Change was in the air. People were open to new ideas like never before. The stuffy conservatism of the 1950s was being replaced by a spiky, vibrant lust for life. Wertham's crusade against the comic book industry the previous decade made the medium very attractive to the youth of the '60s, willing to flip the bird to the stuffy conservatives and their prudish ways. More than this, the characters and stories that were being hammered out by Marvel tapped into society's fresh interest in the more 'out-there' creative concepts which pushed the boundaries of the imagination.

Unwittingly or not, Stan found the balance and struck a chord that resonated with the people while also reflecting the changing times. As ex-Marvel writer John Tomlinson says:

> The youthful look and feel of Marvel's … output was surely a major contributory factor to its success at the time, as was its popularity in schools, on campuses and with the Hippie counterculture. Inspired by the work and notoriety of Roy Lichtenstein (his art often dismissed as a crude parody of comic book artwork), Stan even (briefly) rebranded Marvel's comics of the mid-'60s as 'Marvel Pop-Art Productions'. During those first crucial five years of the decade, Stan was unstoppable.

On the surface, the Fantastic Four may seem pretty generic. In those first few comics, they fought extra-terrestrial perils, fantastical beasts and possessed remarkable powers. The key element that made them stand out was that they were a family. They squabbled and bickered just like any family. Stan confirmed the significance of this in a 1968 interview with Ted White: 'I think we were probably the first to break … the cliché of all the superheroes being goody-goody and friendly with each other … we had our Fantastic Four argue among themselves. They didn't always get along well.'[3] The very first panel we see in the Fantastic Four origin story in the very first issue shows a full-on row between the quartet. This was a feature of the characters from their inception, as evidenced in Stan's initial synopsis which he gave to Jack Kirby: 'To keep it all from being too goody-goody,' Stan instructed Jack, 'there is always friction between Mr. Fantastic and The Thing, with Human torch siding with Mr. F. Also the other three are always afraid of The Thing getting out of their control.'[4]

Even back then, Stan was aware his creative team was breaking new ground. Times had changed since the archetypical superheroes of the '40s and '50s. The twentieth century had hauled itself over the halfway line, bruised and battered by a global Depression, two world wars and Cold-War paranoia. The water had grown murky. Stan's new champions reflected this. They were complicated, conflicted, fallible and faced real issues. The fact that one of the early rejected ideas was to have The Thing insanely jealous of Reed and Susan's relationship shows how far Stan was prepared to push the tension among the characters. This was a marked difference from the roster of superhuman characters in the DC comic book stable, who were essentially gods. As acclaimed social commenter Roz Kaveney observes: 'DC is all about heroes and Marvel is all about heroes and their feet of clay.' DC held an optimistic view of the world and human nature, but Marvel represented that more cynical attitude that was so prevalent from the 1960s onwards.[5]

Beyond the Fantastic Four, other Marvel heroes were equally blessed and cursed with humanity. Stan knew he had to make the man inside Iron Man much more compelling than his tin-can alter ego. Anthony Stark was not only an arrogant, ruthless millionaire businessman in the vein of Howard Hughes, but also a weapons manufacturer. A bold move, given the current mood of the nation against the Vietnam War. In his comic book debut, however, Stark is a man 'soon destined to become the most tragic figure on Earth!' He travels to Vietnam on a military operation only to be injured by a piece of shrapnel embedded near his heart. Surviving the attack, Stark is kidnapped by a Vietnamese guerrilla chief. He is then aided by a captured Chinese scientist, and escapes inside a crudely crafted weaponised metal suit with built-in pioneering technology that prevents the shrapnel from fatally entering his heart. Traumatised, Stark realises that 'to remain alive I just spend the rest of my life in this iron prison!!'

The metaphor of a man with a literal change of heart may be heavy-handed, but it is potent. Stark was the man who had everything, but now he is cursed. Compelled to fight injustice using his greatest invention, Stark must reject his selfish ways and become truly altruistic. This is his burden. Stan later said he challenged himself to create a deeply unsympathetic character, a weapons dealer exploiting the Vietnam War no less, and see if he could make him someone the audience would root for. With this tale of redemption, he succeeded. The prototype suit Kirby designed is far removed from the streamlined yellow and red number that is now so iconic, but this ugly, grey, functional suit of armour cleverly reminds us that Stark is trapped in a prison of his own making.

Stan Lee and Jack Kirby also found a way to imbue their more fantastical Marvel creations with a profoundly human touch. For the Incredible Hulk, Stan plundered classic gothic novels such as Robert Louis Stevenson's *The Strange Case of Dr Jekyll and Mr Hyde* (1886), H. G. Wells' thriller *The Invisible Man* (1897) and borrowed ideas from Universal Pictures' monster movies *Frankenstein* (1931) and *The Wolfman* (1941). Combining elements of the literature and cinema he loved so much growing up, Stan wrote a tragic story of how Dr Bruce Banner befalls an overexposure to gamma radiation that turns him into a raging ogre. What makes the character compelling, however, is that Banner doesn't enjoy being a monster. The Incredible Hulk is essentially a Freudian psychodrama; its central character tormented by the dual nature of his personality. Banner is constantly battling the raging id unleashed beyond his control. Part three in the very first issue ends with Bruce Banner confessing his fears to his young friend Rick:

> How do I know I won't keep changing … into that brutal, bestial mockery of a human – that creature that fears nothing – which despises reason and worships power! Soon the sun will set again! And here I sit, helplessly, fearing I may again become – The Hulk!!

As Banner says these words over the three panels, Kirby masterfully draws a dark and ominous shadow creeping across our protagonist's traumatised face. This is no superhero. This is a man fighting for his sanity and his soul.

Stan and Jack even managed to humanise the God of Thunder. Thor's first two appearances (*Journey into Mystery #83* and *#84*), introduced the audience to crippled doctor Donald Blake, who stumbles upon an enchanted cane in a cave that transforms him into the all-powerful Norse deity. Blake is secretly in love with his assistant nurse Jane, but lacks the courage to confess his feelings. Soon Blake and Jane find themselves caught up in a battle against communist mercenaries in South America, where the pair volunteered to give medical aid. Blake saves the day, and the girl, by becoming Thor once more, but afterwards we discover that Jane did have feelings for Blake. When asked about his whereabouts during the fight, Blake tells Jane he could do nothing but hide – a lie to preserve his new heroic identity. The story ends with a disappointed Jane wishing Blake were more like the brave, handsome and strong Thor. 'But no,' she concludes, 'that would just be too much to hope for!' The interesting dimension to Stan and Jack's reimagining of Thor is that, while Blake can become an all-powerful god, his physical deformity is matched by a crippling sense of self-doubt. Blake is a fundamentally good person, dedicating his life to helping others, even placing himself in mortal danger to do so. Thor can be seen as a physical manifestation of Blake's inner strength. He is as brave as any superhero, but the tragedy is, those closest to him cannot see beneath the surface.

With Spider-Man, Stan and Steve Ditko took the human drama in and out of the classroom, exploring the pains of adolescence and social exclusion. Much like Tony Stark, Stan and Steve took care to fully realise Spidey's far more interesting alter ego. Peter Parker is a poor, intelligent, angst-ridden orphaned teenager lacking in social kudos and friends. The very first page of *Amazing Fantasy #15* shows Parker being ridiculed and excluded from a dance, the one social activity all American kids in the early 1960s embraced as part of their adolescent ritual. One guy suggests inviting Peter, to which another snorts, 'Are you kiddin'? That bookworm wouldn't know a cha-cha from a waltz!'

As the story unfolds, we discover Peter's relationship with his Aunt May and Uncle Ben, the former showing striking parallels with Stan's own doting mother. On the same page Peter is presented as a 'clean-cut, hard-working honor student', who gets rejected by girls and teased by the jocks for being a bookish science nerd. All this essential backstory is vividly realised, with perfect visuals from Ditko, himself a rake thin, bespectacled and, by all accounts, awkward young man. No doubt Parker was modelled on himself. From the moment Peter Parker's life is transformed, thanks to a bite from a radioactive spider, the young teen has to not only grapple with his newly acquired super powers, but also deal with the everyday hormonal and emotional problems that are part of being an adolescent in high school: girls, study, family, money, self-confidence… these are all challenges that being able to climb up walls really cannot fix. When Peter selfishly chooses not to use his new powers to foil a robbery, that same thief goes on to murder his Uncle Ben, the man who gave his nephew the now immortal piece of advice: 'With great power comes great responsibility.' Although a tragic coincidence, Ben's murder carries karmic weight. Peter now blames himself for not doing the right thing when he had the chance, and this guilt becomes his primary motive for choosing the life of a costumed hero.

Arguably the most sophisticated creation in this fertile period was the X-Men. They were mutants. They were freaks; those who exist on the fringes of society. Under the leadership of the incredibly powerful but invalid mutant Professor Xavier, this ragtag team of heroes was offered sanctuary, being taken in and trained in his mansion. X-Men's most famous member, Wolverine, was yet to be invented. The Adamantium-clawed warrior with weaponised healing abilities may now be one of Marvel's most iconic characters, but he would not make his first appearance until the final panel of *The Incredible Hulk #180* in 1974. The original Lee/Kirby line up, debuting in *The X-Men #1* (cover date September 1963), featured the quintet of Angel, Beast, Cyclops, Iceman, and newcomer Jean Grey/Marvel Girl, led by Professor X. The comic also introduced their nemesis, Magneto. Their respective superhuman powers made them liabilities unless properly controlled. They were always a hair's breadth away from being rejected by a society that cannot accept people who are born different. In the very first issue, Professor X inducts Jean into the school. In a typical Stan monologue, the wheelchair-bound mutant lays out the ideology behind the entire comic:

> When I was young, normal people feared me, distrusted me! I realised the human race is not yet ready to **accept** those with extra powers! So I decided to build a haven … a school for X-Men! Here we stay, unsuspected by normal humans, as we learn to use our powers for the benefit of mankind … to help those who would distrust us if they knew of our existence![6]

In contrast, Professor X's arch enemy Magneto believes that normal humans 'no longer deserve dominion over planet Earth'. For Magneto, his kind, 'homo superior', shall fight to rule over homo sapiens. Stan was aware of the cultural threads he was pulling from. Avid fans would approach and tell him that these young mutants were synonymous with being gay. Others reckoned that X-Men was a metaphor for the civil rights movement. Truth is, Professor X's team of teen mutants stood for something wider. 'When I was creating the title back in 1963,

I was looking for a subtle anti-bigotry theme,' Stan explained in 2015. 'Dedicated to **all** the people in the world who have been mistreated because they were different in any way.'[7]

Subsequent X-Men stories and film adaptations have explored themes such as anti-Semitism and homophobia. Of all the allegories, the civil rights movement is perhaps the most potent. On 28 August 1963, Martin Luther King Jr delivered his famous 'I have a dream' speech to 200,000 protesters during a march on Washington. At the same time, confrontational activist Malcolm X was clamouring for direct action, even advocating violence in the name of black empowerment. It's not hard to see the parallels. Replace black rights with mutant rights and Professor X is clearly King to Magneto's Malcolm X.

Throughout the comic's history, the relationship between these two mutants has been the cornerstone of the saga. They are two sides of the same coin, one calling for unity through peace, love and understanding, the other drawing a line in the sand, shouting thus far and no further; now is the time for empowerment and domination by any means necessary. This argument has been perhaps retrofitted a little over the years, but it is rather a tight fit. A natural marketing and advertising man, it's a reasonable assumption that Stan was influenced by the current climate. However, Stan's explanation that X-Men was about *any* prejudice was clearly painted in that very first issue. On page seventeen, Kirby draws a powerful panel revealing the restraining belts that Angel is forced to wear to hide his wings under his civilian clothes. When he dons his X costume, Angel unfurls his mutation, declaring, 'I feel like myself again!' However you interpret the symbolism of the X-Men characters, it's clear that once again, Stan was adding an extra layer of social commentary to his otherwise fantastical creations.

Another Stan Lee master stroke was placing all his heroes in a real city. Superman and Batman existed in the fictitious urban sprawls of Metropolis and Gotham respectively, but many of Stan's creations were firmly rooted in New York. In the Marvel universe, gods and monsters literally walked among us. In a 1965 article for Greenwich Village newspaper *The Village Voice*, Sally Kempton observed that 'there are approximately 15 superheroes in the Marvel Group, and nearly all of them live in the New York area.'[8] Kempton wasn't wrong. Spider-Man lives with his Aunt May in Queens. Doctor Strange broods on Bleecker Street in the heart of the village. The Avengers' HQ is on Fifth Avenue. Professor X has his excusive X-Men private school in a grand mansion upstate in Westchester County. Daredevil, the blind lawyer with heightened senses, created in 1964 by Stan with Bill Everett, launches himself majestically from the rooftops of Hell's Kitchen. The Fantastic Four didn't even hide behind masks. Everyone knew them by name and that they lived and worked in the Baxter Building. First mentioned in *Fantastic Four #3* (cover date March 1962), this thirty-five storey office building was the first comic book superhero HQ to be well known to the public. They paid rent. In *Fantastic Four #9* (cover date December 1962), the team go bankrupt, can't pay their rent and are evicted from their superhero lair.

By grounding these superheroes in real homes on real streets, a lot of them pretty grubby, Stan could write about what he knew, thereby injecting extra details and nuanced touches that made his storytelling come alive. In retrospect, New York was the perfect choice. During the 1960s, the city was dirty and crime-ridden. Social and economic rot had begun to set in. And yet, its glistening Art Deco skyline of glass, chrome and steel served as a potent reminder of prosperity. The geography and architecture of Manhattan, which Stan knew so well, proved a visually striking backdrop that set the city apart from the majority of others on Earth. Most people reading these comics had never been to New York, so the city was still glamorous enough to transport the reader into another world, while also being the perfect breeding ground for the kind of danger, threat and chaos that could only be fought by heroes who knew every rooftop and every alley. New York needed heroes, and Stan gave that city enough to spare.

It is this level of interconnectivity that helped make all the superhero titles Marvel produced during this time so groundbreaking. It was not in itself a new idea. DC had got there first in *All-Star Comics #3* (cover date Winter 1940-41), which introduced the Justice Society of America, featuring DC headliners Doctor Fate, Hour-Man, the Spectre, the Sandman, the Atom, the Flash, Green Lantern, and Hawkman. *All-Star Comics #3* later paved the way for the much more iconic Justice League, which teamed up Batman, Superman and other more memorable DC characters. However, Stan Lee interwove his characters in a way that was far more ambitious. As writer and editor, Stan wanted all these Marvel heroes and villains to regularly meet, interact, fight side by side and even fall out in spectacular fashion.

Of course, this was partly a commercial decision. Stan was savvy enough to know this. A reader who may have only bought one comic book might buy a second if their favourite character's latest exploits crossed over multiple titles. Stan also moved away from self-contained 'one-shot' stories to story arcs across several issues. Nothing keeps audiences howling with frustration but so keenly on tenterhooks like the three dreaded words: 'To Be Continued…'

This crossover soap-opera approach not only strengthened the Marvel brand and fan loyalty, but also allowed Stan to build worlds on a scale hitherto unseen in the comic book industry. Superheroes would make frequent cameos in each other's titles, as part of a rich tapestry; a living, breathing world readers could get lost in. In the Fantastic Four alone, the worldbuilding on display was astonishing. While still able to keep things grounded with their New York base, the cosmic dimension of the characters allowed Marvel to have the team meet with pretty much anyone in the Marvel universe, while also construct parallel and alternate universes interwoven seamlessly into each other. As veteran British comic book creator Tim Quinn rightly concludes, Stan 'created a whole new mythology for our times. A universe of Marvels. Looking back on his work across the '60s, I feel he was doing in comics what the Beatles were doing in music. There is nobody else in comics to compare him to.'

But it wasn't just the bold ideas for new characters or impressive worldbuilding that set apart Stan's work during this period. It was also the writing. That was Stan's gift. He had spent his entire life immersed in literary classics, rich in nuanced characters with distinct voices. For the previous twenty years, Stan had honed his ability to write dialogue in just about any tone and genre. And he was fast too. It took Stan a day to write a comic script, start to finish. All this experience and on-the-job training came to a head when he was finally allowed to unleash his creative powers. 'The dialogue is the most important thing,' Stan stated in a 1968 interview with *The Baltimore Sun*. 'Good dialogue can make a very banal plot seem very important and very profound, but I think bad dialogue can make the greatest plot in the world seem corny and hackneyed.'[9]

Stan's dialogue was striking, at times, verbose, but always sharp. From the pseudo-Shakespearean proclamations of Thor and the angst-ridden obsessive ramblings of Bruce Banner to the 'Noo-Yawk' tough-guy slang of The Thing and the snarky wisecracks of Spider-Man, Stan gave each character a strong voice and personality. 'In my experience of UK comics of the time, one character sounded pretty much like any other,' says former Marvel UK writer John Tomlinson, 'but even without the artwork, it's impossible to mistake Spider-Man's dialogue for that of The Thing, say, or Reed Richards for Doctor Doom. Every character had a distinctive voice, which was also, unmistakably, Stan's own.'

What many people forget about Stan's writing style was that he was often very funny. 'Stan had a great reputation as a humorist,' remarked Joe Sinnott, another Marvel veteran who worked with Stan as an inker for almost seven decades on titles including *The Fantastic Four*, *The Avengers*, *Thor* and *The X-Men*. 'He was always on. He should've been a gag writer.'[10] Stan channelled much of it in the sharp comebacks Spider-Man would quip as he dispatched another villain, reflecting how nerdy introvert Peter Parker could unleash a more confident sense of bravado when hiding behind a mask. The Thing often got great lines as well, his street smarts often used to puncture the po-faced seriousness of Reed Richards' science and logic-driven personality.

You could throw a dart in a pile of Marvel comics produced during the 1960s and it would hit a great example of what made them so innovative and fresh. But, if I were to recommend one single story that just might be the perfect encapsulation of all that Marvel – and Stan – stood for, while showcasing a creative team firing on all cylinders, I would be happy to. And, since you asked, True Believer, I shall.

The perfect distillation of all that made these early Marvel comics stand out is *Fantastic Four Annual #3*. Published in 1965, this king-sized annual ticks all the boxes. The cover is awash with Stan's trademark alliterative superlatives; 'featuring the world's most colossal collection of costumed characters, crazily cavorting and capering in continual combat! This is the big one!' Kirby's cover art is an explosion of colour, showing literally every single Marvel superhero created since the Fantastic Four. Inside its '72 big pages', the lucky reader finds 'Bedlam at the Baxter Building', the tale of Reed Richards and Susan Storm's sensational wedding, 'written by Stan Lee', 'drawn by Jack Kirby' and 'catered by the Bullpen Gang!' When a rogues' gallery of supervillains crashes the ceremony, there is an almighty tussle. Fighting for space within the panels of a single story, we find – deep breath – the Fantastic Four, the X-Men, Captain America, Iron Man, Thor and the rest of the Avengers, Doctor Strange, Spider-Man and Daredevil. Phew!

Seriously, this one has everything. Action, romance, humour, monsters, aliens, street fights in Manhattan and a quick jaunt through the fourth dimension thrown in just for jolly. In a single story, Stan Lee and Jack Kirby showcase all they can do and everything Marvel have achieved in just five years. This annual is almost a victory lap; an event publication to mark how far Marvel had come. Right there, in these vibrant and kinetic pages, is the blueprint and the prototype for what would follow some forty years later, when the Marvel Cinematic Universe became the most successful and lucrative franchise in the history of cinema. But of course, you don't build universes overnight. And Stan had plenty more tricks up his sleeve.

Chapter Nine

Master of the Universe

Stan was always looking to evolve what he believed Marvel stood for. This wasn't just a business. It was a universe unto itself. A cavalcade of characters, worlds, galaxies and dimensions. As editor, his complex and sophisticated crossover policy allowed him to realise this universe, as former Marvel UK writer Simon Furman observes:

> He knew his audience. He understood what they wanted before they even knew it themselves … drawing the readers in, continually cross-referencing other titles, guest starring this or that hero, producing dual headliner books. So that period allowed Stan/Marvel to consolidate their roster of characters and also foster that clubhouse feel and personal touch. You always felt he was talking directly to YOU.

Sally Kempton's 1965 *Village Voice* article reflected Marvel's growing appeal. She wrote: 'College students interpret Marvel Comics. A Cornell physics professor has pointed them out to his classes. Beatniks read them. Schoolgirls and housewives dream about the marvel heroes.' Marvel were now targeting an older audience. The fact the company had drawn attention from *Village Voice*, itself a typical East Coast liberal, intellectual publication and a platform for New York's creative community, indicated that Marvel had begun to find their new target demographic. 'We don't cater to any special age group,' Stan remarked in 1968. 'But we do cater to a special intellectual level. Our readers, no matter what their ages, have proved to be bright, imaginative, informal and sophisticated.'[1] The widespread appeal of their comics ensured that in just five years, Stan and the Marvel bullpen were already making a sizeable dent in popular culture.

Stan took great care to nourish and sustain his bullpen with formidable talent; his own universe of creative wonder. Aside from brother Larry Lieber and the one-two punch of Jack Kirby and Steve Ditko, the bullpen was a roster of revered artists and writers Stan felt honoured to work with. Some were Timely veterans such as Gene Colan and *Sub-Mariner* creator Bill Everett, the latter also taking shared credit of creating *Daredevil.* Wally Wood, formerly EC Comics (of *MAD* magazine fame), also ran with that torch to much success. Another was Don Heck, an Atlas staff artist during the 1950s, who helped create *Iron Man*. Then there was the formidable Marie Severin, a truly pioneering woman playing in what was very much a man's sandbox. Marie was an accomplished artist and colourist who had made her name in EC then Atlas. She also knew a thing or two about production, so she successfully bridged the gap between creatives and the suits. She was also brilliantly funny. In 1968, she wrote and pencilled a short story for *The Amazing Spider-Man Annual #5* called 'Here We Go A-Plotting'. Across three pages, we find caricatures of Stan and a few of his bullpen associates as they thrash out a Spider-Man story. The banter here is Abbott and Costello meets The Marx Brothers; the team portrayed as wisecracking chancers flying by the seat of their pants. It's silly, fast-paced and just one example of Marie's excellent comedy chops.

Of course, many other veteran creatives contributed to Marvel's early success. We cannot cover them all, but we must raise a glass to Artie Simek and Sam Rosen. These unsung heroes were responsible for the word balloons and 'sound effects' for virtually every Marvel title during this Silver Age. It's something many readers take for granted, but their work is just as important as the rest of the artwork. Here's to you.

Marvel's offices soon upgraded to 655 Madison Avenue in Midtown Manhattan. This must have been of particular pride to Stan, given his admiration for the advertising industry. Now here he was, rubbing shoulders with the Mad Men. Stan liked to paint a picture of the Marvel bullpen toiling together under one roof, but many still worked from home, so the idea that everyone collaborated in one space is not entirely accurate. Still, the Marvel offices were indeed a hub that ultimately produced extraordinary work, and they were always on the lookout for fresh blood.

Joining the bullpen in 1966 was former commercial agency artist John Buscema. An all-rounder, John could turn his hand to anything. He soon became one of Marvel's most valued players, pencilling on every major Marvel title, but his work on *Silver Surfer* deserves special mention. The year Buscema joined, Jack Kirby had created the character, a naked, completely silver figure astride a cosmic surfboard, for 'The Galactus Trilogy'. Many consider this not only the greatest Fantastic Four story ever told, but also Kirby's creative high point with Marvel. Two years later, Stan launched *Silver Surfer #1* (cover date August 1968) with Buscema on pencils, exploring the character's origins and motivations. A former herald to Galactus, various acts of rebellion lead to exile on Earth. There the Surfer observes man's inhumanity to his fellow man. *Silver Surfer* is significant because it best showcases Stan's more introspective and thoughtful writing. The character is basically a philosopher, frequently given to Shakespearean-style existential soliloquies. With Buscema's powerful but elegant artwork, Stan used the Silver Surfer for beautifully bleak observations about justice and humanity. It's cracking stuff and, while not a barrel of laughs, the Silver Surfer remains this writer's favourite Marvel character.

Other notable greenhorns during this time include Jim Steranko and Roy Thomas. A former stage magician who fell foul of the law on more than one occasion in his youth, Steranko brought his unique magic and a rebellious streak to the pages of much-lauded title *Nick Fury, Agent of S.H.I.E.L.D.* His work during the latter half of the 1960s deserves a separate chapter to itself, but sadly there's no time. Influenced by the darlings of fashion and pop art, Steranko remains unique among his Marvel peers at the time because he fused traditional comic book art with graphic design, especially photo collages. He truly pushed the boundaries of how a comic book should look, enriching the pages of *Nick Fury* with ideas that were literally outside the box. He would even incorporate imagery across double-page spreads that only made sense if you laid two comics side by side. Steranko became a comic book historian and created conceptual art and character designs for films including Steven Spielberg's peerless *Raiders of the Lost Ark* (1981) and Francis Ford Coppola's visually stunning *Bram Stoker's Dracula* (1992).

Roy Thomas first moved to New York aged 24 to write for DC, but Marvel hired him in July 1965 as Stan's assistant editor. There he worked on several titles, writing on *X-Men*, *The Avengers* and *Doctor Strange*. Thomas co-created many popular characters you may know from Marvel's various big-screen adaptations, including Wolverine, Vision, Carol Danvers, Ultron and Valkyrie. He also brought legendary hero Conan the Barbarian into the Marvel stable. Roy is most notable for being Stan Lee's first successor as Marvel editor-in-chief, taking over the reins in 1971. Unusually for the major players in Marvel's Silver Age, at the time of writing, both Jim Steranko and Roy Thomas are still with us.

Finally, worthy of mention are two figures who operated the Marvel machinery from behind the scenes. The first is production manager Sol Brodsky. A few months younger than Stan, Brodsky was a fellow New York native who also served during the war in the Signal Corps. He began his professional association with Stan round about that time too, writing and drawing for Timely. Throughout the 1950s, he contributed occasional cover art and stories for Atlas' many genre titles, and when Martin Goodman had Stan fire everyone in the comics division, Sol was brought in to handle production. Goodman fired Brodsky in 1957, but he formally came back to Marvel in 1964, where his organisational skills proved essential. Together, the two-man team of Stan and Sol held everything together. Stan wrangled the artists and stories while Sol handled delivery of materials, scheduling with the printer and other vital duties. In many ways Sol was Stan's right-hand man for a very long time.

The second essential staffer handling production was Stan's secretary and Marvel receptionist 'Gal Friday' Flo Steinberg. This Boston native moved to New York in 1963 and was hired when the only two other permanent staffers in Marvel were Stan and Sol. Between them, the trio made up the first true bullpen, long before it became cluttered with creative egos. And unlike the romanticised version, these three were actually in the office. Flo ensured Stan and the other creatives met their deadlines. She sent comics to the Comics Code Authority for approval and helped Stan respond to Marvel's mountain of fan mail. After a few guest appearances in the comics themselves, Flo began receiving her own fan mail. She left Marvel in 1968 and become a major player in the independent comic scene, working with veterans Wally Wood and Marie Severin on Big Apple Comix. But she never broke ties with Marvel, and will always be remembered as the heart of the company during a crucial time in Marvel history, ensuring Marvel strengthened ties with their readership.

Throughout the decade, so many made their mark and uniquely contributed to Marvel's meteoric rise. But yet again we're getting ahead of ourselves. Where were we? Ah yes. Let's pick up somewhere in 1963. OK with you? Goodie.

Stan felt there was always more that could be done. More to share, more to involve and more to reward loyal readers. As editor-in-chief of an entire comic book division, he had a powerful tool at his disposal to showcase a heightened version of his personality that fed his ego, while also giving fans 'secret' insider knowledge. It wasn't enough that they simply read the comics. They had to feel 'in' on something special. To do this, Stan broke the fourth wall as much as he could. Sometimes this was just a throwaway line or visual nod to the reader on the page. Other times Stan went full-on meta. After all, the Marvel bullpen was filled with big characters. How cool would it be, Stan thought, if he could let the readers meet the guys and gals who created all these wondrous adventures?

Marie Severin's aforementioned 'Here We Go A-Plotting' is a great example of this, but it wasn't the first. In *Fantastic Four #10* (cover date January 1963), Stan puts himself and Jack Kirby in the actual story. The pair feature on the cover, talking about how exciting this issue will be. Inside, the evil Doctor Doom turns up at Marvel's offices, demanding that if Jack and Stan value their lives, they call Fantastic Four leader Reed Richards this instant. His wicked plan to lure Richards there is to force Stan to pretend they need help with their latest Fantastic Four story. This was a completely original approach within the comic book medium. Unlike their competition, Marvel had opened their doors, presenting the staff as characters in their own universe.

Stan ramped up his mission to involve the readers in his universe with the creation of the 'Marvel Bullpen Bulletins'. The idea was inspired by a boys' own adventure series that Stan loved as a child called *Jerry Todd*. Each issue saw author Leo Edwards answer readers' letters in a relaxed and informal style that Stan adored. In the summer of 1965, Stan launched his own version, tucked away at the back of the comic, called 'The Merry Marvel Bullpen Page'. The page was soon refined into the 'Bullpen Bulletins'. With its distinct newspaper design laid out on a yellow background, Stan talked directly to his readers. Here he could answer fans' questions, promote upcoming titles with 'The Mighty Marvel Checklist' and feature profiles celebrating members of the bullpen. For Stan, honesty was always the best policy when talking to the fans. If a reader wrote in to complain about the poor quality of a specific story, Stan would agree and thank them for writing in, promising the bullpen would try harder next time.

Most famously, every issue of Bullpen Bulletins featured a regular editorial, 'Stan's Soapbox', in which he shared his opinion on just about anything. Crucially, Stan did not use this to push a specific political or social agenda. 'The only credo we espoused was "Do Unto Others as You Would Have Them Do Under You",' he said.[2] The soapbox was Stan firing on all cylinders. Each edition saw him go crazy with alliterative subtitles, such as, 'More mirthful, monumental, mind-staggering memoranda from your Marvel madmen'[3], and 'A Profound Potpourri of Perplexing Pronouncements and Preposterous Philosophy, all Portending Practically Nothing!'[4]

Stan would also reward fans who sent in letters with a 'Marvel No-Prize', which was literally just that. One lucky reader would receive a letter officially telling them that they hadn't won anything at all. The bulletins also introduced us to Stan's more memorable turns of phrase. 'Face Front, True Believer', 'Make Mine Marvel', 'Nuff Said' and 'Excelsior!' all got frequent use until they became enduring catchphrases.

Stan even used the Bullpen Bulletins, and especially Stan's Soapbox, to fire potshots at the competition. It was irreverent, anarchic and perfectly in sync with the rebellious streak of the times. As Stan biographer Bob Batchelor observes, 'For teens and college-aged fans, the wink-wink, tongue-in-cheek tone spoke to their anti-establishment notions and seemed discernibly different from the voice they were used to hearing from adults.'[5]

Bullpen Bulletins threw shade on all other comic book companies in every sense. It showcased Marvel's unique, playful nature, talking to fans as if they were close friends. It also gave Stan an opportunity to elevate his status as the face of Marvel. He used his larger-than-life personality to great effect, portraying himself as a constantly overworked but impossibly positive editor. Stan would finally relinquish control of Bullpen Bulletins in the early 1970s, when he stepped down as editor-in-chief, but he still contributed his soapbox as and when he could. In the late 1990s, Stan returned to create the page, but Marvel finally discontinued Bullpen Bulletins in 2001. During that time, it underwent various different iterations, tones and styles, reflecting whoever was editor-in-chief, but nothing quite compared to those early days. Quite simply, the industry had seen nothing like it. 'The fact is,' wrote Sally Kempton in 1965, 'that Marvel Comics are the first comic books in history in which a post-adolescent escapist can get personally involved.' They weren't just reading a comic, they were in the club.

It was only a matter of time before Stan created a Marvel club readers could actually join. Again, this wasn't a unique idea. During the 1940s, DC had both 'The Junior Justice Society' and the 'Supermen of America' clubs. During the Timely days, Stan had resisted the idea for fear of appearing as if they were jumping on that bandwagon. By 1964, however, Marvel had received so much fan mail and created such a distinctive house style, they felt the time was right.

Stan cannily teased the name of the club, M.M.M.S., throughout Marvel's titles before even saying what the letters stood for or, indeed, what it even was. As he hoped, fans were intrigued. They wrote in with their own interpretation, such as 'Make Mine Marvel Stan', or the brilliantly more cynical 'Marvel's Money Making Scheme'. It was a classic marketing move. Pique their interest, lure them in, then – POW! The big reveal. In the autumn of 1964, the Merry Marching Marvel Society was unveiled in all its glory.

For one dollar, plus a seventy-five-cent returning annual fee, the club offered a welcome letter, membership card, stickers, badge and a certificate on which fans would state a pledge of allegiance. Most interestingly, membership included a one-sided 33½ rpm vinyl record titled *The Voices of Marvel*. Stan later boasted:

> In a moment of inspiration, I marched the whole gang out of the office one day to a recording studio about five blocks away. In those days you could press a very cheap vinyl record for less than a penny each. Since it was so affordable, we made a record for our fans, ad-libbing the whole thing.[6]

You can still listen to this recording. It's on YouTube, although of course, other video streaming websites and apps are available.[7] Underneath the pops and crackles are the voices of Stan Lee, Flo Steinberg, Jack Kirby, Sol Brodsky, Artie Simek, Sam Rosen, two of Jack Kirby's leading inkers Chic Stone and Dick Ayers, Wally Wood, Don Heck and colourist Stan Goldberg, with honourable mentions to those unable to attend the recording. It's forced and stilted and in no way ad libbed – none of them is a good enough actor to cover that up – but it is sweet. It's a perfect, cheesy distillation of Silver Age Marvel right there in the grooves. They take cheap shots at each other, complain they're not getting paid enough and riff on Stan's lousy memory; each person playing an exaggerated version of their personalities, including Steve Ditko being too shy to say anything and ducking out of the window like Spider-Man.

This record was a real treat for those who had signed up to be one of the mighty Marvel's merry marchers. The record literally put Stan in people's living rooms, echoing those radio shows that gripped him during his formative years. Sadly, Martin Goodman wasn't so tickled and before the decade was out, the M.M.M.S. was given its final marching orders. Despite its value as great PR, the club was not, in the eyes of the ever-thrifty Goodman, financially viable.

Throughout the 1960s, the relationship between Stan and Martin cooled slightly. Some have suggested Goodman didn't like Stan increasingly being seen as the guy who runs the show. Stan may have been the face of Marvel, but it was still Martin's company. He held the purse strings and pulled all other strings for that matter. It was easy for Stan to get carried away, and every so often Martin would need to remind him who was really in charge. As much as the effervescent Stan would always like to pretend it was just one great big party in the bullpen, way before Goodman shut down the M.M.M.S., there was trouble in Stan's Universe.

Not everyone was happy with the Marvel method. Again, the blurring of lines between writer and artist made it hard to give credit where credit was due. While this suited most, some found it frustrating to breaking point. In June 1965, veteran Wally Wood quit Marvel. He felt he had been contributing too much to storylines and not being paid accordingly.[8] He also felt Stan was taking liberties in his role as editor. 'Remember that issue of *Daredevil I* wrote?' Wood said in a 1978 interview with Jack Kirby biographer Mark Evanier. 'Stan said it was hopeless and that he'd have to rewrite the whole thing. Then I saw it when it came out and he'd changed five words, less than an editor usually changes. I think that was the last straw.'[9] Months later another departure caused even more upset.

Relations between Stan and Steve Ditko had been floundering for a while, due to many disagreements over the direction to take Spider-Man. Steve had been diligently working away on his own with Doctor Strange, but Stan had seemed less interested in that title. Steve's brilliantly skewed psychedelic imagery was the perfect fit for any Strange tale to be told. But Steve had also taken more control of Spider-Man story lines and wanted to push the title in directions that made Stan uncomfortable. At the time, Steve was becoming greatly influenced by the writings of Ayn Rand and had begun to play with some of her objectivist philosophies in his Spider-Man stories. The objectivist idea of pursuing self-interest at all costs was turning Peter Parker into a more assertive but less sympathetic character. When Steve allegedly started ignoring Stan's suggestions and requests, tensions rose to the point that by early 1965 the two men weren't speaking. Steve would submit his work to Sol Brodsky, who would then pass it on to Stan. For someone as reclusive and private as Steve Ditko, this was understandable. For someone as gregarious and open as Stan, this was odd behaviour.

Then one day, Steve handed in his work for *The Amazing Spider-Man #38* and *Strange Tales #146* and quit. Most sources, including Stan, say this happened in January 1966, but John Morrow's meticulously collated account of the relationship between Stan and Jack Kirby places Steve Ditko quitting Marvel on 22 November 1965. There's no independent source available to verify this. *The Amazing Spider-Man #38* and *Strange Tales #146* were indeed Steve's final contributions for Marvel Comics. Both were cover dated July 1966, which means they actually hit the stands in April. One thing is clear. Steve Ditko was already out of the door.

Steve remained enigmatic about the whole matter for most of his life. He did go on record to say, 'I know why I left Marvel but no one else in this universe knew or knows why. It may be of mild interest to realise that Stan Lee chose not to know, hear why, I left.'[10]

Naturally, there was much speculation about Steve's departure, as 'creative differences' didn't quite cut it. With Spider-Man, he was practically given free rein to do what he wanted. Steve's cryptic remark is true, in that Stan dealt with it by not dealing with it. Stan would admit as much during a 2004 interview with Tom DeFalco. 'I was angry over the way Steve Ditko quit,' he said. 'He left in such a way that I wasn't tempted to call him and ask him why.'[11]

In later years, Stan suggested that Steve was disgruntled because he never got the recognition he deserved. He said, 'He wanted to be known as Spider-Man's co-creator. And that was OK with me. I started calling all the artists who did a first issue with me my co-creators. But despite that, by 1966, I'm sorry to say, he was gone.'[12] For years this was presented as what drove Steve away, and this may be partly true. We'll never know. Fifty years later, three years before his death in 2018, Steve Ditko gave his most explicit account of why he departed. The interview suggests that it was actually Stan's conduct towards him that proved the real issue. 'Why should I continue to do all these monthly issues, original story ideas, material, for a man who is too scared, too angry over something, to even see, talk to me?' demanded Steve.[13]

Stan knew how vital Steve was to the initial success of Spider-Man and he was nervous for the future. So he turned to former DC artist turned recent bullpen regular John Romita. At that moment in time, Romita had just started regularly pencilling *Daredevil.* Funnily enough, Stan had only just written him a crossover story in which Romita had to try his hand at drawing Spider-Man. Was this Stan cannily testing the water for Steve's replacement should relations break down completely? Probably. Stan was too sharp not to have a contingency plan in the works.

Despite initially not much caring for Steve Ditko's work on Spider-Man, which he thought to be rather unheroic, Romita agreed to take over *The Amazing Spider-Man.* Those were big shoes to fill, so he initially copied Ditko's style. Soon after, Romita went on to make the role his own. His Peter Parker was confident, capable and even a little bit cool. Physically he was bulkier, more square-jawed, more akin to a matinee idol than the skinny, nebbish Ditko original. John also brought back the likeability so vital to the character. He also introduced the neighbour, Mary Jane Watson, as a fiery redhead, no doubt reminding Stan of his own wife, who had similarly coloured hair, and made supporting characters such as Gwen Stacy and Flash Thompson more glamorous. It is impossible to overstate the role Steve Ditko played in creating Spider-Man, but John Romita's run, which lasted over a decade, evolved the character and his world. John refined Spidey into the hero we all know and love to this day. In the most recent big-screen adaptations, you can see the legacy of both Ditko and Romita in there. Any argument over which Spidey artist was 'best' feels trivial and redundant. They both brought something truly great to the table and together, their work helped create a true pop-culture icon.

With Spidey in the safe hands of John Romita, it was hoped things would settle down. Guess again. In January 1966, the *New York Herald Tribune* ran an article that caused major friction between Stan and Jack Kirby. Unlike Ditko, Kirby clearly had no real trouble working with Stan – their astonishing collaborative output reflects this – although their personal relationship was fractious at best. It never took much for tensions to ignite. When the article came out, Jack's wife Roz saw it as a slight on her husband. It not only diminished his role in the creative process, but also personally attacked Jack's appearance; a fat slob all 'baggy eyes', who looks like he should be 'the assistant foreman in a girdle factory'. The piece angered Roz Kirby so much, she got straight on the phone to give Stan a piece of her mind.

Stan and his wife Joan have both gone on record saying this angle was created entirely by the journalist, but certainly Stan knew that after losing Wood and Ditko, he couldn't afford to lose the ace up his sleeve. Time for damage limitation. Shortly after the article was published, Jack Kirby's involvement in the comics was made clearer. *Fantastic Four #56* (cover date November 1966) is the first of many to feature the credit, 'Produced by Stan Lee and Jack Kirby'. This is no coincidence.

This peace offering smoothed things over, but many feel that the *Herald Tribune* article triggered the rift between Stan Lee and Jack Kirby that would ultimately tear apart their working relationship. For now, things were rosy once more. The Marvel universe continued to swell and blossom. Stan took his brand out to the people. He capitalised on his formidable presence and charisma by conducting talks, lectures and pressing the flesh at college campuses, where M.M.M.S. chapters had started forming around the country. This connected him further with his newfound, more mature audiences. Stan would soon extend these public appearances to more random places, including a rather bizarre drop-in at Burachio Bros, a drive-in cleaning company on Long Island. Then again, he may have just been picking up some slacks on the way home.

That year, Martin Goodman moved his expanding comic book division down the block to 635 Madison Avenue. This literally gave Stan more distance from his boss, which he appreciated. By the end of that year, sales of Marvel Comics had swelled to thirty-three million copies.

Something else happened in 1966, more significant than Stan popping up at his local cleaning firm. The same month as the notorious *Herald Tribune* article hit the stands, DC Comics delivered a major coup. Their brand-new, live-action TV series was broadcast on ABC on 12 January. Starring Adam West and Burt Ward, *Batman* crashed on the small screen with a big bang. It was a huge hit. A home run for the network, the studio and Marvel's arch rivals. Stan had to up his game.

Chapter Ten

A Brave New World

There are two types of people in America. Those who have seen the 1966 *Batman* television series, and those who haven't seen television. To say it was one of the biggest television phenomena of the 1960s is an understatement. To say it's one of the most distinctive TV shows ever made is pretty accurate too. And with good reason. It was – and still is – a singular piece of entertainment. There's really nothing like it. *Batman* was so influential it cemented popular perception of the Caped Crusader for decades. It would take over twenty years before Batman was brought back to his darker roots with Tim Burton's all-conquering 1989 blockbuster.

Burton's movie owed more to the darker Batman comics of the 1970s by Dennis O'Neil and Neal Adams, then the adult graphic novels of the 1980s, especially Frank Miller's *The Dark Knight Returns* and Alan Moore's *The Killing Joke*. *Batman* '89 was a noir-drenched fairy tale of psychosis and revenge, framed by Anton Furst's Oscar-winning grandiose 'dark deco' production design. This is the version of Batman that has endured to this day. Any attempt to brighten up the character or – whisper it – bring back Robin the Boy Wonder tends to be met by a huge outcry from the fans. For 2012's *The Dark Knight Rises*, director Christopher Nolan challenged himself to see if he could introduce Robin in a way that wouldn't have fandom spitting feathers. He succeeded, but only by making the character so removed from the comic book version he was barely recognisable. Nolan's Boy Wonder was John Blake, a young and optimistic orphan turned incorruptible police officer who never lost faith in all that Batman stands for. It is only at the very end of the film, when Blake inherits the keys to the Batcave, that we discover John's real name is Robin. The reveal is such a stretch from its source material, it illustrates just how wary filmmakers are of re-introducing Batman's sidekick into the franchise.

But for many years, and for an entire generation, Batman meant only one thing – actors Adam West and Burt Ward, wrapped in unflattering leotards, prancing around vibrant sets in broad daylight, earnestly exchanging puns and quips as they foiled the dastardly plan of whichever faded actor from the Golden Age of Hollywood played the guest villain that week. The show is gloriously camp and over the top, but it works due to the cast playing it completely straight and giving it their all. The witty, tongue-in-cheek scripts came from a team of writers led by Lorenzo Semple Jr. Semple would later work on the screenplays for paranoid political thrillers *The Parallax View* (1974) and *Three Days of the Condor* (1975).

Batman's rise was meteoric. The same year the TV show launched, a film was released in cinemas, the first full-length, non-serialised theatrical adaptation of the character. At its height, *Batman* was one of only two prime-time[1] shows (the other being soap opera *Peyton Place*) to be broadcast twice in one week as part of the regular network schedule. Part one went out on Wednesday at 7:30 pm, and usually ended with the Dynamic Duo trapped in a preposterous and overly elaborate death trap, 'to be continued…'. This nail-biting cliff-hanger would be resolved on Thursday, same Bat Time, same Bat Channel.

The *Batman* TV show was much welcome. Its delirious visuals tapped perfectly into 1960s psychedelia, compounded by the show's use of Dutch angles, a cinematographic device from German Expressionism whereby shots are filmed off kilter to suggest things are not quite what they seem. The beats of each storyline were essentially the same every week, so viewers reassuringly knew what they were in for. It was easy, it was throwaway and it was fun. After one murdered president and thousands of reluctant patriots being slaughtered in the jungles of Vietnam, this kind of safe escapism was just what America needed.

Batman's success boosted comic book sales, not only for DC but in general. But while Marvel's star continued to ascend, in sales terms, DC were still ahead in the game. DC also had the good sense to never really drop the ball when it came to quality of their output. Marvel's bullpen was formidable, but DC too had solid talent. There was veteran artist Carmine Infantino, who in 1956 helped revive the Flash, a move seen by comic book historians as being just as important in heralding the Silver Age of Comics as anything Marvel created. In 1960, writer Gardner Fox, together with artist Mike Sekowsky, created the Justice League of America. Fox then worked with Infantino on *The Flash #123* (cover date September 1961), a landmark DC story because it introduced the concept of the multiverse. Marvel's complex, interwoven universe was more elaborate and impressive than DC's, but we shouldn't overlook the efforts of DC to expand their own. The 'distinguished competition', as Stan dubbed DC in his Bullpen Bulletins, was making impressive creative strides of its own.

Even before the TV series aired, DC's star editor Julius Schwartz had ensured Batman was already enjoying a renaissance. Like Stan, Schwartz was a native New Yorker of Romanian-Jewish descent. He also greatly influenced the Silver Age of Comics. Batman's success on the small screen only added to the popularity of what Schwartz was doing on the page. As a direct result of the *Batman* TV series, its comic book counterpart become the first title in decades to sell more than one million copies. Martin Goodman knew he needed to get Marvel on television right now.

Stan knew it too. As a child, he had devoured radio and film, and was aware of the transformative power of this relatively new medium. Crucially, he also knew that Batman co-creator Bob Kane had made a lot of money from the TV show. By this time Stan and Bob were very good friends, both New Yorkers in the same game from the same high school. Stan and Joan frequently met up for dinner with Bob and his second wife, the actress Elizabeth Sanders, who would go on to make cameos in the three *Batman* live-action films of the 1990s. Bob had struck a deal with Jack Liebowitz at DC back in 1946 that not only gave him a cut of the licensing, but also allowed him to claim sole creator credit on Batman, much to the chagrin of co-creator Bill Finger.

Bob Kane's profile rose immeasurably in the wake of the *Batman* television series. Now able to publicise himself as 'the Man who invented the Bat', he featured in many newspaper and magazine articles as well as on talk shows. Bob moved to LA to act as a consultant on the show, living the Hollywood lifestyle as much as he possibly could. Meanwhile, poor old Bill Finger could do nothing but watch as his erstwhile creative partner lived the high life off the back of a luxuriously massaged truth. To really rub it in, Kane renegotiated his DC contract when the TV show was at its height, securing even more rights and much more money. Finger went on to write for several TV shows, including his first public credit on any Batman story, for a two-part episode in season two of the

1966 show. Bill Finger died in 1974, aged only 59, largely forgotten, forever in the shadow of Bob and the Bat. It has only been in recent years that Bill Finger's invaluable contribution to the creation of Batman has been deservedly recognised. But that is another story.

Back to 1966, and it hadn't escaped Stan's attention that this new *Batman* series, ironically, seemed more in line with the Marvel sensibility. With its heavy use of puns and alliterations, the TV show frequently felt like it had leapt directly out of his head. Keen to strike while the Bat-iron was hot, but not prepared to fight the Bat-behemoth for prime-time audiences, Marvel made their play for television glory. But the first-ever TV series based on their characters would not be a prime-time live-action spectacular like *Batman*. Marvel's televisual debut was a cartoon. A bad one.

Saturday morning was always the favoured slot on American television networks for kids' cartoons, But, from the mid-'60s onwards, commissioners and advertisers began to truly exploit its commercial potential. There was literally a captive audience, sitting cross-legged on the floor, transfixed to their sets. Why not have a block of programming around which these impressionable little tykes could be bombarded with products and services?

The first true powerhouse of TV animation was the partnership of William Hanna and Joseph Barbera. This pair of American animation directors would enjoy a partnership that spanned six decades, their names forever seared into the minds of kids everywhere as they sat through the end credits of so many cartoons. During the 1940s, they created the wickedly violent cat-and-mouse capers of *Tom and Jerry*, before dominating the American television animation industry from the late 1950s onwards. Their characters would become known across the globe, with cartoons such as *The Huckleberry Hound Show*, *The Yogi Bear Show*, *The Flintstones*, *Top Cat* and *The Jetsons*. *The Flintstones* was the first animated series to be awarded that coveted prime-time slot. Much of the initial Saturday morning scheduling was repeats of these cartoons, alongside shorts that had previously appeared in cinemas, featuring Bugs Bunny, Daffy Duck and the rest of Warner Bros' *Looney Tunes* and *Merry Melodies* characters. As the decade progressed, Hanna-Barbera Productions, Inc. began making cartoons specifically for the booming Saturday morning schedules, including *Wacky Races*, *Laurel and Hardy* and *Scooby-Doo, Where Are You!* to name just a few.

Other animation houses soon cashed in on the weekend madness. DePatie-Freleng Enterprises created *The Pink Panther*, a silent-but-smart character that began life in the title credits of Blake Edwards' classic 1963 comedy film of the same name. Jay Ward Productions also deserves a mention if only for giving the world the wonderful *Rocky and Bullwinkle*. Satirical and self-referential, there's never been a better cartoon about a flying squirrel and a moose.[2]

All these studios used a budget-saving production technique called 'limited animation'. This meant the animators did not redraw entire frames every time, but reused the same elements. The finished product looked decidedly cheap, but because quantity not quality was the name of the game, this became the norm. These cartoons were about as far as you could get from the delicate beauty and hand-drawn attention to detail you'd find in classic Walt Disney, but the kids didn't care and many of these shows became huge hits.

For Marvel's first foray into television, Martin Goodman hastily struck a production deal with Grantray-Lawrence Animation, a studio co-founded by Grant Simmons, Ray Patterson and Robert Lawrence. Between them, Simmons and Patterson had an impressive pedigree. Together they had worked for Disney on *Fantasia* (1940) and *Dumbo* (1941), before contributing to several Oscar-winning cartoons for Hanna-Barbera at MGM Studios. They founded their own production company in 1954. When Martin Goodman approached them, Grantray-Lawrence Animation was mainly making commercials, but its track record revealed talent and Goodman felt these were the guys up to the challenge of bringing Marvel's superheroes to the small screen.

Seeing the success enjoyed by his friend Bob Kane, Stan made sure he was as involved in the production of this new Marvel TV series as much as possible. At that time, the Lee family was still living on Long Island, so producer Robert Lawrence rented Stan and Joan a penthouse apartment at 30 East 60th Street, near the Marvel offices on Madison Avenue. There Stan could work after hours as a consultant on the show.

Goodman's strategy was simple. Make a load of short cartoons that could either be cut into filler segments, or edited together to make thirty-minute episodes, then syndicate them across the country. A total of sixty-five half-hour shows were produced, each comprised of three seven-minute chapters. *The Marvel Super Heroes* featured Captain America, the Incredible Hulk, Iron Man, Thor and Sub-Mariner.

Marvel placed promotional ads in their comics, telling readers to check their local paper for broadcast schedules. But would it be a hit?

The very first episode of *The Marvel Super Heroes* aired on Thursday, 1 September 1966, but depending on where you were in the country, you could watch it every night, five nights a week. A syndicated kids cartoon could never have the same impact as the live-action prime-time *Batman*, but it didn't help that Grantray-Lawrence's 'limited animation' techniques were even more shoddy than average. *The Marvel Super Heroes* was produced using xerography – photocopied images used directly in the animation – and the only moving parts were the lips, or sometimes the limbs. It was crude and clunky. An original theme song was written, but it lacked the kitschy charm and catchy melody of the '66 *Batman* theme (which I bet you can hear in your head right now. You're welcome). This forgettable Marvel ditty kicks off with a weird, dated fanfare, even for 1966, before we get the opening line: 'Meet the sulky, over bulky, kinda Hulky superhero!' Not exactly an earworm for the ages.

In its defence, *The Marvel Super Heroes* should be credited for using the original stories from the comics. Plus, the voice actors give it their all and, by lifting the original artwork directly from the comics, the cartoon preserved and celebrated the original artwork of Kirby, Heck, Ditko and others. Both the X-Men and the Avengers make a surprise appearance in a couple of episodes, as do established foes such as the Mandarin, Loki, Baron Zemo, Doctor Doom and the Red Skull. Overall, Marvel's first animated series never truly captures the complex universe, nor the anarchic charm that existed in the comics. Despite the show not setting the world alight, as Stan would have liked, Marvel's reputation was not damaged by this unremarkable debut. Once the show was on air, Lawrence whisked Stan on the road to continue speaking engagements at college campuses, which Stan always loved as he got to be the showman, raconteur and star of the show.

At the same time, DC Comics had not been idle either. Hot on the heels of *Batman*, Marvel's rivals had been cooking up something with another animation studio, Filmation Associates. On Saturday, 10 September 1966, less than two weeks after the premiere of *The Marvel Super Heroes*, *The New Adventures of Superman* debuted on CBS.

Like the Marvel strategy, Filmation was commissioned to produce a raft of short segments that could be used either as fillers or together as a longer programme. It too kept faithful to the comic book source, but also borrowed heavily from previous incarnations. Veteran actors Bud Collyer and Joan Alexander – Superman and Lois Lane in the 1940s radio series and the Fleischer Studio cartoons – reprised their roles with relish. The first episode lasted thirty minutes, with two Superman stories either side of a single *Adventures of Superboy* short. This version of the Man of Steel never achieved the same level of praise as the older Fleischer cartoons, but *The New Adventures of Superman* proved highly popular.

Meanwhile, Marvel's cartoon output had a bit of a wobble when Grantray-Lawrence Animation went bankrupt in 1967. Fortunately, it wasn't before they'd managed to deliver another animated Marvel adventure. This time, it was a solo outing with *Spider-Man*. This time, they hit closer to the mark. A co-production with Canada, the show first aired on ABC on 9 September 1967 – finally in the coveted Saturday morning slot. This time, they also nailed the theme tune. It was written by Bob Harris with lyrics by Paul Francis Webster. Harris' other notable credit was the theme to Stanley Kubrick's 1962 adaptation of *Lolita*, but Webster was a three-times Academy award-winning lyricist,[3] with sixteen further nominations under his belt. In hiring such a heavyweight musical wordsmith for *Spider-Man*, Marvel wanted to come out swinging. Like the 1966 *Batman* theme tune, the song relies on catchy repetition and contemporary arrangement. The end result became permanently lodged in the brains of a generation, especially the opening line: 'Spider-Man, Spider-Man, does whatever a spider can.' You can tell a theme song has made it when people know the theme but never saw the show. You'll know it. Even if you don't think you do. Go online and look it up. Decades later, most of the modern Spider-Man films feature a nod to that theme. And for many, Canadian actor Paul Soles will always be the voice of Spider-Man.

Again, Stan served as story consultant, but this time with additional input from John Romita. Limited animation was the order of the day and there's a lot of repetition; that same shot of Spidey swinging across New York appears far too often. Spider-Man's costume is mainly red and blue, with far less detailed webbing than in the comics, as that would be too costly and time-consuming to animate. In the first season the spider on his chest only has six legs, but who's counting, right?

Like *The Marvel Super Heroes*, the limited animation does allow for the essence of Steve Ditko's original artwork to shine through. Stories and characters from the comics were deployed, including villains Doctor

Octopus and the Green Goblin, and of course J. Jonah Jameson, the irascible editor of *The Daily Bugle*, where Peter Parker struggles to earn a living as a freelance news photographer. The first season of *Spider-Man* remains true to the spirit of the Marvel character and his universe.

When Grantray-Lawrence Animation went under, Krantz Films took over, appointing American filmmaker Ralph Bakshi as director and executive producer on *Spider-Man*. Bakshi would go on to make 1972's subversive *Fritz the Cat*, which has the dubious honour of being the first animated feature film in the US to land an X rating. In 1978, he adapted J.R.R. Tolkien's *The Lord of the Rings*. Mixing live action with animation, the film is otherworldly and disconcerting, which is apt for such an epic fantasy. With a cast including John Hurt as Aragorn and *Star Wars* stalwart Anthony Daniels as Legolas, Bakshi's adaptation was a critical success despite compressing the source material to such an extent that the film is an ambitious but confused oddity.

Bakshi certainly didn't apply the same ambition to *Spider-Man*. Seasons two and three were made on an even smaller budget than the first. The decision was made to completely ignore all the classic Marvel villains and storylines. Instead, Spidey tackles generic beasts and monsters. To economise further, some episodes, such as 'Revolt in the Fifth Dimension' and 'Phantom from the Depths of Time', were just repurposed episodes of another Krantz Films/Bakshi animation, *Rocket Robin Hood*, which was a re-imagining of Robin Hood in a futuristic sci-fi setting. Bakshi literally dropped Spider-Man in scenes from this odd little cartoon, complete with gigantic robot beetles. Still, by this time, they'd given the spider on his chest the right number of legs so it's not all bad. Despite this 'inventive' approach to cost-cutting, with its bad animation and curious storylines, the show has become something of a cult favourite, resulting in Spider-Man memes proliferating across the web. Fitting really.

When *Spider-Man* premiered on ABC in 1967, Marvel badly wanted to win the battle for Saturday morning supremacy. Marvel also knew they were going up against *The New Adventures of Superman*. Spidey couldn't defeat the Man of Steel alone, so they played four aces they had up their sleeve. On the same morning as *Spider-Man* swung into action, so too did *The Fantastic Four*. For this cartoon, Marvel brought in the big guns. The show was produced by the mighty Hanna-Barbera and featured character design by DC Comics' veteran Alex Toth. Although he had recently worked with Stan and Jack on *The X-Men*, this was a bit of a coup. Stan may have personally requested Toth after collaborating with him on *X-Men*, but it wouldn't have gone unnoticed that one of DC's old guard was now storyboarding a Marvel production.

The Fantastic Four storylines were also lifted faithfully from the original comics, and more characters from the Marvel Universe made their TV debut, including Galactus, the Silver Surfer and a shape-shifting alien race known as the Skrulls. While still relying on limited animation, the show remains a strong entry in Marvel's televised output. *The Fantastic Four* lasted twenty episodes before being cancelled in 1968. It perhaps would have lasted longer were it not for a grassroots, non-profit child-advocacy group, Action for Children's Television (ACT). The spiritual successor of Wertham's crusade in the 1950s, ACT dedicated itself to 'improve' the quality of children's television by targeting several cartoons it believed to feature high levels of violence. ACT was, at the time, a powerful lobby and *The Fantastic Four* was one of the shows it managed to drive off the air, despite not being any more violent than other cartoons made at the time. By this point, *The New Adventures of Superman* had transformed into a more general showcase for other DC characters, including the Justice League of America, but in 1969 that too was cancelled. Not even Superman could survive the stern eye of conservative America.

As the 1960s drew to a close, the bubble had apparently burst on superhero TV shows. The game-changing live-action *Batman* series, once so adored by so many, suffered a huge drop in ratings during the third season and was canned in 1968, only two years after its stellar ascension. Rival network NBC agreed to take over production from ABC, but when it transpired that many expensive sets built for the show had already been destroyed, NBC abandoned the project. The Bat was dead.

Spider-Man was the only one to survive into the next decade. After three seasons, the final episode aired on 14 June 1970. A fourth season of *The New Adventures of Superman* did last until that September but all its episodes were repeats. The changing public appetite, combined with the efforts of ACT, had put an end to this short-lived raft of TV superheroes.

As for Stan, he had used the late 1960s to take his friend Bob Kane's example and raise his public profile even higher. He made several televised appearances to discuss the success of superhero comics, at times credited well above his actual job title. In one round-table discussion, Stan was dubbed 'creator of the Marvel Comics Group'.[4] When writing about the upcoming *Fantastic Four* TV show, Ohio-based *Akron Beacon Journal,* stated that 'the characters are the brainchild of Stan Lee, who is the fearless leader of the Marvel comic book empire'.[5]

Did Stan ruthlessly strive to elevate his status? Put it this way. He didn't exactly correct these incorrect job descriptions. Rightly or wrongly, he let others cement his reputation as the face of Marvel. This trend would continue for the rest of his life, reviving his fortunes on more than one occasion. Little did he know there was a firestorm coming.

As sad as it was to see *Batman* cancelled in 1968, that year will probably be remembered by Americans for more tragic moments with the assassinations of Senator Robert Kennedy and Dr Martin Luther King Jr. The end of the Vietnam War was nowhere in sight, and America's clamour for change continued to boil over into the streets, loud, angry and violent. But change was coming for Stan Lee. Martin Goodman's company was about to undergo the biggest upheaval in its history. And Stan would soon lose the one person who helped keep it together.

Chapter Eleven

Stan Lee Presents

In 1968, Martin Goodman sold Marvel. The offer he couldn't refuse came from a corporate lawyer who specialised in mergers and acquisitions, Martin S. Ackerman. This ambitious entrepreneur had started investing in the publishing industry through the conglomerate he had founded in 1962, Perfect Film and Chemical Corporation. Ackerman was keen to build on an empire that now included pulp paperback book company Popular Library which, in turn, owned the Curtis Publishing Company. Ackerman had then zeroed in on Goodman's empire and made his play to strengthen his position as a publishing giant. He offered to buy both the parent company that produced Goodman's entire magazine range, and the jewel in the crown, his comic book division Marvel Comics.

Regardless of Ackerman's advances, Goodman had already been thinking about his company's future. He had ambitions to install his son, Charles 'Chip' Goodman high up in its ranks, but was initially reticent about walking away himself. This was, after all, the house that Marty built. Ever since the days of Timely, decades of blood, sweat and ink had gone into the presses, developing a successful publishing business model that was agile and resilient enough to weather any economic storm and the fickle appetites of the general public. Marvel had lit up the once-derided comic book division like a roman candle, sparking huge sales and making a dent in popular culture in ways no one saw coming.

Goodman was many things, but an idiot he was not. Despite such a vibrant renaissance, the dip in superhero popularity at the end of the 1960s was also a factor. The freewheeling counterculture of the Love Generation had failed to overthrow the establishment. The superhero revolution, it seemed, would not be televised. Comic book sales had dropped overall, but Marvel were still enjoying success. Goodman knew it was time to sell up while his business still had currency. It didn't hurt that the deal Ackerman proposed was more than generous. It was finalised in July 1968, and Perfect bought Martin's publishing empire for $15 million in cash. That's just over $110 million in today's money.[1] Not too shabby.

The terms of the deal included Goodman staying on as president and publisher, which he would for four more years. Another benefit from the deal was that Goodman's prohibitive distribution deal with Independent News was replaced by a contract with Ackerman's own Curtis Publishing, allowing Marvel to publish as many titles as they wanted for the first time in a decade. As hoped, Chip Goodman was installed as editorial director, but there was another term of the deal that Martin may not have seen coming. Perfect insisted Stan sign a contract to stay on as figurehead and spokesperson of Marvel Comics. This cemented Stan's conviction that he truly was the face of Marvel and that all those little personal touches he had devised throughout the 1960s had been the right thing to do. The Bullpen Bulletins, Stan's Soapbox, the college campus appearances, random meet and greets, televised interviews, even lending his voice to Marvel's fledgling animated output, had all paid off. Prior to the takeover, Stan had muscled through to becoming Marvel personified; here was an official endorsement right from the top. Stan Lee was good for business.

The transition to new ownership did not go without a few hiccups. At one point, Martin Goodman took Stan aside and promised him that the company buyout meant his editor-in-chief would receive valuable stock options or 'warrants' in the company. He reassured Stan that he and Joan would never have to worry about money for the rest of their lives. Stan had never thought himself shrewd when it came to financial dealings, that he was 'too casual with money', and this moment was a prime example. As he was one of the terms of Perfect's buyout, Stan could easily have renegotiated a better employee contract for himself, but instead he trusted Martin's assurance that he would be up to his eyeballs in stock options. But the warrants never materialised. All he got from the contract he so eagerly signed without question was a small pay rise. After the deal went through, Martin never spoke of these stock options again, nor did he make good on his word to see Stan right for the rest of his life. 'Yep, that was me,' Stan later shrugged, 'sharp negotiator, shrewd judge of character, and trusting soul.'

Martin Goodman, on the other hand, had made a very astute business decision. That year, comic book publishers raised prices from twelve cents to fifteen cents a copy, which resulted in a further dip in sales. Martin Goodman pocketed a vast fortune, while his staff, Stan included, were left wondering what the future would hold under new owners.

But don't think for a minute that Stan and his family were slumming it. Stan once wrote that around this time, just after his father died in early 1968, he sold the Long Island home in Hewlett Harbor to buy a two-bedroom condo in Manhattan, 'somewhere in the East 60s'.[2] The family would stay around that area until 1980 'because Joanie, my little black-belt, world-class shopper, didn't want to live anywhere that wasn't within walking distance of the Bloomingdale's department store at Sixtieth Street and Third Avenue,' said Stan. The truth is, however, Stan also owned that house on Long Island until 1980.[3] Here we have another case of our hero being more than a little vague about dates or, at the very least, playing down his wealth. Despite what he says in his autobiography, by the end of the 1960s, Stan owned more than one property. He was doing more than OK.

In 1968, Jack Kirby was planning a move of his own. His daughter, Lisa, suffered from chronic asthma and in May, Jack borrowed $2,000 from Martin Goodman to help relocate him and his family to Los Angeles. He would still be working for Marvel, but replacing lungfuls of New York smog with fresh West Coast sea breeze that would hopefully alleviate her condition. Stan announced 'with mixed emotions' via the December 1968 Bullpen Bulletin that Jack was moving to LA and in January 1969, the Kirbys began their new life in Orange County.

Later that year, another departure brought yet more change to Marvel. None other than Martin Ackerman, the man responsible for buying Martin Goodman's publishing house, found himself out on his ear. Turned out he had some unhealthy lawsuits churning over, which both the shareholders and the board didn't find in their best interests, so they forced him to resign. Ackerman was replaced with basically the same person, albeit in a different suit. Former Revlon senior executive, Sheldon Feinberg seamlessly slotted into the space once occupied by Ackerman and, despite a new CEO, nothing really changed for Marvel Comics.

The last year of the 1960s proved tough for Jack Kirby. Since the move west, he had struggled to keep up with his obligations to Marvel and the decade ended with Kirby failing to renegotiate more favourable terms of his contract. What Marvel didn't know was that when he was visiting New York to discuss the contract, he had also met with DC Comics' superstar Carmine Infantino, who had recently been promoted to editorial director. Jack had three ideas cooking that he later claimed he didn't want to serve up for Marvel, including a high-concept adventure of all-powerful alien entities he called New Gods. Another version of events plays out that Kirby had actually wanted to introduce these characters to Marvel, but Stan had vetoed this. The story goes that Kirby wanted to shake things up for the *Thor* title, wipe everyone out in the comic and start afresh with this new order of supreme beings. Whether Kirby had always intended to hold New Gods back for DC or Stan had thwarted Kirby's ambition is anyone's guess. Regardless, Jack Kirby was now distinctly disgruntled with his Marvel employers and clearly had other irons in the fire.

Meanwhile, Stan was fighting his own battles within the company. The continued dip in sales led Martin Goodman to further tighten the Marvel belt, including cancelling *Doctor Strange*, only a year after the Master of the Mystic Arts had finally landed his own solo title. It was round this time that Chip Goodman, now fully ensconced in management within the Marvel machine, canned the Merry Marvel Marching Society fan club. Stan was not happy. He knew the value of M.M.M.S. to maintaining a direct line of contact between the Marvel Universe and its more loyal readership. For Goodman, it was just too costly to keep sending out these membership packs containing exclusive material. Instead, merchandising rights were sold off to an independent company based in California, run by a business man named Don Wallace. At the end of 1969, Wallace launched a new fan club called Marvelmania.

Like its predecessor, the Marvelmania membership kit featured a card, newsletter and custom artwork. The first kit cost one dollar seventy-five cents plus twenty-five cents shipping, and the first 5,000 came with a test issue of brand-new fanzine *Marvelmania Magazine*. The first proper edition of this was released in spring 1970 and featured a black-and-white illustration of Black Bolt, leader of the Inhumans, by his creator Jack Kirby. Despite this, Stan was not a fan of taking such an important aspect of the Marvel personality out of house. He was neither publisher nor editor of *Marvelmania Magazine*, with those duties given to Don Wallace and Mark Evanier respectively. This is not to say Evanier didn't do a bang-up job. He was a former president of a Los Angeles comic book club before becoming Kirby's production assistant. Evanier definitely had the insider knowledge and experience to oversee *Marvelmania Magazine*, but that was not the point. Since inception, this had been Stan's domain. He had spent years nurturing the public voice of the company. No longer being able to oversee and control Marvel's tonality must have made him very uncomfortable.

Stan wasn't the only major Marvel player to find himself not as involved as he used to be. By 1970, Jack Kirby was only supplying art for *The Fantastic Four* and *Thor*. His physical absence to warmer climes had rendered him conspicuous by his absence. That March, Jack Kirby quit Marvel and signed a three-year contract with DC.

As has been seen previously, it's fruitless to establish the exact causes for these turning points in the history of Marvel Comics. While others within the bullpen had made invaluable contributions to building the brand, two men had long towered above all else. Stan was 'The Man' and Jack was 'King'. These nicknames were not attributed without merit. So, when arguably the most celebrated creative partnership in the history of comic books finally broke down, to this day people still want to know why. And we'll never really know for sure.

We do know that Jack and Stan enjoyed a volatile relationship from day one, although Stan had always insisted it was not as fractious as the gossipmongers and professional speculators would have the world believe.[4] Bottom line, you cannot work so closely with another creative person for as long as they did without there being some collaborative spark, some sense of mutual admiration and respect. It is also safe to assume that there was not one single factor that led to Kirby quitting Marvel.

Stan was now officially the face of the brand, which would definitely have placed some colleagues' noses out of joint, Kirby perhaps more than most. Recent corporate decisions had also unimpressed him. Several sources close to the bullpen at that time later observed that the artist was fed up of not only a lack of proper credit and recognition, but also his inability to control corporate use of his creations. Another contributing factor was the meeting he had held with Carmine Infantino at DC. They liked his ideas and would naturally relish reeling in such a monumental talent. Given Jack had failed to negotiate a better contract with Marvel two years earlier, and if Stan had indeed vetoed his New Gods idea, his ego would have been heavily bruised. His current company didn't respect him and his editor undermined his ideas. Why wouldn't he jump ship and swim to a shiny new company that promised to treat him well?

In hindsight, it's no surprise Jack left, but at the time it came as a bolt from the blue.

Jack's defection to the Distinguished Competition reverberated throughout the Marvel bullpen. 'I'll never forget when I walked into Stan's office and heard that Jack left,' recalled John Buscema in 1997. 'I thought they were going to close up! As far as I was concerned, Jack was the backbone of Marvel.'[5] Roy Thomas recalled that, 'Stan was very upset and a little depressed when he called me and Sol into his office to tell us Kirby had just called to quit.'[6] The professional and personal loss to Stan would have been profound. He would later often lament losing Jack, wishing that his star collaborator had agreed to a permanent role as Marvel's art director, but this had never appealed to Jack, who enjoyed the freelance life. Imagine a Silver Age Marvel Comics officially run by Stan Lee and Jack Kirby. Would a secure staff position, high up the Marvel food chain, have prevented the rift that led to Jack's departure? Surely a *what if* moment worthy of the Marvel title of the same name![7]

Jack Kirby wasn't the only departure that year. Stan's dutiful production manager, Sol Brodsky, left to co-found Skywald Productions with entrepreneur Israel Waldman. Together they published black-and-white magazines, mainly within the horror and western genres. While Sol would return to Marvel a few months later, it did nothing to boost Stan's feelings about the loss of Kirby.

Still, the show must go on. And, indeed, it did. Stan named John Verpoorten as Brodsky's replacement, determined as he was that nothing would stop the Marvel freight train. But who would take over Kirby's output? He was arguably Marvel's most valued creative force. His were enormous shoes to fill, but it was not an impossible task; the bullpen was brimming with talent. Besides, Stan had found a solution when Wally Wood left. And when Steve Ditko left. If anyone could keep the Marvel ship on course, it would be Stan Lee. Stan chose John Buscema to handle regular pencil duties on both *The Fantastic Four* and *Thor*. The man who most helped Stan build Marvel was gone, but the company forged ahead. Around this time Sheldon Feinberg, perhaps keen to distance the organisation from Ackerman's legacy, rebranded Perfect Film as Cadence Industries. Despite the rebrand, yet again Marvel Comics just carried on, churning out monthly issues to solid sales.

Meanwhile, Stan continued to promote himself and the industry. He felt that comic books deserved greater recognition as both a literary and art form, so he came up with the idea of creating a professional organisation, like a comic book version of the Academy of Motion Picture Arts and Sciences. With DC's Carmine Infantino on board, Stan set up the Academy of Comic Book Arts (ACBA). Naturally, Stan wasn't only elevating the prestige of comic books and their creators, he also had his marketing hat on. Later, he recalled:

> I felt that if we had an awards ceremony every year, we could probably get it on the radio and eventually, after we got a little more prestige, even have it televised. I knew there were a lot of celebrities who were into comics, and that's all you need to get something on television.[8]

The ACBA received support from many across the industry and also set up the Academy of Comic Book Arts Hall of Fame award, with Superman creators Jerry Siegel and Joe Shuster the first to be inducted.

In 1971, Stan was approached by the Department of Health, Education and Welfare to write a comic book warning kids about the dangers of drugs. He obliged and chose to feature this in a brand-new Spider-Man story. Together with penciller Gil Kane, and John Romita on inking detail, Stan devised a three-issue story arc beginning in *The Amazing Spider-Man #96* (cover date May 1971). The idea was simple. Spidey would get caught up in the New York drugs scene. Despite the story unequivocally condemning drug use, the comic depicted drugs and addicts strung out on illegal substances. This was in total breach of the Comic Book Authority Code, who refused to approve the issue. Undeterred, Stan and Martin Goodman decided to put the comic out anyway. 'I said, "Screw it",' Stan later recalled, 'and just took the Code seal off for those three issues.'[9] This was the first mainstream comic book ever published without code approval, with no stamp on the cover. It was a risk for sure, but one they felt was worth taking.

The story arc, which follows Peter Parker's dear friend Harry Osborn overdosing on unidentified pills,[10] was a triumph. The story received much praise in the press, and sold exceedingly well. This not only raised awareness of the Marvel brand, but also demonstrated the power of using the medium of comics to warn impressionable kids of the dangers of illegal drugs. The storyline's success actually led to a revision of the comics code itself. One of the most significant changes was that the code now permitted stories about werewolves and vampires, previously considered too adult and violent for mainstream comic books.

Stan continued to position himself as the spokesman of the comic book industry. In January 1971, he made a notable appearance on the panel at the National Cartoonist Society and hosted the wildly ambitious 'A Marvel-ous Evening with Stan Lee' at Carnegie Hall in January 1972. Unfortunately, with its shambolic dramatic readings by random actors and curious musical interludes, the event proved a rather chaotic and disappointing affair that failed to make its money back.

Despite his lauded status flying the flag for comic books, Stan once again grew conflicted about the direction of his writing career. Consequently, he sought to try other media where he could flex his literary muscle. Stan had struck up a friendship with French art house director Alain Resnais, and the pair collaborated on a never-completed film project called *The Monster Maker.*[11] To undertake the project, Stan took his first ever sabbatical from writing comic books. The industry had begun to frustrate him. Like Jack Kirby, he didn't like that he did not own the characters he helped create. Hollywood, therefore, proved a highly attractive option, and he confided with Resnais that he even considered bringing others with him, specifically Jack Kirby and John Buscema: 'These men are so talented that I think if I do movie work, I could take them with me,' he said.[12]

Around this time, both Marvel and DC raised the number of pages in their comics from thirty-two interior pages to forty-eight and bumped prices from fifteen to twenty-five cents. However, in a canny move, a few months later, Martin Goodman returned Marvel's comics to thirty-two pages but charged twenty cents. DC kept their prices at twenty-five cents, but now, comic book fans could buy five Marvel comics for the price of four from DC. The move paid off. Stan returned from his sabbatical to find that Marvel's sales had overtaken DC. The war, it seemed had been finally won.

In 1972, there was another major turning point for Stan Lee and Marvel. It was the year that Martin Goodman retired, fully expecting son Chip to become publisher of Marvel Comics. But Chip had little comic book experience, having only really worked within other divisions of his father's company. In March, Cadence promoted Stan Lee from editor-in-chief to publisher and editorial director of Marvel Comics.

It's not known whether the Cadence executives had sensed Stan was getting twitchy and wanted to make sure he didn't jump ship, or they had simply decided this was a perfect step up for him. But while the promotion was seamless, Martin Goodman was not pleased. Despite being an increasingly remote figure within the company, he took it as a professional and personal snub. He even accused Stan of betraying him after all that he had done for his younger relative. Stan never seemed to hold any bad blood for Martin's rather melodramatic remarks, which perhaps reflected how he felt about his new position. No longer answerable to his old boss, he had been elevated to a role that couldn't be topped. 'By this time,' he later wrote, 'I didn't care what Martin said or thought. I was finally free to do what I always felt could and should be done with Marvel, and that was all that mattered.'[13]

However, the price Stan had to pay for the role was that he would no longer be writing any stories. The final flagship titles that Stan Lee scribed were *The Amazing Spider-Man #110* (cover date July 1972) and *Fantastic Four #125* (cover date August 1972). He then walked away from comic book scripts and turned his attention to cue cards. Not that he needed them. Stan was now to go forth into the world and spread the gospel according to Marvel, something he had been doing for years. This no doubt sated Stan's already considerable ego, tapping into his gifted oratory skills and passion for entertaining a room. Unfettered, now he could go full throttle. Having already established a highly personal profile with the press, Stan was now regularly called upon by feature writers to lend his view on the cultural impact of comic books, either as having a bad influence on the day's youth, or as a true American art form. 'After a while, many writers started referring to me as "Mr Marvel",' he said. 'I kinda liked that.'[14]

Before stepping down as editor-in-chief, Stan handed over the reins to the one man he felt possessed all the right attributes to continue the so-called Marvel style: Roy Thomas. The perfect blend of editorial savvy, go-getting enterprise and creative firepower, Thomas had also been single-handedly responsible for obtaining rights to iconic hero Conan the Barbarian, whereupon Marvel reimagined the mighty Cimmerian for the comic book generation. Initially sceptical about introducing author Robert E. Howard's muscle-bound creation to a Marvel audience,

Stan was won over by Roy's hard work and persuasive confidence. Conan proved a hit, launching a trend in sword and sorcery epics in the comic book industry. Stan was convinced this young lad from Jackson, Missouri was his heir apparent. From then on, everything at Marvel Comics would be different. From then on, all their titles were prefixed with three simple-yet-powerful words: 'Stan Lee presents'.

It was a fitting legend for a man who was now just that. With John Romita promoted to art director, Stan and Roy set to work. Hand in glove, together they rolled out a bold and ambitious plan to shake things up like never before. Steve Ditko was gone. Jack Kirby was gone. Stan was no longer writing. Phase two of the Marvel Age of Comics was about to begin.

Chapter Twelve

The Long Dark Road to Hollywood

America in the 1970s was a far murkier place than during the previous decade. Progressive ideas that had germinated in 1960s counterculture did continue to grow – political awareness, women's economic freedom and cultural diversity – but a sense of unease crept across the country. Vietnam would drag on for five more years, ending in a humiliating defeat for America. The once-mighty nation, that had failed to flex its considerable muscle abroad, returned home with many people scratching their heads wondering what it was all for. Rising tensions and conflict in the Middle East led to an oil crisis in 1973 that struck hard in the American heartland, then in 1974, the Watergate scandal saw President Richard Nixon resign in shame to avoid an inevitable impeachment. The USA felt that little bit less united. Political paranoia and the huge dent in national pride after the fall of Saigon was reflected in the new wave of American cinema that cut jaggedly through to the mainstream.

At the same time as newly minted Marvel publisher Stan Lee was spreading the love across America, a posse of brash, young American filmmakers emerged, ripping back the shining veneer of his beloved New York, exposing the city's fetid underbelly. Directors such as William Friedkin, Francis Ford Coppola and Martin Scorsese crafted dark tales of morally corrupt antiheroes operating within the city's broken social and political systems. Friedkin's slick 1971 thriller *The French Connection* was inspired by a true story of how far NYPD narcotic detectives will go to bring down their prey. In 1972, *The Godfather* exploded into cinemas to worldwide critical and commercial acclaim. Coppola's masterpiece expertly immersed audiences among the dynastic tensions of immigrant crime families in New York, fighting tooth and claw for the soul of the city. Scorsese's more intimate, but no less profound, take on New York crime in 1973's *Mean Streets*, explored the broken and conflicted lives of low-level criminals with ties to the Mob. This trio of films perfectly captures the rotten side of the Big Apple, where inhabitants struggle in an unforgiving and indifferent metropolis. Where horrific acts of violence, betrayal and murder are justified in the name of one thing that all immigrants in this city either longed for or clung to whatever the cost: respect.

Despite the frequent depictions of sadistic violence, these films were well received by the critics and public because they tapped into the increasingly cynical mood of the nation. For the first time since the Great Depression, the US had been forced to doubt itself and the values that it previously held so dear.

Entertainment in 1970s America not only celebrated moral ambiguity, but also ethnic diversity through a rise in multicultural genre films. *Shaft*, in 1971, exemplified the Blaxploitation genre, in which African American actors were, for the first time, cast as impossibly cool heroic leading men and women, no longer relegated to novelty villains or sidekicks. Martial arts movies also proved popular, the most successful being 1973's *Enter the Dragon*, starring the iconic Bruce Lee. A joint American and Hong Kong production, this landmark film successfully blended chopsocky action with Blaxploitation to huge success.

This public hunger for more gritty and diversified storytelling was also reflected in Marvel's output. While not leading the charge, Stan knew that Marvel had to be in the fight. Stan wanted the changing times to be present within the comic book universe and, as publisher, he worked hard with protégé Roy Thomas to realise that ambition. The bullpen started this decade with a raft of much younger talent than it had ten years ago, keen to take things as far as they could.

Fortunately, the recent revisions to the comics code meant they could. Stan himself was never interested in comic book stories crammed with lashings of sex, gore and violence, but at least now Marvel were able to push the boundaries further than ever in a bid to grab older readers. The early 1970s saw the resurrection of the horror comics, with titles such as *The Tomb of Dracula*, *The Monster of Frankenstein*, *Werewolf by Night*, *Man-Thing* and *The Living Mummy*. In 1971, Roy Thomas even added the morally ambiguous vampire Morbius into Spider-Man's rogues' gallery. Morbius proved so popular that he was later rewarded with his own title. After publishing *Tale of the Zombie* #1 (cover date July 1973), Marvel even trademarked the word 'zombie' in comic book titles, which it held onto until 1996.

Marvel went darker still with *The Amazing Spider-Man # 121* (cover date June 1973). Written by 20-year-old newcomer Gerry Conway, with pencils by Gil Kane, this bold storyline saw the Green Goblin kill the woman Spider-Man loved. This was a major turning point in Marvel Comics. Some comic book historians, including Marvel's own Roy Thomas, believe that 'The Night Gwen Stacy Died' marked the end of the Silver Age of Comics. It was a tragic story that shocked readers, simply because, in comics, characters never normally died and actually stayed dead. This dramatic denouement was symbolic of the bold directions this new wave of writers and artists wanted to take mainstream comics.

Marvel's welcome play for diversity led to the creation of new characters with different ethnicities. Marvel's first black superhero, Black Panther, actually made his debut back in *Fantastic Four #52* (cover date July 1966) and their first African-American superhero was the Falcon, debuting three years later. Luke Cage, however, was the first African American to grace the front cover of a mainstream comic book in *Hero for Hire #1* (cover date June 1972). Then there was Native American masked hero Red Wolf, and a duo of martial arts warriors, Master of Kung Fu and Iron Fist.

This new breed of Marvel characters was more complicated than ever before, and the morally conflicted antihero was reflected no better than in the Punisher. This was a vigilante who walked the same New York streets currently being explored in cinema. Created by Gerry Conway in 1974, the Punisher is the alter ego of Frank Castle, an ex-military veteran whose entire family is gunned down by the Mob. Castle works through his trauma and grief by declaring war on organised crime, savagely punishing the New York underworld with his own personal arsenal. Stan Lee has said he came up with the name of the character, but really this is Conway's brutal world. The Punisher is very much a product of his time. While his lack of super powers and quest for familial revenge could be dismissed as a more brutal version of Batman, the character was actually inspired by American author Don Pendleton's monthly action-adventure book series *The Executioner*. In it, a Vietnam veteran called Mack Bolan becomes a serial killer of criminals after the Mafia kills his family. Like *The Executioner*, Frank Castle is an even more pulpy distillation of his country's growing rage, frustration and alienation at that time. His military backstory reflects years of failure and slaughter in Vietnam, while his vigilante methods allude to the distrust many Americans had developed in the law and the justice system, and also the power of the New York mob as explored so vividly on the big screen at the time.

When it came to vice and corruption, Marvel rarely took a political stance. That wasn't Stan's thing. But after Watergate, writer Steve Englehart made a bold statement. In *Captain America #175* (cover date July 1974), everyone's favourite patriot follows a criminal conspiracy leading directly to the White House, and after a confrontation, the president commits suicide. Even though his identity is never revealed, the parallels are blatant. 'I was writing a man who believed in America's highest ideals at a time when America's president was a crook,' Englehart later reflected, 'I could not ignore that.'[1] His story, with its especially brutal climax would have been unthinkable during previous decades, especially for a comic book. It further reflected where the comic book industry had found itself, and the identity crisis America was experiencing during these troubled times.

That year, a face from Marvel's past emerged, seeking retribution and justice of his own. In a move that smacks of spite more than anything else, Martin Goodman came out of retirement. Still sore from what he saw as a personal slight by Cadence for not electing his son as publisher, Martin resurrected Atlas Comics as direct competition to Marvel and installed Chip at the helm. He also managed to lure several writers and artists from the Marvel bullpen, including the elusive Steve Ditko and even Stan's own brother, Larry Lieber. Stan never seemed too bothered by the fact his brother was working for Atlas, perhaps because he had moved on to such an elevated status he could easily roll with the potential punches. Fortunately for Marvel, and despite this talent on board, Atlas was a commercial and financial failure. A lack of compelling characters undermined Goodman's ambition and his company completely crumbled less than a year after it began.

In 1974, Roy Thomas stood down as editor-in-chief. He missed the life of a writer at the expense of too many business compromises. Happily returning to his original role, the position was filled by a rapid succession of talented souls who continued to steady the ship. These included Wolverine co-creator Len Wein, then Roy Thomas' protégé Marv Wolfman, best known for co-creating with Gene Colan the half-undead vampire hunter Blade. After Wolfman, the Punisher co-creator Gerry Conway stepped up to the plate, but he only lasted a few months before being succeeded by Luke Cage co-creator Archie Goodwin.

A major coup under Goodwin's tenure came in 1977 when Marvel landed the rights to produce a comic book adaptation of a quirky little indie flick by the name of *Star Wars*. Despite this success – some say the deal actually saved Marvel from financial strife – Goodwin also proved to be a temporary fixture. In 1978, he was replaced by the prolific scripter Jim Shooter. This amiable slugger from Pittsburg had been with Marvel as a teenager during the late '60s. The revolving door of Marvel's editors-in-chief throughout the 1970s gave Jim the opportunity to, ahem, shoot to the top. Stan absolutely loved Shooter, who made significant but controversial strides during his nine years in the role.

Despite this high turnover of staff, there seemed to be an inexhaustible supply of reliable creatives lined up to keep things moving along. By now the Marvel method had long been interwoven into the fabric of the company. Stan had cultivated not just a way of working but an ethos and philosophy that made the creative part of business extremely resilient to change. With Marvel's comic book output in many good hands, Stan Lee spent the second half of the 1970s assuredly developing new projects. This confidence was bolstered by the excellent rapport he shared with the new CEO of parent company Cadence, Jim Galton. Stan and Jim liked and respected each other, which made for far smoother sailing than under Ackerman and Feinberg. Stan also attributed his savvier business decisions over the years to Jim Galton's professional advice.

After becoming publisher, Stan had bought a summer house in the Hamptons where the family would spend weekends. The sociable and charismatic Lees soon established close friends in that idyllic part of Long Island. Not that Stan had much time to laze around. Now free from the office-bound shackles of running the Marvel bullpen, he accelerated his travels through campuses and university halls across America, then in Canada, Europe and the Far East. Before long, he was racking up an average of one public speaking engagement a week, all year round. Notable excursions included Mexico City where he was issued six bodyguards to protect him for an admiring legion of fans. Another time, while in London, Stan received a call from Paul McCartney. The former Beatle invited Stan over to discuss collaborating on a comic book to support a song written and performed by his then wife Linda. While this never came to fruition, it was clear that the world saw Stan as the go-to guy for comic books.

In 1975, who should come back through Marvel's door but Jack Kirby? During his run at DC, Kirby had been less than kind about Stan. Former Marvel UK writer and *2000 AD* editor John Tomlinson observes how Kirby even went as far as to channel his feelings into one of his creations in his comic book title, *Mister Miracle #6*:

> 'Funky Flashman', an unmistakably Lee-like character, is represented as a verbose and dishonest parasite, skewered pitilessly in the story intro by Kirby the writer: 'In the shadow world between success and failure, there lives the driven little man who dreams of having it all!!! The opportunistic spoiler without character or values, who preys on all things like a cannibal!!! – Including you!!!'

By the mid-1970s however, time had healed wounds enough for Kirby to feel he could come back. His glorious return was announced publicly in New York on the last day of that year's Mighty Marvel Comic Convention. As you'd expect in a room full of comic book fans, the news was met with rapture. A follow-up notice in the April-May Bullpen Bulletins simply read, 'The King is Back. Nuff Said'.

The prodigal son was welcomed back to Marvel with open arms and given a three-year contract. In October 1975, Stan conducted a radio interview in LA and, clearly embracing his celebrity status, arrived at the studio in a Mercedes Limo owned by his friend, *Playboy* impresario Hugh Hefner. The interview was also notable for Jack Kirby appearing to prank call an unsuspecting Stan while on air. Later that year, Lee and Kirby were seen publicly sharing jokes with one another at Miamicon. How much of a professional act this was remains unclear, but at face value there did seem far less animosity between these two than many had previously thought.

Meanwhile, Stan's celebrity status continued to rise. As Tomlinson says, 'Stan was an undisputed master of what he once described as "pandemonious puffery". He even appeared in a TV ad campaign for Personna razor blades, spoofing his former role as Marvel's editor-in-chief and writer with the creation of a new hero – Personna Man.' In 1977, Stan appeared in a print ad endorsing Hathaway Shirts. Looking suave and confident, but still sporting that famous cheesy grin, the pull quote accompanying the image read, 'When you create superheroes, people expect you to look like one. I wear Hathaway shirts.' He was credited as 'Stan Lee, Originator of Marvel Comics'.

After years of touring and presenting, his showman rhetoric became more polished but also more self-aggrandising. It was common to hear Stan wax lyrical about creating the Marvel Universe, about how he tried to make his characters typical Americans with personal problems. When reminiscing about the birth of the Marvel Age, Stan would still laud his fellow artists in the bullpen, but at this point he was equally happy to take all the glory. For example, the July/August 1977 issue of arts and travel magazine *Quest* featured a five-page article by Stan titled, 'How I invented Spider-Man'. The magazine contents page teased the article with 'a bored hack starts writing for himself … and creates the world's most popular hero.'

Stan was always finding ways to reach a new audience. Marvel struck a deal with Fireside Books, a division of publishing giant Simon and Schuster. It was a simple idea that Stan took from cartoonist Jules Feiffer's 1965 book *The Great Comic Book Heroes*: reproduce the origins of classic Marvel characters in full-colour trade paperback format. Featuring the original artwork of Kirby, Ditko and more, readers could now access these stories without spending vast sums on hunting down back issues. The first, *Origins of Marvel Comics*, featured a foreword by Stan, before diving into the origins of the Fantastic Four, the Hulk, Spider-Man, Thor, and Doctor Strange. The book was a success, spawning more *Origins* volumes, as well as activity books and how-to guides. The most famous of these was 1978's *How to Draw Comics the Marvel Way*. Inside, Stan and John Buscema lifted the lid on the so-called 'Marvel style', breaking down how to draw muscular heroes and dynamic action splash pages. *How to Draw Comics the Marvel Way* influenced generations of aspiring comic book creatives and the book is still in print today.

Stan also collaborated with John Romita to launch a daily Spider-Man newspaper strip. Written in a dramatic, soap opera style, Stan wrote story arcs sometimes running up to twelve weeks. They existed within their own continuity, separate from the comic books, but featured many of the same characters. Stan had actually proposed the idea for a syndicated newspaper strip back in 1970 and two weeks' worth were drawn up, but the strip was never commissioned. Seven years later, in January 1977, *The Amazing Spider-Man* strip was picked up for syndication. A contrast from the Marvel method, Stan wrote the entire script on his own. Romita returned as artist on the initial run, but after four years, others carried on the intensive job of churning out strips on a weekly basis. Within the first month of launch, the strip appeared in over 200 papers, increasing to 500 papers a month worldwide. The strip continued with Stan's name attached until beyond the day he died, although Roy Thomas admitted he had been ghost writing for Stan since 2000.[2] The last ever original *The Amazing Spider-Man* strip was published on 23 March 2019, making this the most popular, successful and longest-lived strip about a superhero ever.

Over a decade had passed since Marvel failed to conquer television. Stan had learned lessons from past attempts, and this time he was armed with the savvy guidance of Jim Galton. Now a senior executive at Marvel, Stan would naturally be heavily involved in the development for TV of their key properties, but he would still have to contend with ratings-hungry stakeholders and other creatives in TV production, all huge egos wanting to leave their mark on already iconic characters. As before, the results were a decidedly mixed bag.

The Amazing Spider-Man premiered on 19 September 1977 with a feature-length pilot on CBS, simply named *Spider-Man*. The prime-time live-action show was developed by veteran radio and TV writer Alvin Boretz, with Peter Parker/Spider-Man played by Nicholas Hammond, whose only other notable credit was the eldest Von Trapp son in 1965's *The Sound of Music*. This Peter was older than the original Lee/Ditko creation, a university student navigating his way through part-time work at *The Daily Bugle*. The show was more grounded than the comic in every way. Gone were the flamboyant villains, replaced by organised crime, terrorist threats and common-or-garden thieves. Hammond is fine if a little bland in the role, frequently sporting a natty line in camel-coloured suits, but with all Spidey stunts performed by the show's stuntman, Fred Waugh, it could be anyone under the mask. Hammond didn't quite have the lithe super physique drawn by either Ditko or Romita, and the suit itself, while faithfully replicated, wasn't exactly the super fit. Made way before the invention of CGI effects, any shots of our hero swinging into action tend to look like a man wearing Spider-Man pyjamas dangling from a rope. It hasn't aged well, but it was the first ever live-action television show based on a Marvel character.

Following on from *The Amazing Spider-Man* was *The Incredible Hulk*. This infinitely superior show premiered also on CBS, on 4 November 1977.

The show was developed for TV by writer/producer Kenneth Johnson, who had already made *The Six Million Dollar Man* and spin-off *The Bionic Woman*, so he was experienced in high-concept science fiction shows. Johnson had a distinct vision on how to translate the Hulk from page to screen, not all of it Stan agreed with. The producer had initially been reluctant to make the show but became inspired while reading Victor Hugo's classic 1862 work, *Les Misérables*. Johnson saw Dr Banner as ultimately a tragic wandering figure on an endless quest for redemption. As with *The Amazing Spider-Man*, Johnson rejected the high-concept storylines and supervillains of the comics in favour of realistic and thoughtful plots involving the people Banner encounters on his literal road to salvation, whose misfortunes would inevitably unleash the beast within.

Bruce Banner, played gravely by actor and magician Bill Bixby, had his name changed to David Banner, allegedly because Johnson felt the use of Stan's beloved alliterative names felt too gimmicky outside a comic book. It has also been claimed by Stan that Johnson felt the name Bruce Banner sounded 'too gay'. Which is just weird. For the Hulk himself, they cast bodybuilder-turned-actor Lou Ferrigno. A Brooklyn native, Ferrigno was almost completely deaf and his performance pretty much involved him growling and snarling to terrified guest actors. He wore an appalling fright wig made of dyed-green yak hair that unfortunately looked exactly as I have described. This version of Hulk did not speak, and was nowhere near as powerful as his comic book counterpart. Had Johnson got his way, this Hulk would have been crimson, which he felt was a more accurate human colour of rage. Stan had no problem with much of the creative decisions made for the show, but on this he put his foot down. Hulk was green. No arguments.

The Incredible Hulk is, on the whole, a great show. With his now iconic catchphrase, 'Don't make me angry. You wouldn't like me when I'm angry', Bill Bixby's Banner is warm, sincere and profoundly human. Ferrigno does well with what he is given. Most of the camera angles are shot from below to make him seem even bigger, and in a time before CGI, his huge build and physicality is much more tangible and therefore all the more impressive. During the quieter moments, Ferrigno also conveys a certain childlike vulnerability, further adding depth to the performance. Every episode finishes with arguably the saddest theme music ever made for TV. Seek it out,[3] it makes every ending heartbreaking. The show never goes out with a bang. Instead we are left with a lonely figure on the road, moving on, still haunted by the beast within, from which he can never escape. In this way, *The Incredible Hulk* captured the spirit of the original comic book. More than this, the show perfectly reflected the moral ambiguity of the time, but with enough gloss and sci-fi action to satisfy audiences now living in a post-*Star Wars* age, when big, bold spectacles were the toast of the town.

CBS greenlit more Marvel heroes for the live-action treatment. In 1978, *Dr. Strange* teleported into living rooms across America for a made-for-television film that everyone hoped would get picked up for a full series. Despite a generous special-effects budget, and considerable input from Stan, the film faltered, spluttered and failed. It has since gained a cult following, some claiming it was a camp treat that was ahead of its time. However, it's more accurate to say that the show fell between two stools; too late to piggyback on its psychedelic 1960s origins and too soon to benefit from the fantasy craze of the 1980s. What probably killed *Dr. Strange* was the simple fact it was scheduled opposite a repeat of *Roots*, an immensely popular mini-series based on Alex Haley's 1976 novel *Roots: The Saga of an American Family*. Scooping up oodles of awards, this televisual phenomenon destroyed all other competition in its wake. Not even the Master of the Mystic Arts could beat that. This failure was followed by another TV movie, broadcast in 1979, *Captain America*. A terrible piece of entertainment that took huge liberties with the character, who looks more like Evel Knievel than Simon and Kirby's original creation; this too was exceptionally poor and never made it to series.

The Amazing Spider-Man lasted just two seasons before being cancelled in 1979. *The Incredible Hulk* fared better with five seasons until it was canned in 1982. Rival network NBC picked up the show in 1988 and made three TV movies, *The Incredible Hulk Returns* (1988), *The Trial of the Incredible Hulk* (1989), and *The Death of the Incredible Hulk* (1990). Marvel saw this as an attempt to introduce more characters from the Marvel Universe. *Returns* introduced Eric Kramer as a rather unconvincing Thor, *Trial* brought in Daredevil, played by Rex Smith, who had already garnered cult TV status as Jesse Mach in the fun but short-lived 1985 action series *Street Hawk*, about an unbelievably cool weaponised motorbike. Again, this additional Marvel character fails to convince. *Death* did actually kill off Dr David Banner and, despite there being talks to resurrect the character, star Bill Bixby sadly died of cancer in 1993, aged 59.

A major factor affecting the fate of these superhero TV shows was CBS getting nervous that it would be seen as 'the superhero network'. Stan was always honest about how he felt about these live-action adaptations: '*Dr. Strange* and *The Hulk* were fine,' he reflected in a 1985 interview, '*Captain America* was a bit [of a] disappointment and *Spider-Man* was a total nightmare.' Despite the disagreement over the colour, Stan thought that decisions made in bringing the Incredible Hulk to the small screen were prudent and correct: 'Ken Johnson took something that could have been corny and turned *The Incredible Hulk* into an engrossing show for adult audiences, without losing the younger fans.'[4] He felt the failure of *The Amazing Spider-Man* was due to a complete omission of the trademark humour, personality and human relationships that make the character so memorable. Stan knew that he needed to have even more input in any future projects, ensuring the Marvel magic was sprinkled in all the right places.

In 1978, Jack Kirby left Marvel. Again. It was technically his third departure (if you count being fired from Timely with Joe Simon), but this time it was for keeps. Stan and Jack had only just reignited the fire that fuelled their prolific creativity for a 100-page Fireside paperback, *The Silver Surfer: The Ultimate Cosmic Experience.* To have Marvel's dynamic duo back together was a thrill not only for Marvel fans across the globe, but also no doubt for Stan himself. But the party was short-lived. When Jack's three-year contract came up for renewal he declined, citing a combination of more lucrative offers and employee benefits working in television back in California. Jack never felt Marvel took care of him nor respected his craft. He even felt that during his 1970s tenure, other staffers in the bullpen were out to sabotage his work. 'I see it as a serpent's nest,' Kirby remarked in a 1982 interview in *Comics Scene #2.* 'And in a serpent's nest nothing can survive. Eventually all the snakes will kill each other. Eventually they'll also kill whatever generated them.' Naturally it made sense for Jack to work nearer to where he actually lived, and he was then hired to develop storyboards for the short-lived *Fantastic Four* animation.[5] It was the last time Jack Kirby would ever work for Marvel Comics.

There's no doubt that Jack planting both feet firmly on West Coast soil precipitated Stan's desire to follow suit. That summer, in a telling interview for rock magazine *Circus*, Stan candidly confessed to a major regret:

> I wish I made my move at Marvel 20 years ago, had done different things earlier. I was stupid – for my first 20 years, I did what my publisher wanted … and I think I should have gotten out of this business 20 years ago. I would have liked to make movies, to be a director or a screenwriter.[6]

The other major event of 1978, that impacted the comic industry, came a few weeks before Stan's fifty-sixth birthday. Warner Bros released *Superman: The Movie* with an untested stage actor, Christopher Reeve, in the title role alongside veterans Marlon Brando and Gene Hackman. Director Richard Donner delivered a film that was an absolute game changer, albeit one born from a complicated gestation period. Its original story, written by *The Godfather* author Mario Puzo, endured many rewrites before Donner brought in *James Bond* scriptwriter Tom Mankiewicz as 'creative consultant', chiefly to rewrite what had become a bloated and camp script. Donner and Mankiewicz insisted on a mantra of 'verisimilitude'. That is, *Superman* must feel real. The film must take its world and characters seriously. Despite studio pressure to cast an A-list Hollywood actor as Superman, an unknown actor was crucial to the film's believability. No celebrity, no baggage. It was a master stroke. At the film's heart, Christopher Reeve delivered a warm, vulnerable and layered performance that still makes his on-screen portrayal of Superman the one to beat.

The film was a triumph on all fronts. *Superman* leapt over the competition in a single bound, its impact more powerful than a locomotive. Made with a budget of $55 million and filmed back-to-back with a sequel, *Superman* became the second biggest-earning film of the year, defeated only by retro musical *Grease*. The Man of Steel made $300 million at the global box office, was nominated for three Academy Awards and received a Special Achievement Academy Award for Visual Effects. *Superman: The Movie* is still seen as a high-water mark for how to make a superhero motion picture. In what must have been at once thrilling and frustrating for Stan, the movie's success is largely because the filmmakers took the superhero storytelling approach he had pioneered at Marvel, applied it to the ultimate DC superhero and knocked it out of the park. While Marvel's recent televisual attempts had received mixed fortunes, come Christmas 1978, the entire world believed a man can fly.

Jerry Siegel and Joe Shuster's Kryptonian creation may have been king at the box office, but Stan was still holding onto his crown as the king of superheroes. In January 1979, *People* magazine proclaimed that, 'Stan Lee, creator of Spider-Man and The Incredible Hulk, is America's biggest mythmaker'. Stan and Marvel knew there was more mileage in mining the Marvel Universe for television and, hopefully, cinema. The phenomenal success of *Superman: The Movie* and, to a lesser extent, *The Incredible Hulk* TV show proved that tapping into the humanity behind the superpowers held the key to success. It was also agreed that there was only so much Stan could do if he was constantly shuttling back and forth from New York to LA. He told the other executives he needed to be where the action was all the time. Tinseltown was calling. In May 1979, Stan's Manhattan apartment was robbed, which shook up the family considerably. This disruption also made a big decision even easier to make. In 1980, after forty-one years in New York, Stan Lee packed his bags and moved to Hollywood.

Chapter Thirteen

Development Hell

Not everyone in the Lee family was happy about the move west. Stan had his sights set on finally realising the ambition he had harboured for some time – being a player in the movie business – but for his wife and daughter, this meant being uprooted from the place they loved dearly and leaving behind the city they had called home their entire lives. Los Angeles may project an image of glitz and showbiz glamour, but it was also viewed with suspicion by the more cynical and earthy folk from America's East Coast. Virtually synonymous with Hollywood, LA was often lampooned as a shallow pool of vacuity and self-serving vanity. Even Marvel had satirised the City of Angels in *The Fantastic Four #9 (*cover date December 1962*)*. In that same issue, where the quartet of power are declared bankrupt, they relocate to LA with the promise of a movie contract, only to find the place trivial and superficial. Los Angeles lacked the authenticity and streetwise swagger that made New York so vibrant.

Still, by the time of the move, Stan's beloved hometown had fallen far from grace. The migration of the middle classes to the suburbs and a nationwide economic recession that decimated the city's industrial sector during the 1970s, saw areas of New York decline into squalor and violence. Mass unemployment and cuts in law enforcement allowed the Big Apple to rot from the inside out. Manhattan was now a grimy, edgy and dangerous city. Subway trains were blighted by casual violence and territorial graffiti, women walked around with mace in their purse, and the ransacking of Stan's apartment was a prime example of petty crime that was now commonplace. This New York had been perfectly captured on film with Martin Scorsese's 1976 masterpiece *Taxi Driver*. The broken, beaten and scarred psyche of Robert De Niro's antihero, lonely veteran Travis Bickle, is a fitting cypher for a city teetering on the brink of the abyss. The film was made when New York was itself on the verge of bankruptcy, and in the following years, things had gone from bad to worse. Of course, as with any major city, there were still pockets of considerable wealth and affluence, but by 1980, New York was riddled with many areas so-called 'decent folk' just didn't dare go. Burned out and derelict, an innocent saunter through these festering streets day or night would be suicide. Even for Joan and JC, perhaps it was a good time to see what sunny California had to offer.

After a few months renting a high-rise apartment in Westwood, Stan bought property in West Hollywood; a three-bedroom house with a swimming pool overlooking Sunset Strip. It was a prime spot, with stunning vistas directly onto the iconic Hollywood street on one side, and untamed woodland on the other. The house once belonged to Don Wilson, the long-serving announcer on *The Jack Benny Program*, which Stan must have got a kick out of. The new Lee home was, in short, a palm tree-lined, sun-kissed, Pacific-coast paradise, boasting a view that was literally thousands of miles away from the brick wall he had stared at while growing up in New York all those years ago.

Stan's start in Hollywood was of course, not without incident. On the very first night in the new family home, he and Joan were raising a glass on their terrace to celebrate the next chapter in their life. Suddenly, strains of music could be heard wafting across the lawn from the guesthouse. They were shocked to discover a random gentleman living on the property. Turned out the previous owner had rented out the guesthouse and not bothered to tell the Lees. In the end, it took the police and, eventually, the law courts to remove him. Not the most auspicious welcome to the neighbourhood. Then again, if you can afford to buy a swanky Hollywood property big enough to have a second house on the grounds, squatter or not, you're really not doing too bad.

Stan's move was all part of delivering on his newly appointed role as creative head of Marvel Productions. Live-action, big-screen ambition was always in Stan's sights, but for now the main focus of Marvel's fledgling production arm was animation. A studio was set up for Stan in the beautiful San Fernando Valley, in a rather drab one-storey building at 4610 Van Nuys Boulevard in Sherman Oaks.

Joining him were two animation veterans, David H. DePatie and Lee Gunther. DePatie was the last executive in charge of the original Warner Bros cartoon studio; he later worked for Hanna-Barbera before joining forces with animation director Friz Freleng to form DePatie-Freleng

Enterprises (DFE). Together they created *The Pink Panther* cartoons and animated adaptations of books by Stan's former Signal Corps colleague, Dr. Seuss. In 1981, Freleng and DePatie sold DFE to Marvel Comics – their company renamed Marvel Productions – and DePatie was installed as president. Lee Gunther also cut his teeth at Warners, then at DFE, before being brought on as vice president of production. This trio of talented titans set about trying to conquer Hollywood, one animation cell at a time.

Stan enjoyed the relaxed atmosphere of his new Los Angeles lifestyle. Back in New York, he had worn a tie to work every single day for his entire professional life. Here there was no need for such sartorial formalities, and a multitude of stuffy neckwear was left dangling in the wardrobe. He may have loosened his collar, but he still held a tight grip on a hectic schedule. With a specially commissioned bust of his beloved wife Joan watching over him in his new office, Stan dedicated half the week to writing projects, and half to business meetings and strategy sessions.

Marvel Productions began small, initially working on commercials, but with a view to creating new Saturday morning cartoons featuring Marvel's most popular characters. The first cartoon series out of the gate was *Spider-Man and his Amazing Friends*, broadcast on NBC on Saturday, 12 September 1981. Here Spidey was joined by Iceman and a brand-new female superhero. The Human Torch was originally intended to complete the trio as a fitting contrast to Iceman. Unfortunately, rights to the character were owned by Universal Studios, so they dreamed up the equally flammable female Firestar. A year later, almost to the day, a new animated adaptation of *The Incredible Hulk* hit the schedules. Both shows would inevitably be paired together on NBC schedules and enjoyed brief success until they were cancelled at the end of 1983.

These shows featured more sophisticated animation than previous incarnations, but did still rely on repeating some sequences, such as transformations into super-secret identities. Also, Bruce Banner's ripped clothes would always miraculously return to normal once he turned back from the Hulk. Now that's a true superpower. Both cartoons were narrated by Stan himself, the first time many young comic book fans (the author included) heard the distinctive voice of 'the man behind Marvel'. I still vividly remember watching these shows when I was about six years old, thinking 'this guy has a great voice, and always sounds so damn[1] excited by the story he is sharing.' I didn't know who he was, but Stan made an impression on me even then.

The next Marvel title to be adapted into a cartoon wouldn't be until 1989 with *X-Men: Pryde of the X-Men*. For most of the 1980s, Marvel Productions' slate was dominated by a considerable portfolio of memorable animated titles for other companies. These included *Dungeons & Dragons* (1983-1985), sword and sorcery shenanigans based on the hugely popular role-playing game of the same name, and a couple of animated adaptations from the brilliant mind of the genius that was Jim Henson, *Muppet Babies* (1984) and *Fraggle Rock* (1987). Marvel Productions also struck a deal with another animation studio, Sunbow Productions, to co-produce a cartoon series based on popular lines from toy giant Hasbro. Most successful were *G.I. Joe* (1983-1986), *Transformers* (1984-1987) and *My Little Pony* (1986). These three also enjoyed a feature-length theatrical adventure, the most memorable being 1986's *Transformers: The Movie*. The film boasted an impressive cast, including Leonard Nimoy, Robert Stack, Judd Nelson, Eric Idle and Orson Welles in his final role. The film also traumatised millions of fans by brutally killing off the hugely popular leader of the heroic Autobots, Optimus Prime. Yeah, still not over that one. *Transformers: The Movie* may not have set the box office alight, but many of these series are still remembered fondly as definitive weekend kids' entertainment that enraptured a generation the world over.

Meanwhile, back over on Madison Avenue, Marvel Comics landed in the 1980s with a fair amount of turbulence. Editor-in-chief Jim Shooter hadn't been afraid of making some bold operational and creative decisions, shuffling the deck considerably. Stan's spiritual son and heir, golden boy Roy Thomas, found himself at loggerheads with Shooter over creative control. During a heated meeting, in which Shooter also forbid Thomas from doing any work on the side for DC Comics, Thomas walked. After shrugging to Stan that 'it's been a nice fifteen years', he promptly signed a contract with the Distinguished Competition.

Another disgruntled party was Steve Gerber, who had created one of the more random Marvel characters, *Howard the Duck*. Marvel fired him in 1978 for repeatedly failing to make deadlines, but when, in 1980, Marvel began taking out ads in *Variety*, effectively pimping out their characters for film and television adaptions, Gerber filed a copyright infringement lawsuit. As far as he was concerned, he was the sole creator and owner of *Howard the Duck*. In 1981, Gerber collaborated with none other than Jack Kirby, who was only too willing to bash his former employers. Together they created *Destroyer Duck,* a satirical comic to raise funds for Gerber's court case. The case was eventually dismissed in 1982, but it reflected not only the ongoing battle for intellectual property between creators and publishers, but also how Shooter's Marvel had begun to turn once-loyal staffers into disgruntled enemies.

With such high-profile conflicts, it was time to review the process of how comic book creatives were being paid. After such negative publicity, an overhaul of the model was inevitable. DC made the first move, introducing a royalty plan. After 100,000 copies of a title were sold, four per cent of profits would be split between artist and writer. The hope was that this would incentivise creatives to up their game, that the quality would, in turn, be rewarded by increased royalties from sales. Following DC's lead, Jim Shooter introduced similar plans at Marvel. He trialled the model with the 1982 launch of a new Marvel imprint, *Epic Comics*. Edited by Archie Goodwin, *Epic* was separate from the Marvel Universe, featuring all new and original characters and storylines from the realms of fantasy and science fiction.

Epic was intended to thrive in comic books' rapidly growing direct market. This approach first emerged in the 1970s, as a contrast to the traditional retail model, whereby comics were sold through distributors to appear in their list of local bookshops and newsstands. With the direct market, retailers could now buy direct from the publishers. Despite prohibiting the traditional 'sale or return' model (where unsold titles were sent back to the distributor), the direct market system was seen as lower risk. Publishers could target their audience, and this, in turn, led to the rise of speciality comic book stores. Marvel saw *Epic* as a way to cash in on this. Selling via the direct market also provided a legal loophole whereby comic book publishers could bypass the Comics Code Authority. Free from such constraints, the *Epi*c imprint allowed Marvel to explore more adult themes, thereby widening their potential readership. To this day, the direct market is the dominant network for selling comic books.

Despite apparent tensions under Jim Shooter, this period saw Marvel create more landmark comic books that would sow the seeds for future global success, thanks to the continuing roster of emerging talent that would define what became known as the Bronze Age of Comic Books.

Leading the charge were two British-born men, writer Chris Claremont and artist John Byrne. Both had been doing sterling work for some time on *Uncanny X-Men,* unfolding the mutant world with a dazzling array of characters and sophisticated storylines that transformed the title into a complex sub-universe within Marvel, not seen since Stan and Jack's original run on *The Fantastic Four.* By the '80s, Claremont and Byrne were firing on all cylinders. They unleashed two game-changing *X-Men* storylines, the apocalyptic *Dark Phoenix Saga* (1980) and Wolverine's head-scratching time-travel romp *Days of Future Past* (1981). Byrne would also enjoy a superlative run on *The Fantastic Four*, ending in 1986, but it was his collaboration with Claremont on these two dense, dramatic and emotionally thundering story arcs for which the pair will perhaps be best remembered. They certainly earned their keep. By the mid-'80s, *Uncanny X-Men* became the most consistently best-selling comic of not just Marvel, but of all comic books.

Another Marvel flashpoint at this time was writer and penciller Frank Miller's debut on *Daredevil #168* (cover date January 1981). Young, weird and a distinct voice in the comic book landscape, Miller would go on to create two of the most popular and influential Batman stories ever told, 1986's *The Dark Knight Returns* and, in 1987, *Batman: Year One*. He then created his own universe, the ultraviolent neo-noir series *Sin City,* but Frank Miller's work on *Daredevil* made him Marvel's rising star. His love for hardboiled detective fiction and Japanese culture bled into the comic, adding darker storylines and complex new characters, such as martial arts mentor Stick and assassin love interest Elektra. Miller's more mature approach elevated *Daredevil* from second-tier popularity to firm fan favourite. Miller's run lasted until early 1983, before returning in 1986 for *Daredevil Born Again* with future *Batman Year One* collaborator David Mazzucchelli.

The mid-'80s onwards became known as the Dark Age of Comic Books, not for primitive characters or underdeveloped stories, but because of the more adult and morally ambiguous comics and graphic novels that emerged at the time. Groundbreaking works from seminal creators such as Miller and, over at DC, the peerless British writer Alan Moore. A mercurial magician from Northampton, Moore's works during this period, *V for Vendetta* (1982-1985), *Swamp Thing* (1984-1987), *Watchmen* (1986-1987) and *Batman: The Killing Joke* (1988), still represent perhaps the pinnacle of what can be achieved within the medium. In its collected form, *Watchmen* was the only graphic novel to appear on *Time* magazine's 2005 list of 'All-Time 100 Greatest Novels'.

There were, of course, other notable Marvel creations during the 1980s. Special nod goes to 1982's *The Death of Captain Marvel* by writer and penciller Jim Starlin. With its oversized format, heavier and glossy pages, this surprisingly mature one-shot is celebrated by many as Marvel's first ever graphic novel.[2] Starlin's legacy had already been secured by creating one of Marvel's most iconic villains, Thanos. Introduced in *The Invincible Iron Man #55* (cover date February 1973), the mad titan makes a memorable appearance in this moving tale of frailty, terminal illness and mortality.

In 1982, writer Mark Gruenwald, who had carved out a reputation for meticulously keeping track of the ever-growing Marvel Universe, solidified this encyclopaedic knowledge with the *Official Handbook of the Marvel Universe*. A mammoth fifteen-volume series released each month across thirty-four pages and sold for one dollar, Gruenwald canonised many key character backstories, interactions and key events. Jim Shooter even took to the storyboard in 1984 to write the ambitious *Marvel Super Heroes Secret Wars*. This twelve-part bestseller was a sprawling struggle across the entire Marvel Universe, enveloping crossover titles from all the key characters. A financial success, tied in with a toy line from Mattel, Shooter's *Secret Wars* was not the critical darling he had hoped, and is probably most notable for giving Spider-Man a rather cool black costume.

Talking of Queens' favourite wall crawler, in 1987 *The Amazing Spider-Man Annual #21* saw Peter Parker start a new chapter in his complicated life, marrying the fiery redhead Mary Jane Watson. For this major storyline, written by David Michelinie with cover art by John Romita, Marvel once again embraced the cross-publication approach, after Stan suggested they celebrate the big day simultaneously in both the comic book and his weekly *Spider-Man* news strip. Shooter doubled down on the marketing, sending out actual invites to the most amazing wedding of the decade. There was even a live-action performance of the wedding in front of 55,000 screaming fans at Shea Stadium in Queens, home of the New York Mets baseball team. Introducing the event was, naturally, Stan The Man.

Aside from this marital celebration of Marvel's favourite son, and a fascinating 1988 collaboration with French artist Moebius under the

Epic imprint, *Silver Surfer: Parable*, Stan's creative input at Marvel Comics was minimal. His role at Marvel Productions meant that his college campus tours had to take a back seat in favour of larger and more high-profile events, such as comic book conventions and television and radio appearances. Despite the success of Marvel Productions on the small screen, Hollywood was proving a tough nut to crack. Sure, there were plenty of irons already in the fire. As far back as 1979, riding on the crest of *Superman: The Movie's* success, Stan had been in talks to make a Silver Surfer movie with Lee Kramer, boyfriend of *Grease* star Olivia Newton-John. The budget was even set at $25 million, but the film never materialised. Many Marvel characters found themselves trapped in an unbreakable prison from which even their varied superpowers could not escape: development hell. Projects that failed to get off the ground included a live-action *Daredevil* show for ABC, a *Dr. Strange* remake starring *Magnum P.I.* himself, Tom Selleck, and a *Fantastic Four* movie produced with German impresario Bernd Eichinger.

Studio sharks circled superhero scripts with black, lifeless eyes, but rarely took a bite. Hollywood is a fickle mistress and genres fall out of favour as rapidly as they bust open box offices. *Superman: The Movie* in 1978 was a cinematic leviathan, but only five years later, 1983's *Superman III* underperformed financially and critically. Nowhere near as strong as the first two instalments, the superhero genre, once seen as the future of cinema, was now being dismissed by some film studios as a passing fad. Stan enjoyed myriad meetings with Hollywood executives but there was one thing holding him back. Many studio types had grown up reading his comics and were slightly star-struck upon meeting the Man behind Marvel, but as a scriptwriter and live-action producer, Stan Lee was an unknown quantity and far from bankable in Hollywood. TV cartoons were one thing, but history was repeating itself; Marvel just couldn't land the big deals. The first live-action Marvel adaptation to hit the big screen was, randomly, *Howard the Duck* in 1986. The film tanked at the box office. Despite being produced by George Lucas' production company and directed and written by the team who gave the world *American Graffiti* and *Indiana Jones and the Temple of Doom*, *Howard the Duck* is often referred to as one of the worst films ever made. And you know why? Because it is. It has since amassed a cult following, presumably among those who like seeing a duck being romantically involved with a human being.

Stan grew increasingly disillusioned with the Hollywood system. Marvel Productions had more than enough work to keep the business ticking over, but it had failed to become a major player in town. More scripts that had been developed under other studios fell into obscurity. Frustrations were clear and doubt grew over Marvel Studios' ability to break into the big leagues. There was uncertainty over in New York too. Marvel's parent company Cadence was in trouble.

The 1980s had begun well with the phenomenal success of those early iconic storylines and, in 1982, Marvel had moved thirty blocks downtown to bigger offices at 387 Park Avenue South. But in 1986, Cadence Industries was liquidated. Later that year, Marvel Comics and Marvel Productions were sold to New World Pictures, an outfit founded by king of the B-movies, director Roger Corman. New World had started life making exploitation films, before making waves in the slightly more reputable TV industry. The comic book and film divisions were combined and rebranded Marvel Entertainment Group. Jim Galton, Stan's boss and trusted business adviser, survived the Cadence collapse and continued as Marvel Entertainment Group's president and CEO. And, as is tradition whenever there is a corporate shake-up, the deck was shuffled yet again. In 1987, executives fired long-standing editor-in-chief Jim Shooter.

Despite so many huge successes, morale under Shooter had been dwindling for some time. The bullpen had become fractured. There were those who respected how the big man had grown Marvel Comics, but there were others who resented a work culture that had veered from frivolity and hi-jinks to ruthless business. Shooter's dismissal was met with rapture by several former Marvel creatives such as Steve Gerber, Gene Colan, Marv Wolfman and Don Heck, who happily returned to the fold under newly installed editor-in-chief, Tom DeFalco. A New York native, hopes were pinned on DeFalco as the man who could heal Marvel Comics. He was generally well-liked and respected by everyone, so his promotion proved to be a prudent decision. He appointed *Marvel Handbook* mastermind Mark Gruenwald to executive editor and together they created their own plan to expand the Marvel empire. Things looked rosy in the bullpen once more. Then, on 19 October 1987, the stock market crashed.

Black Monday, as it became known, hit hard and businesses big and small were left on the verge of bankruptcy. The corporation limped along for a spell but was soon forced to sell off some of its assets. In January 1989, Marvel Entertainment Group was sold for $82.5 million to Andrews Group, owned by media mogul Ronald Perelman. Andrews was a behemoth of a company that held among other interests, cosmetic giants Revlon. Soon he would buy up the rest of New World, but first, Perelman wanted Marvel. He wanted it so badly, he put up $10.5 million of his own money towards the purchase.

The sale went through and once again instability hung over the heads of the Marvel employees. What would this mean for their future? That year a live-action, big-screen theatrical adaptation of *The Punisher* starring Dolph Lundgren came and went. It wasn't the first character that springs to mind for a Marvel cinematic breakthrough, but the late 1980s box office was ruled by muscle-bound action vehicles and Lundgren was very much of that ilk.[3] However, the film strayed too much from the source material and was let down by sub-par writing and acting. *The Punisher* proved to be enough of a turkey to rival a certain duck, and Stan inevitably wondered about his position within the company. He had been tasked to make waves in Hollywood. Now, a decade later, Marvel Productions had failed to cause so much as a ripple. Surely, the fallout from this latest big-budget failure would land on his shoulders?

To make things worse for Marvel, only a few months earlier in 1989, DC had played another mighty trump card. Director Tim Burton's *Batman* was more than a film. It was a phenomenon. 'Batmania' swept through the world. A stunningly effective marketing campaign proved just how iconic a character the Caped Crusader was. Bold and super-confident posters appeared everywhere that simply showed a bronzed version of the instantly recognisable Bat symbol. It was all that was needed to whip fans into a fury. With a just-past-his-prime Jack Nicholson cast as the Joker and Michael Keaton in the title role, this was to be THE summer movie. Warner Bros promised to deliver an adult retelling of the Batman story that would blow away any memory of Adam West camping it up in 1966.

Burton went on record stating he was never a comic book fan, but for inspiration he devoured the darker tales such as Frank Miller's *Dark Knight Returns* and Alan Moore's disturbing *The Killing Joke*. Despite an initial uproar and subsequent angry fan petition about casting Keaton as Batman – then only known for broad comedy – Burton delivered a sweeping and stylish action melodrama of revenge, duality and psychosis.

Despite not being given much to work with, Keaton proved to be the right man for the job. He delivered a quiet but brooding performance of obsessive determination, while Nicholson howled and whooped around the sets, chewing up everything he could. The grandeur was elevated further by composer Danny Elfman's orchestral score, arguably his finest, and Anton Furst's glorious 'dark deco' sets, for which the late production designer won an Oscar. As with *Superman: The Movie*, Tim Burton's *Batman* restored Hollywood's faith in superheroes, legitimised the genre as entertainment not 'just for kids', and made an absolute killing at the box office. Fighting off the return of Timothy Dalton's James Bond in *Licence to Kill* and sequels to *Back to the Future* and *Ghostbusters*, *Batman* was the highest grossing movie of 1989 in the US. Worldwide, it was only beaten by the sublime *Indiana Jones and the Last Crusade. Batman* was a stupendous way for DC Comics to close the decade. They had thrown down the black-leather gauntlet to Marvel, whose response had been a dull, unfaithful adaptation of a character deemed too violent for mass audiences, one that limped over the finish line with bad reviews and weak sales. Stan was in awe of what Warners had achieved with *Batman*, and the conversation must have come up at one of the many Los Angeles dinners Stan enjoyed with his old friend, Bob Kane. Why couldn't Marvel get it right in the movies? What was missing?

In October, Jim Galton retired as CEO of Marvel Entertainment Group, aged 65. Stan Lee was 67. Was it time for him to also bow out gracefully? Spend the rest of his days relaxing by the pool and reflecting in past glories? He could dedicate time to his beloved wife and proudly support his daughter, who was now showcasing her flair for painting at various exhibitions around Los Angeles, and had published her first novel, *The Pleasure Palace*. But Stan didn't want to retire. That's the thing about writers. They don't know how. And Hollywood misfires aside, Marvel were doing well. Very well in fact.

By 1990, overall sales were over $70 million, with an extra $11 million from licensing characters to eighty companies worldwide. Marvel Comics was now the largest comic book company in the world. Everything was fine. And last time he checked, Stan was still the public face of the brand. The way he saw it, he still had a valuable role to play. He could never have guessed that in just six years, the Marvel Universe he had helped build would come crashing down.

Chapter Fourteen

Rack and Ruin

Now is the time, True Believer, to make my own appearance in Stan's story. Necessary? Probably not. Self-indulgent? No question. But I ask you also to indulge me. And given Stan's proclivity for making brief cameos in his work, I feel he would approve. Besides. I feel it's justified, because I played a teeny tiny part in the downfall of Marvel Comics. Let me explain.

I first got into comics in early 1990. I was 11, going on 12. For reasons I can never recall, my school friend Jack had gifted me *Silver Surfer #36* (cover date April 1990). The bold cover was a single image: the Surfer looking straight at me, horrified, screaming 'OH NO! NOT **YOU**!' It really popped. I was instantly drawn in by the dazzling and vibrant artwork of Ron Lim, and then the story, written by cosmic king Jim Starlin, knocked me for six. It introduced to me the unforgettable character of Thanos, via a backstory that featured most of the main Marvel superheroes from the Silver Age. It also hinted at the mad titan's dastardly quest to destroy the universe with the 'Soul Stones'. I was also struck by how funny this issue was. The second half featured a surreal encounter with the Impossible Man, a cheeky, exasperating emerald shape-shifter who teases the Silver Surfer while morphing into a plethora of forms, much like the late, great Robin Williams' scene-stealing genie in Disney's smash hit *Aladdin* – although that wouldn't come out for another two years. The Impossible Man's many incarnations included Charlie Chaplin, Groucho Marx, Yoda, a custard pie, hot air balloon and a tidal wave. It was brilliantly inventive, bold and anarchic. I'd never read any comic book like it. I was hooked.

For my thirteenth birthday, my parents arranged a trip for me and five friends to visit London's largest comic book store, Forbidden Planet. Walking through the hallowed doors in hushed awe, I scrambled to the 'S' section and bought as many *Silver Surfer* comics as I could afford.

I started collecting other titles, including *The Amazing Spider-Man* and *Batman* (I wasn't completely a Marvel boy) and soon I had a veritable treasure trove of back issues. My friends and I were poster children for the generation that voraciously devoured comic books on a weekly basis. We all had our favourites, but we also had an interest in collecting the various limited-run stories, spread over a handful of issues. One of the biggest was 1991's *The Infinity Gauntlet*, also by Starlin, with art by former DC regular George Pérez and then *Silver Surfer* regular Ron Lim. This six-issue limited storyline, a multi-character cosmic crossover slugfest, was all we talked about when it came out. It was a huge success, and the strength of its story would be reflected in the fact that the saga of Thanos, the Infinity Gauntlet and an evolution of the six Soul Stones formed the overarching narrative connecting the recent run of Marvel Cinematic Universe movies.

At the time, there were so many new comic books being launched, both by Marvel and DC, often with multiple covers of the same first issue. Pocket money permitting, we tried to collect them all, partly to gain peer prestige but also in an obligation to our more compulsive and completest tendencies. We had heard that several first-issue comics in mint condition were selling at auction for tens of thousands. Perhaps, if we completed the set of any given series, then kept them pristine in a box, it was a nest egg for the future and we'd never have to get a job! We all got rolls of clear comic book bags that you had to buy in bulk from your nearest comic book shop. Getting a roll of them was almost as satisfying as buying a comic itself. Sometimes you even bought a comic then never read it. Why sully your investment with grubby, oily finger smudges? They went into our ever-growing collections. It wasn't unusual to buy two copies of exactly the same comic, one for reading, one for collecting. It was just what you did.

After a spell, however, it just got too much. There were too many issues coming out, all aggressively competing for our attention. This was pre-internet, and it was hard to keep track of all the tie-in issues that fed into whatever prestige limited-edition mini-series was being launched that week. We had to rely on what the guys who ran the comic book shop told us, and they were only too keen to push some exciting new release. It soon became too expensive to buy all six variants of the first issue of the latest *X-Men* reboot. We couldn't afford all the different-coloured versions of yet another *Incredible Hulk* title – now with hologrammatic cover. Pretty soon, we grew fatigued. It felt relentless and a little cynical. The titles kept coming, but we ran out of pocket money. Interest waned. We discovered girls. And we stopped buying comics.

And that, in a nutshell, is largely why Marvel filed for bankruptcy in 1996.

Not only because of me. I'm important, True Believer, but not *that* important. My friends and I merely exemplified the relationship between comic book publishers and the fans throughout the first half of the 1990s. There were, of course, other factors. The '90s created a perfect storm that engulfed the comic book industry. 'It's still hard to believe,' Stan reflected later, '[it was] probably the first time in history that an entire industry hit bottom because of increased customer demand.'[1]

For Marvel, it was a classic case of boom and bust. They'd hit the decade as top dog in the business, with phenomenal sales and critical acclaim. This winning streak continued largely thanks to a triumvirate of impossibly precocious artistic talent, Todd McFarlane, Rob Liefeld and Jim Lee. McFarlane's distinctive artwork had transformed Spider-Man into a much more angular and animalistic creation. Marvel had increased the number of separate monthly Spidey titles to one a week. McFarlane's *Spider-Man #1* (cover date August 1990) was a sensation, selling four million copies, not least because it was released with eight different versions, to appeal to the burgeoning collectors' market.

A year later, Rob Liefeld's equally striking artwork graced the pages of mutant spin-off *X-Force #1* (cover date August 1991). Double-sized and priced at one dollar fifty cents, each issue came with one of five trading cards. Sales outstripped *Spider-Man #1*, then a few months later came the juggernaut. Chris Claremont and Jim Lee's *X-Men #1* (cover date October 1991) was unleashed with four different covers, then a fifth version featuring a special gatefold cover, showcasing the quartet of previous covers in one long tableau of mutant mayhem. It sold close to eight million copies and remains the biggest-selling comic book of all time. And yes, I bought all five. In 1992, Marvel proved that they was still as fresh and progressive as ever, giving the world the first openly gay superhero, French-Canadian mutant Northstar, in *Alpha Flight #106*. It may seem quaint today, but back then this was a bold but welcome move. By this point, Marvel could do no wrong. The 'house of ideas', as it had long been known, was unstoppable.

Stan himself wasn't doing too bad either. At the start of the decade, he was given a new title and, to his amazement, his salary tripled. It was all part of overlord Ronald Perelman's master plan. He was aware Stan was still an invaluable asset to the Marvel brand so keeping him on was a no-brainer. He had to keep him sweet. This massive pay increase was all part of the plan, as was making Stan head of another new set-up, Marvel Films. Perelman had greater ambitions for the company than all his predecessors. He wanted to turn Marvel into the new Disney.

Perelman predicted that Marvel's bright future lay in acquisitions, licensing and merchandising the characters to reel in the big bucks. The Marvel Universe was there to exploit, and while previous suits at the top had spotted this potential, Perelman took it further than anyone before. He hired a man called Bill Bevins to run the show. A former chief financial officer for Turner Broadcasting, with extensive experience in acquisitions, Bevins upgraded the comics. Using better paper and slicker packaging, prices were raised from seventy-five cents to one dollar. Capitalising on the collectors' boom, and thanks to the excellent work of the current bullpen, print runs soared. Two years after Perelman and Bevin took over, Marvel's revenue was up by thirty-five per cent to $81.1 million, with profits jumping to $5.4 million.[2]

After a curious incident where the music icon and professional eccentric Michael Jackson allegedly tried to buy Marvel just so he could star as Spider-Man in any future feature-film adaptation,[3] Perelman sold most of New World's operations to Sony. He then took Marvel Entertainment public, retaining sixty per cent of the company for himself. While investors bought up shares, Perelman made $40 million in the first public sale of stock. He then went on a spending spree.

In July 1992, a month after the death at 84 of Martin Goodman, the man who started it all, Marvel purchased Fleer, the world's second-biggest maker of trading cards, for $286 million. The following year Perelman targeted Toy Biz, a toy company owned by two Israeli Americans, businessman Isaac 'Ike' Perlmutter and toy designer and self-proclaimed comic book enthusiast Avi Arad. The Toy Biz deal involved trading a royalty-free licence of Marvel characters in exchange for Perelman's forty-six per cent controlling stake in Toy Biz. In 1994, Marvel bought collectible stickers giant Panini and, in 1995, another trading card company, Skybox International. Perelman was betting all on the collectors' market, which had been going great guns thanks to the booming direct market. And then the bubble burst.

Looking back, it was amazing no one saw it coming. There were several voices of caution, signalling the writing on the wall. Writer Neil Gaiman, acclaimed creator of the *Sandman* comic book series and later the author of many incredible dark fantasy novels including *Stardust*, *Neverwhere* and *American Gods*, called it out at a comic book convention in 1993. In front of his industry peers, he likened the comic book boom to the tulip craze of seventeenth-century Holland: 'You can sell lots of comics to the same person, especially if you tell them that you are investing money for high-guaranteed returns,' he declared. 'But you're selling bubbles and tulips, and one day the bubble will burst, and the tulips will rot in the warehouse.'[4]

True enough, the market was being driven by consumers stockpiling comics that they believed one day would be worth a small fortune. But these comics did not go up in value. Yes, some comics had been auctioned off for a lot of money, such as issues of *Batman* and *Superman* from the Golden Age, but that was because they were decades old and very rare. During the mid-1990s, publishers doubled or tripled their print run. They had saturated their own market, and the collectors had run out of money. When collectors started trying to sell their comics, they were horrified to discover their piles of mint-condition issues preserved in the cellophane bags were worthless.[5] Meanwhile, speciality comic shops couldn't pay for all they had ordered. Soon a great many comic book stores closed down which, of course, reduced the outlets for publishers to sell their titles. To make matters worse for Marvel, industrial action plagued professional sports in the US. This absolutely hammered the trading card business, in which Marvel had heavily invested when it bought Fleer and Skybox.

Marvel suffered more blows from the many more comic book publishing houses that had sprung up following the direct market boom. Smaller and more agile than Marvel, these were eager and talented pretenders to the throne. The triumphant trio of Todd McFarlane, Rob Liefeld and Jim Lee had defected to form their own independent publishing house, Image. Another notable example was Topps Comics. Formed in 1993 and operating over the bridge in Brooklyn, Topps specialised in licensed titles, run by a Marvel veteran Jim Salicrup. He recruited a roster that was a veritable who's who from Marvel's Silver

Age, including Steve Ditko, Roy Thomas, Gerry Conway, Dick Ayers, Don Heck and John Severin. Not only that, Topps also published comics based around ideas from the now-retired Jack Kirby. Marvel were rapidly losing their share in a market that at the same time was shrinking fast.

Comic book fans suffered a major loss in 1994. On 6 February, Jack Kirby died of heart failure. He was 76. He was buried at the Pierce Brothers Valley Oaks Memorial Park in Westlake Village, California. Stan attended the funeral, but kept a low profile. According to one report, Jack's widow Roz tried to speak to Stan after the service, but he had already slipped away.[6] If true, this is a sad way to draw a line under the most famous creative partnership in comic book history. They endured a fractious and complicated relationship but their fates are forever intertwined. Neither one would have achieved his success without the other. You'd think Stan, ever the showman, would have served up some poignant and fitting eulogy to the life and talent of his former Marvel collaborator, but this was not the case. The King was dead, and the Man was nowhere to be seen.

There is comfort in the fact that in later years Stan worked hard to ensure Jack got the credit he deserved, and that while Jack never lived long enough to see the characters he helped create blast their way into cinemas, there was some recognition before he died. As former Marvel UK editor John Tomlinson observes:

> Kirby lived long enough to be feted on the convention circuit, where fans queued to pay homage to his talent, imagination and stellar back catalogue. By all accounts he was unfailingly courteous and polite. That this fan culture now exists and thrives, however, is due at least in part to the tireless human PR offensive that was Stan Lee.

Hulkbuster and War Machine creator Kev Hopgood also remembers a sweet moment at the premiere of *Avengers: Age of Ultron* in 2015. 'We were sat in front of Kirby's widow and his two daughters,' says Hopgood. 'When the credits rolled we discovered that this was the first time Stan Lee and Jack Kirby shared joint credits for creating the Avengers. A huge cheer went up in the audience which I'm sure the Kirby girls appreciated.'

Marvel continued to struggle on, despite receiving so many punishing slings and arrows. Comics had taken a back seat to the many other divisions within Marvel, a fact that did not go unnoticed by those left in the bullpen. 'They wanted to make us a merchandising empire,' remembered John Romita. 'They told us we were worth ten per cent of their time.'[7] Late 1995 was the turning point. Marvel reported their first annual loss under Perelman's watch, to the tune of $48 million, despite sales of $829 million. Their debt was an eye-watering $581 million. In 1996, the dominoes truly fell. January saw 275 employees laid off. Shares worth thirty-six dollars only three years ago had dropped to a pitiful two dollars. The comic book industry had imploded and Marvel had to rely on their other outlets, otherwise they would go under forever.

By now, Toy Biz co-owner Avid Arad was a senior executive at Marvel Films. A hands-on creative, Arad fast became a major player. He had worked alongside Stan on two weighty animated series for television. Launching on Halloween 1992, *X-Men* became the number one-rated kids' cartoon, and in November 1994 a brand-new version of *Spider-Man* was unveiled on Fox. Both cartoons were slick and exciting, finally reflecting a budget that could realise the colourful and dynamic adventures fans expected to see. Live-action adaptations during the early '90s had proved, predictably, terrible. In 1990 the world was blighted by another terrible stab at Captain America. It was originally intended to be helmed by British director and all-round bounder Michael Winner, who worked with Stan on the script. When Winner left, the project languished for a time before finally being made. The film struggled to find a release slot and made a rather meek debut straight to video, on cable and with a *very* limited theatrical release. *Captain America* is utterly forgettable and one for Marvel completists only. The film's sole interesting nugget of trivia is that the actor playing the eponymous hero is Matt Salinger, son of J. D. Salinger, the revered but reclusive author of seminal novel *The Catcher in the Rye*.

Marvel stock rose during the summer of 1991 when *The Terminator* and *Aliens* director James Cameron announced, during a press junket for the phenomenally successful sequel *T2: Judgment Day,* that he was about to tackle adapting Spider-Man for the big screen. Alas, it was not to be and eventually Cameron walked away from the project to devote his time to a small film about a certain ship scraping an iceberg. A sequel to *The Punisher* was also mooted, despite the original's poor performance, and plans were afoot for a She-Hulk film starring statuesque Danish actress Brigitte Nielsen. Neither came to fruition.

Perhaps the weirdest ever cinematic adaptation of a Marvel title – yes, even more so than *Howard the Duck* – was 1994's *The Fantastic Four*. This film is singular for the simple reason that to this day it has never been released.

The story goes that production company Constantin Film, which had owned the rights to the characters since the early 1980s, was in danger of losing those rights in 1992. Constantin was owned by German entrepreneur Bernd Eichinger, who knew he did not have the budget to make the epic Hollywood version he had intended. To keep the rights, he turned to former New World founder and B-movie impresario Roger Corman with a plan. They would make a cheap version, on a shoestring budget of under $2 million, then bury it without telling anyone involved. So they made the film, which looks impossibly cheap by the way, cast a bunch of unknowns and got a stuntman to play The Thing, lurching around in a foam suit. Trailers ran in American cinemas during 1993. The actors hired their own publicist. The date for a world premiere was set as 19 January 1994. This never happened. Suddenly the cast received a cease-and-desist order and the studio confiscated the negatives. Eichinger refuted any rumours that the whole endeavour had been a backroom deal to retain rights, and Avi Arad stepped in to purchase the film, keeping it forever locked up in the Marvel vault. This curious entry in Marvel's cinematic history has since developed a cult following and it can be viewed, but only via bootleg copies. In 2014, film studies professor Marty Langford released a feature-length documentary about the whole debacle, *Doomed!: The Untold Story of Roger Corman's The Fantastic Four.* To date, this writer can neither confirm nor deny if he has seen the film.[8]

With yet another decade filled by Marvel cinematic failure, Avi Arad stepped up and took charge. In 1996, Marvel raised money by selling off Toy Biz stock to create their own completely autonomous production company within Marvel Films, called Marvel Studios. Arad was put in charge of Marvel Films and he had a clear plan of attack. 'When you get into business with a big studio, they are developing a hundred or 500 projects; you get totally lost,' he told *The New York Times* that year. 'That isn't working for us. We're just not going to do it anymore. Period.' The idea was to control every stage of pre-production, from scripts to hiring directors and casting actors. Once put together, the assembled product would be handed over to a movie studio for production and distribution. Marvel Studios arranged a seven-year development deal with 20th Century Fox and were making headway in realising characters including X-Men, Daredevil and a proper version of the Fantastic Four for the big screen. Despite these big plans, by the end of 1996, Marvel filed for bankruptcy.

Whenever a major company looks like it's going under, the corporate raiders appear. These are financiers who step in and make hostile takeover bids, usually to resell for profit. One such character to enter at this point was Carl Icahn. He bought Marvel bonds at twenty per cent of their value and tried to block Perelman's plans. There then followed an ugly high-profile legal tussle between two financial leviathans: Icahn v. Perelman.

Stan distanced himself from this very public spat, dismissing it as some entertaining piece of fantastical whimsy. 'I found it exciting,' he wrote in his autobiography, 'sort of like reading a comicbook [*sic*] about a couple of super-powered titans who were battling to control a galaxy.'[9] In a sense, he was not far off. The soul of the Marvel empire was indeed up for grabs. In 1997, Icahn won the bankruptcy court's approval to take control of Marvel's stock and he replaced the entire board, including the mighty Ronald Perelman. Icahn installed former Marvel executive Joe Calamari (what a name) as the new president and CEO of Marvel Entertainment Group. Stan was fine with this news, chiefly because he and Calamari were old friends. Stan also considered him 'a bright, hard-working dynamo of a guy, and, even though I was doing my own thing in Los Angeles, I looked forward to things picking up under his management.'[10]

Calamari's rule was short-lived. During the post-bankruptcy reorganisation phase, Toy Biz waded in with a counter offer. Protecting their prior agreement with Marvel, Perlmutter and Arad came to a new agreement with the banks to buy Marvel for $400 million. The offer was accepted and Marvel changed hands again. June 1998 saw Toy Biz and Marvel Entertainment Group combine into Marvel Enterprises. This merger not only saved Marvel from bankruptcy but also secured Isaac Perlmutter and Avi Arad on the throne. Calamari was promptly fired and replaced by veteran Toy Biz suit, Joseph Ahearn. The fight to save Marvel was, it seemed, finally over.

So where was Stan in all this? Well, he was sunning himself in Los Angeles, floating above it all, still the face of the corporation. Towards the end of the 1990s, he had tentatively branched out by setting up his own production company with old friend Larry Schultz called Lee Schultz Productions, but nothing of note materialised.

In 1998, Stan fell out with Marvel, when his new boss Ike Perlmutter terminated all existing employee contracts and issued new ones. Stan had been sitting pretty with a lifetime contract and more than comfortable salary. This too was torn up. The new contract Stan received no longer covered the rest of his life and halved his salary. This is a very interesting moment in Stan's career as it may be one of the rare occasions in which he publicly bared his teeth. For all his avuncular patter, presenting himself as always removed from the corporate skulduggery, the incident showed a different side to Stan. He contacted his powerful lawyer friend Arthur Lieberman who successfully renegotiated a similar contract as before: $800,000 annually for life, $125,000 a year for his beloved Spider-Man strip, a $500,000 annual pension for his wife and a ten per cent stake in all future Marvel film and TV profits.[11] This was proof that, when he had to, Stan could swim with the sharks. As John Tomlinson acutely observes: 'It wasn't goodwill or sentimentality that stamped the byline: "Stan Lee Presents …" on the title page of every Marvel title, years after Stan himself had quit writing comics and left the building. Behind that toothy PR grin was a core of steel.'

Following these aggressive renegotiations, Stan was rebranded as chairman emeritus, with a clause in his contract that he could do any work anywhere with anyone. This suited him just fine. Stan had secured his legacy as the spiritual head of Marvel forever but even though he was in his mid-seventies, it was time to seek out new opportunities. Besides, he had been working less and less with the development of Marvel movies, cartoons and TV shows. Avi Arad was now in charge of all that and things were starting to happen. Elsewhere in Hollywood, the finishing touches were being applied on the first of Marvel Studio's licensed deals. *Blade* (1998) was a modest, live-action film for New Line Cinemas, starring Wesley Snipes as one of Marvel's lower-tier characters. No one predicted it would be a game changer. But it sliced through Hollywood with enough force for people to take notice. The Marvel Movie Age was about to begin.

Chapter Fifteen

Marvel Rising

By 1998, the superhero movie was dead. The once triumphant DC were out of the game. The Batman franchise had derailed the previous summer with Joel Schumacher's truly abysmal *Batman and Robin.* This almost-wilful cinematic pile-up threw out all that was great about Tim Burton's 1989 original and its sequel, the grotesque expressionist fairy tale, *Batman Returns* (1992). Instead, Schumacher doubled down on the garish Day-Glo sugar fest he'd applied all over the second sequel, the wildly-uneven *Batman Forever* (1995). Not even the easy charisma of George Clooney or the star power of Arnold Schwarzenegger could breathe life into a major motion picture made by people who, collectively, had forgotten how to make a major motion picture. Meanwhile, Superman had long since been banished to the Phantom Zone after 1987's space oddity *Superman IV: The Quest for Peace*. By this point, the franchise had fallen far from Richard Donner's initial 1978 smash. Thanks to terrible effects, too much noble but misguided creative input from star Christopher Reeve, and a truly awful supervillain who dressed like a WWF wrestler and was played by a bouffant actor called Mark Pillow, Superman found his Kryptonite was the cinema-going public. In 1996, Tim Burton was hired by Warner Bros to make the ill-fated *Superman Lives*, starring everyone's favourite maniac Nicolas Cage as the Man of Steel. This baffling endeavour never got made, but if you search online you can see Cage in a really bizarre costume test, while its many strange behind-the-scenes tales from the people involved almost rival those of Roger Corman's never-seen *Fantastic Four* effort.

In 1997, another comic book movie fell face down in the dirt. *Spawn* was based on Todd McFarlane's most celebrated creation for his own Image Comics, but failed to convince its loyal fan base, nor win over a new audience. Only the summer release of *Men in Black* bucked the downward box office receipts of late '90s comic book adaptations.

This enjoyable left-field caper, directed by Barry Sonnenfeld and carried by Will Smith and Tommy Lee Jones as secret agents who regulate alien life on Earth, was well received by both critics and the public. The film was adapted from Lowell Cunningham's comic book series *The Men in Black,* originally created in 1990 for Canadian publisher Aircel Comics. Aircel was bought out by Malibu Comics, which itself was acquired in 1994 by Marvel. So, you could say *Men in Black* was the first successful feature film based on characters appearing in Marvel Comics. You *could.* If you were feeling generous. But the superhero that can truly claim to have kick-started Marvel's cinematic domination was a very different man in black.

Written by future *Dark Knight* trilogy scribe David S. Goyer, and directed by Stephen Norrington, *Blade* adapted the story of the half-human, half-vampire hunter created by Marv Wolfman and Gene Colan in 1973. New Line Pictures produced the film: they would hit pay dirt a couple of years later with Peter Jackson's *The Lord of the Rings* trilogy. Despite rather entry-level CGI effects, *Blade* is a slick actioner that pulls no punches. From its opening blood-soaked set piece in a vampire-infested nightclub to its preposterous gladiatorial climax, Norrington delivered a stylish adult romp that is funny and tongue in cheek, while at the same time explores vampire lore in a fresh light. As the eponymous 'daywalker', possessing all of the vampire's strengths and none of its weaknesses, Wesley Snipes is an effortlessly cool action hero, ably assisted by the one-liners and arsenal of sidekick Whistler, played by a crumbly and cranky Kris Kristofferson. *Blade* is not perfect, but it was a hit. 'The movie came out the second weekend of *Saving Private Ryan*,' said producer Peter Frankfurt in a 2014 interview with SyFy.com, 'and it opened at number one. It knocked *Private Ryan* off number one. Everybody was like, "What? Are you kidding?"' With a budget of $45 million, *Blade* made $131 million.

Blade followed the template of all successful superhero films and took its source material seriously. It was as grounded as a vampire fantasy action film can be, but also never forgot to have fun all along the way. *Blade* spawned two sequels and proved there was a mature audience for superhero films once more. Studio executives watched the healthy box office returns roll in. Their eyes sparkled. DC's heroes were either floundering or had fallen out of favour. The success of *Blade* made studios sit up and take note of Marvel Studios.

Back in New York, Marvel were enjoying their recent salvation from bankruptcy and subsequent rebirth as Marvel Enterprises. The company was now organised into four major units: Marvel Studios, Toy Biz, Licensing, and Publishing. With Marvel Studios making headway under Avi Arad, the publishing output was undergoing a drastic change. In 1998, four mid-level titles, *Black Panther*, *The Punisher*, *Daredevil* and *The Inhumans* were outsourced to a pair of talented creatives who ran their own publishing house, Event Comics. Penciller Joe Queseda and inker Jimmy Palmiotti were tasked with breathing new life into this quartet of second-tier characters under a glossy new imprint, *Marvel Knights*. Queseda was made editor of the whole shebang and dutifully brought in a raft of new talent, including Hollywood writer/director Kevin Smith on *Daredevil*. A gregarious and verbose comic book geek, Smith had actually given Stan a cameo playing himself in the 1995 comedy *Mallrats*, and had been hired by Warner Bros to work on the script for Tim Burton's *Superman Lives*. He was hot property in Hollywood at the time and choosing him to revitalise the Man Without Fear reflects Marvel's fresh approach of looking outside their industry for talent. *Marvel Knights* took the bold move of delivering stand-alone stories, which freed up the writers to take these titles wherever they wanted. It was a refreshing change that paid off and *Marvel Knights* was a huge success. Throughout the 2000s, all the Marvel heroes received the *Marvel Knights* treatment to critical acclaim.

Inevitably, Marvel continued to branch out in unusual directions. MarvelMania Hollywood restaurant opened its doors to the public. Despite offering 'Blazing Beverages', 'Astonishing Appetizers' and 'Pulse-Pounding Pizzas', the restaurant closed after only two years. Better received was the launch, in 1999, of Marvel Super Hero Island, part of Universal's Islands of Adventure theme park in Orlando, Florida. At the time of writing, that one is still going strong. That same year, Marvel freed up a bit of cash by selling off their trading card company, Fleer/Skybox for $30 million. In 2000, Fleer's former president Bill Jemas was appointed Marvel's President of Consumer Products, Publishing and New Media. Despite not having a creative background and being very much another high-end 'suit', Jemas demonstrated unbridled enthusiasm and wanted to be very involved in steering the Marvel ship into uncharted waters. His first notable decision was installing *Marvel Knights* editor Joe Queseda as editor-in-chief. It was a smart move. Together, Queseda and Jemas would be largely responsible for turning around the fortunes of Marvel Comics.

The most radical innovation Queseda and Jemas brought to proceedings was abandoning the long-standing and much-lauded Marvel continuity. They felt that this vast, interconnected universe, once the key to Marvel Comics' success, had actually become a hindrance to younger or newer readers. After all, would you really want to start reading a comic if you had to swat up on decades of that character's history? Of course, they knew there would be an outcry were they to abandon classic Marvel continuity altogether, so together they launched the *Ultimate* comic book line. Not a reboot as such, these comic titles existed on an alternate timeline, retelling Marvel's finest heroes' stories from scratch, but with a few twists. This frequently included modernising characters along the way and altering familiar relationships. Much like *Marvel Knights*, pretty much all the top-tier Marvel characters enjoyed this reimagining, kicking off in 2000 with *Ultimate Spider-Man*. Particularly memorable was edgy Scottish writer Mark Millar's *The Ultimates*, a mature reworking of the Avengers that saw Nick Fury, the once-Caucasian general of counter-terrorism and intelligence agency S.H.I.E.L.D.[1] transformed into an impossibly cool African American. In fact, this Fury was deliberately drawn to look exactly like Samuel L. Jackson. There is even an inspired moment in the comic when the characters discuss who should play them in a movie adaptation of their lives; Fury just replies, 'Mr. Samuel L. Jackson, of course, no discussion.' How prophetic.

Stan had pretty much stepped away from Marvel during this time to focus on new projects. He did occasionally pop up here and there, just to remind people he wasn't dead, and very much still the unofficial face of Marvel. He appeared as himself in cartoon form during the final episode of the latest *Spider-Man* animated series on Fox Kids TV channel. Broadcast in early 1998, the touching scene saw Stan taken web-swinging by Spidey as thanks for helping create him. There were many new Marvel animated series either on air or in development throughout the noughties, but Stan was not heavily involved. His revised Marvel contract had left him completely unfettered and energised to explore fresh avenues.

Stan cautiously moved towards multimedia projects, harnessing new technology and platforms to continue telling stories that excited him. Like so many turning points in his life, it was impeccable timing.

The exponential rise of the internet resulted in those historically on the fringes of societal grouping now being given the confidence to collectively raise their voice, and a powerful platform on which to be heard. Online culture has always been a realm of the geek. Within that culture thrives a great enthusiasm for comic books, fertile ground in which to cultivate the same sense of community that Stan had nurtured with Bullpen Bulletins and M.M.M.S. all those years ago. Online was the next logical domain to grow an even stronger bond between Stan and his fans, especially now he was stepping out from the shadow of Marvel. It was such a shame, then, that Stan's first major business venture online would end in total disaster.

In early 1999, Stan launched Stan Lee Media Inc (SLM) near his Hollywood home in Encino's Ventura Boulevard. The business was co-founded with a man called Peter F. Paul, whom Stan had met ten years earlier via ludicrous leonine model Fabio, who had been circling any future role of Thor. Peter Paul had founded several non-profit organisations, including one with veteran Hollywood actor James Stewart. A consummate smooth talker and showman, Paul soft-soaped Stan by offering him an award at one of his glitzy showbiz bashes, where Stan was thrilled to be rubbing shoulders with the likes of ex-US President Ronald Reagan. The following year, Paul emerged as the largest contributor to Hillary Clinton's senatorial campaign. Paul was clearly a high-stakes player the likes of which Stan could only dream to be. SLM was intended to be a creation, production and marketing company. At the centre of this enterprise was www.stanlee.net, where Stan could continue to have his creative voice heard, undiluted and uncompromised, and on a scale and scope unlike anything that had gone before.

Things at SLM started very well indeed. Stan created a new breed of superheroes for a high-profile web series *The 7th Portal*, which in February 2000 was launched in a gala presentation at a cost of $1 million. The dot com boom saw the company thrive; at its peak, it was a multimillion-dollar multimedia studio and home to over 150 employees. In November 2000, Marvel appointed a new media president to oversee their website, but that same month SML won Best of Show Web Award for Best Entertainment Portal, beating the likes of Disney and Warner Bros. While Marvel tried to make inroads online, their veteran employee was streaming ahead at high speed.

Then everything crashed.

At the end of 2000, Stan Lee Media ran out of money. Peter Paul would later blame intervention by Bill Clinton as a factor; that the former president had allegedly persuaded companies not to invest in SLM, but there is no evidence to support this. Besides, the dot com bubble burst, leaving many online enterprises dangling in the wind, no matter how successfully they had grown. And the problem with Peter Paul was that he was a career criminal. Before he worked with Stan, he had served time for cocaine possession and fraud, and in 1983 was sent to prison for travelling under the identity of a dead man. In February 2001, SLM filed for bankruptcy, prompting Paul to do what any conman would: he fled to Brazil. Later that year he was indicted on one count of manipulating stock prices in SLM. The law finally caught up with him and he spent four years under house arrest. In 2009, he was indicted for committing a securities regulation felony. He pleaded guilty and was sentenced to ten years in prison.

As you'd expect, Stan was not proud of the whole messy business. No criminal accusations or charges were lobbed his way, but the wool had been truly pulled over his eyes by his corrupt business partner. It was utterly humiliating and embarrassing for Stan, both personally and professionally. Undeterred, he ploughed on with his other projects. His first novel, a World War II sci-fi romp *The Alien Factor* was published in 2001. Not the Great American Novel he had always hoped to write, this is another one for Stan Lee completists only.

Less than a year after SLM went under, Stan joined forces with producer Gill Champion and lawyer (wise choice this time) Arthur Lieberman to form POW! (Purveyors of Wonder) Entertainment. POW! was set up to develop film, television and video game properties, with Stan as chief creative officer, determined not to let things go belly up as it did with SLM. Clearly there was a personal need for redemption after the disastrous collaboration with Paul. 'I just wanted to show that I can succeed,' Lee later reflected, 'working with people who are honourable and competent.'[2] Fortunately for Stan, there were plenty of friends in high places keen to help him regain his confidence. In 2001, he struck a deal that for decades would have been unthinkable: Stan Lee, the face of Marvel, went to work for DC Comics.

This surprising collaboration came about when *Batman* producer and comic book scholar Michael E. Uslan invited Stan to re-imagine several of the Distinguished Competition's finest heroes. Superman,

Batman, Wonder Woman, Aquaman, Green Lantern and the Flash all received the Stan Lee treatment in a line that was christened *Just Imagine...* . This twelve-issue series gave Stan free rein to mess about with long-established origin stories of the original superheroes. In this universe, Superman is the weakest member of the Kryptonian police force; Batman is an African American called Wayne Williams; and the Flash is a woman. In a typically arch Stan flourish, he even changed characters' names to be alliterative, just as he had so frequently done for Marvel. Working with artists John Buscema and Jim Lee, he had a lot of fun in this new sandbox. One cannot help but wonder what his former colleagues from back in the day, many of whom had now passed on, would have made of the definitive Marvel poster boy working for the Distinguished Competition.

POW! allowed Stan to create characters across different media to which he actually retained the rights, a luxury he never enjoyed at Marvel. The quality of these creations varies wildly. For every conventional romp, such as *Starborn* or *Soldier Zero*, there were also plans for a new superhero series starring the Beatles' second-best drummer, Ringo Starr. Suffice to say, this never happened, and the world is a little poorer for it. Stan collaborated with *Playboy* lothario and old friend Hugh Hefner on an animated show for MTV called *Hef's Superbunnies*. Think *Charlie's Angels* but with more boobs and you're on the right lines. And yes, it's as classy as it sounds. Then there was *Striperella*, a risqué animated superhero series made for Spike TV, starring the inflatable *Baywatch* star Pamela Anderson. Stan didn't write the series, but was happy to make it and have his name above the title. These last two projects seem curious choices for Stan, rather more lascivious than his usual fare. Then again, if you can't enjoy a bit of sex in your work just before you turn 80, when can you?

POW! also embraced talent from around the world, creating Manga series *Karakuri Dôji Ultimo*, a collaboration between Stan and celebrated Japanese artist Hiroyuki Takei. In India, POW! created the animated series *Chakra: The Invincible*. Stan even hosted, co-created, executive-produced, and judged a reality game show called *Who Wants to Be a Superhero?* for the Sci-Fi Channel. It's worth pointing out that despite expert guidance and advice from Stan himself, no one, sadly, became an actual superhero. Which is a shame.

Things were back on track for both Stan and Marvel. POW! was proving to be a lucrative, bold, surprising and original creative force, while Stan was enjoying a second wind of pure imagination. Meanwhile, Marvel Comics had become a much more agile beast, thanks to Bill Jemas and Joe Queseda cutting ties to the past and freeing up their creatives from Marvel's own lumbering lore. Both *Marvel Knights* and the *Ultimate Marvel* line ran successfully throughout the decade. Other titles worth mentioning include *Wolverine: Origin*, which finally unravelled the hugely popular mutant's mysterious past; and Neil Gaiman's *1602,* which transplanted Marvel characters into an Elizabethan setting. Queseda also managed to remind readers of the unpredictable and subversive values that inspired the Silver Age with two notable crossover storylines. *House of M* saw mutants made to feel like a vulnerable persecuted minority once more, while heroes were pitted against one another in the epic *Civil War* storyline.

In another canny move, Marvel also broke long-standing ties with the Comics Code Authority. This allowed them to publish adult titles under a new imprint, MAX. This new line introduced more complex characters, most notably troubled former superhero turned private investigator Jessica Jones. Elsewhere, the injection of successful creative minds from TV and film into the Marvel bullpen proved an effective way to refresh the brand. In addition to Kevin Smith, *Babylon 5* creator J. Michael Straczynski, and *Buffy The Vampire Slayer* mastermind Joss Whedon wrote extensively for *The Amazing Spider-Man* and *The Astonishing X-Men*, respectively.

Despite this period of renewed creativity, Stan did have to endure more legal skirmishes. Only this time, he was right in the epicentre. In 2002, Stan performed another unthinkable act and sued Marvel. The seeds of this dispute were sown back in the 1990s. After decades of not delivering in Hollywood, Marvel had promised Stan ten per cent of any future profits if his characters appeared on TV and film. Fast forward to the early 2000s and several of Stan's co-creations had proved hugely successful at the box office (more on that to come). Trouble is, Marvel had failed to pay him the share they had promised, so he took legal action. It took three years before Stan and Marvel finally reached a settlement. He didn't win the rights to his creations, but he did land an undisclosed seven-figure sum.

Stan's legal woes continued two years later. In March 2007, SLM somehow resurfaced and filed a lawsuit against Marvel Entertainment, to the tune of $5 billion. Turns out that Stan's internet company had survived both bankruptcy and Peter Paul doing a runner, been bought up, and spent years mired in litigation. Under new management, the company that rose from the ashes of SLM claimed that back in the late 1990s, Stan had allegedly handed over the rights to several Marvel characters in exchange for stock and a salary. Later that year, the resurgent SLM sued Stan and his new company POW! Entertainment. It all seems a bit ridiculous in hindsight. To be sued by a company long shut down that has your own name in the title must have been, for Stan, rather strange to say the least.

What these legal shenanigans do demonstrate is what an enormously valuable commodity these Marvel characters had become. These were not just superheroes, they were super-lucrative properties that were a licence to print money, if handled correctly. And there's the rub. For the most part, Marvel characters had been underserved by media outside of the comic books. That was all about to change. And change the world.

Chapter Sixteen

The Oldest Posterboy in Town

Poland 1944. Filthy, worn boots wade through grey slurry in sheet rain. An armed guard perches in his watchtower, surveying this slow, sorry procession. We see yellow stars of David crudely stitched on sodden clothes as people trudge towards vast gates of rusted metal and barbed wire. From the huddle, a young boy spies, through the ragged fencing, numbers tattooed on a female prisoner's arm as she toils in the filth. Suddenly, angry soldiers with rifles intercept the group, dividing men and women from the children. The boy is torn from his parents. The gates swing shut behind the boy's mother as she screams for her son. The distraught boy howls in anguish, reaching out with both arms. Through sheer will, he forces the gates to buckle open. Soldiers pile on in an attempt to detain the boy but he is too powerful. Despite their combined might, the boy is propelled like a magnet towards the twisted iron, until a swift crunch to the face by the butt of a soldier's rifle renders him unconscious. The screaming stops. They all collapse in the mud. Silence. Confused soldiers rise from the mud. What just happened?

This was not your average superhero film.

If the success of *Blade* allowed Marvel to finally be heard hammering on the gates of Hollywood, 2000's *X-Men* ripped them off their hinges. After two critically acclaimed feature films – the stylish neo-noir crime thriller *The Usual Suspects* (1995) and taut Stephen King adaptation *Apt Pupil* (1998) – director Bryan Singer's take on Marvel's iconic mutants didn't pull any punches. Its arresting opening scene in a Nazi concentration camp was a bold mission statement. This is a comic book film dealing with profoundly serious, real-life issues. The film expertly taps into the central theme that made the source material so compelling: the emotional torment of being feared, persecuted and cast out by society just by virtue of being different. *X-Men* boasted a roster of great talent, with British thespians turned Hollywood pros

Ian McKellen and Patrick Stewart leading both sides of the 'mutant problem' and a breakout performance of pure power and charisma by then-unknown Australian actor Hugh Jackman as Wolverine. The film is lean and efficient, rattling along for its 100-minute runtime and is a solid but brisk adaptation of Marvel's most successful comic book title. *X-Men* cost $75 million to produce, peanuts for a modern-day summer superhero blockbuster, and it went on to make $296.3 million at the box office. Its runaway success sowed the seeds for a fully formed Marvel franchise for 20th Century Fox. Most importantly, of course, it also featured the first of Stan's many cinematic superhero cameos,[1] as a dumbstruck hot-dog vendor.

Marvel had a second global smash on their hands. As head of Marvel Films, Avi Arad, who served as producer on *Blade* and executive producer on *X-Men*, had triumphed where Stan had failed, delivering not one but two hugely successful theatrical adaptations of a Marvel comic in a row. In 2001, Arad created a short-lived and forgettable TV show for syndication called *Mutant X*, but that fell foul of legal troubles because 20th Century Fox felt it was too similar to *X-Men*, to which they owned the rights. Arad needed another hit. More than this, he needed to prove that the recent Marvel successes weren't a fluke. March 2002 saw Mexican auteur Guillermo del Toro deliver the underrated *Blade II*, netting over $150 million on a budget of $54 million, but that summer was the big one. The face of the brand, almost as much as Stan himself. The single most important adaptation that had to succeed, to finally secure Marvel as a major player in Hollywood: *Spider-Man*.

It was a miracle that old Web Head found his way onto the big screen at all. Ugly legal tussles had grounded the character in development hell until the late 1990s. Cannon Films, under misrule of Israeli cousins Menahem Golan and Yoram Globus, had obtained the film rights for Spider-Man from Marvel back in the late 1970s. Golan and Globus had a reputation for cost-cutting to the detriment of their films, as had been the case when they buried the Superman franchise with the fourth entry, *The Quest for Peace.* They were not best positioned to deliver the Spider-Man film everyone deserved.

Despite Cannon being subsequently swallowed up by another company, Menahem Golan hung onto his precious spider-rights, which were due to expire in 1990. By the time that date arrived, Golan was now head of a set-up called 21st Century Film Corporation, and he found a way to extend the rights contract. To raise the vast sums of money Golan predicted he needed to get Spider-Man off the ground and he sold off subsidiary rights to other media companies, including MGM, Viacom, Tri-Star and Carolco Pictures. Due to Carolco's global success of *Terminator 2: Judgment Day*, the aforementioned James Cameron had entered the frame as writer/director. Never one to do things by half, Cameron bashed out a mammoth fifty-seven-page treatment. He was also given final say on everything, which made Menahem Golan livid. That's when it got messy. As in five lawsuits over eighteen agreements messy. For the next six years, the battle for Spider-Man raged in and out of the courts. Everyone sued everyone. At one point, three studios claimed they had the rights to make the film. During this period, several of the companies involved went under, including Marvel. In 1997 the dust finally settled, as did everyone involved. Columbia Pictures, owned by Japanese giant Sony, stepped up and agreed to make the film on a big budget using the latest special effects. Finally, Spidey would have his time to shine.

While a Spider-Man film made by James Cameron at the height of his creative powers remains one of the great 'what if' moments in modern Hollywood, the film Columbia did deliver, directed by Sam Raimi, remains a delight and a solid adaptation. Stars Tobey Maguire and Kirsten Dunst have great chemistry as Peter Parker and Mary Jane Watson, and *Jurassic Park* script writer David Koepp clearly went back to source. After studying Stan's punchy words and Steve Ditko's angular art, he knew that to make the film engaging, it had to sell Peter's mixed-up life. Despite the still baffling decision to have Willem Dafoe's Green Goblin suit look like a cheap reject from *Power Rangers*, the film is a faithful origin story, buoyed by Oscar-nominated special effects that allowed Spidey to swing through New York just as he had done in the comics. No more chubby stuntmen in pyjamas on string. Yes, it may have relied a little too heavily on CGI, but it looked and felt like Spider-Man. Again, its success lay in treating the characters and their world seriously and with respect. The premise may feel ludicrous and childish to some, but that doesn't mean it shouldn't feel real.

Stan was thrilled. Of course, he pops up in the film; this time in a much more heroic cameo, playing a man who saves a little girl from falling debris. When Raimi was announced as director, Stan was confident that the *Evil Dead* director would do the character justice.

He was right. The world premiere took place in Hollywood on 29 April 2002, and Stan was there to soak up every moment from the red carpet. *Spider-Man* proved a spectacular hit. It was the first ever film to take in more than $100 million in its opening weekend. With a budget of $139 million, Sony's *Spider-Man* reaped a colossal $821.7 million worldwide.

While Stan continued his various projects with POW!, Marvel's licensed films gained further traction through Hollywood. They drew in huge audiences, even if they were a mixed bag. In 2003, there was a trio of Marvel adaptations – 20th Century Fox released Mark Steven Johnson's *Daredevil* starring Ben Affleck, Bryan Singer's *X-Men* sequel, *X2*, and Universal produced Ang Lee's *Hulk*.

Despite mining the very best of Frank Miller's run on the comics, *Daredevil* is not good. It feels disjointed, Affleck is hammy and the tone is all over the place. It also co-stars, in a supporting role, Jon Favreau. Keep an eye on that one, he'll prove significant in this story. *X2,* however, is brilliant. Singer built on the original to make a larger, deeper exploration of mutant existence, boasting excellent performances and two truly exceptional set pieces: the opening presidential assassination attempt by teleporting mutant Nightcrawler, and the exhilarating attack on Professor X's mansion where Wolverine fights intruders with full-on beserker rage. There's also a wonderful scene in which Bobby Drake, AKA Iceman, goes home to tell his parents he is a mutant, deliberately crafted to mirror a teenager coming out as gay to their parents. The dramatic climax also teased Chris Claremont and John Byrne's classic *Dark Phoenix* comic arc, causing much whooping from fans in multiplexes.

Then there was *Hulk.* Significant for being the first film to bring the angry green giant to life entirely through CGI, *Hulk* is a divisive oddity. Oscar-winning Taiwanese director Ang Lee brought an ambitious and distinct art house style to proceedings, and visually it's gorgeous; Lee saturates every frame with hues of green, and presents the action in moving panels as if the film is a living version of the original comic. Sadly, the action gets bogged down in theatrical melodrama, the cast, led by Eric Bana as Bruce Banner, doing their best with overlong scenes stuffed with heavy-handed and overblown dialogue. *Hulk* proves there's a fine line between treating the source material with respect and laying on the histrionics too thick. In this case it felt like some overwrought Greek tragedy. It just wasn't fun. However, Stan's sensational cameos continued. He was 'Old Man at Crossing' in *Daredevil*, and in *Hulk*,

'Grumpy Security Guard #1', alongside original TV Hulk, Lou Ferrigno. For some reason, Stan didn't make a cameo for *X2*, and to date it is one of only four Marvel films without a Stan Lee cameo. What was clear, however, was that people had an appetite for Marvel movies. The three releases of 2003 collectively cost over $300 million to make, but together they pulled in box office receipts to the tune of over $800 million.

Around this time, entertainment executive David Maisel approached Avi Arad in his office on Santa Monica Boulevard with a proposition. He pitched a way for Marvel Studios to stop licensing their titles to studios and become an actual production company that made its own films. As Arad had tried to negotiate further creative control with his licensing deals back in the 1990s, he was more than interested. Arad had been growing increasingly frustrated because these licensing deals meant Marvel were only getting a percentage of profits from films about characters that were 100 per cent their own. For instance, *Spider-Man* and its 2004 sequel *Spider-Man 2* made a total of $3 billion dollars[2], but a Lehman Brothers analysis showed that Marvel 'only' got $62 million from both.[3] After a second meeting with Arad's old Toy Biz partner and Marvel top dog Isaac Perlmutter, Maisel was hired as president and COO of Marvel Studios. Now all he had to do was untangle a raft of characters whose rights had been sold to various Hollywood studios across several decades and reel them all back in to the Marvel cinematic bullpen. It would take time. Time and money.

While this was going on, further Marvel-licensed adaptations continued to perform well, but increasingly suffered from poor critical reception. With the exception of Raimi's superior *Spider-Man 2*, still one of the strongest superhero films ever made, cinema audiences in 2004 had to endure a raft of sub-par adaptations. *The Punisher* was reimagined as a rather nasty modern revenge western and, although Tom Jane is great as Frank Castle, the film is inexplicably set, not in dark, grimy New York, but bright sunny Florida. The third *Blade* film saw writer David S. Goyer step up to direct what turned out to be a mess of a film, in which TV's *Prison Break* and *Legends of Tomorrow* star Dominic Purcell is woefully miscast as Dracula taking on the daywalker. The final result underachieved all round.

In 2005, the *Daredevil* spin-off *Elektra* totally misfired, and *The Fantastic Four* finally got a shot at the title. It missed wide of the mark, but is notable for the fact the Human Torch is played by

Chris Evans, who would go on to shine as another Marvel character, Captain America. That year Christopher Nolan struck gold for DC with the excellent *Batman Begins*, while Marvel characters continued to struggle. Was history repeating itself? Not even the *X-Men* franchise could sustain its own winning streak. When Bryan Singer left the project to reboot the Man of Steel with *Superman Returns*, jobbing director-for-hire Brett Ratner stepped in to deliver 2006's *X-Men: The Last Stand.* It's a muddled, uninspired and ultimately generic action film that undid all of the previous two films' goodwill. Its worst crime was to drop the ball on the absolute gift of a storyline, the *Dark Phoenix Saga*.

In 2007, Nicolas Cage's *Ghost Rider* crashed and burned; no one noticed. *Spider-Man 3* was ruined by creative clashes between executives and director Sam Raimi about who the film should have as its main villain. Raimi ultimately delivered a convoluted, half-hearted action film overstuffed with far too many bad guys and a woeful subplot where Peter Parker goes emo. *Fantastic Four: Rise of the Silver Surfer* was utterly inconsequential, at the same time managing to botch this writer's favourite Marvel character's cinematic debut. Still not over that.

A major reason so many of these films failed was because Marvel did not have enough creative input. Many of their beloved characters were being mangled by studio interference. Every so often, they got it right, as with the first two *X-Men* and *Spider-Man* films, but more often than not, decisions by committee had watered down or detrimentally deviated from the original vision. That's the thing about adapting hugely successful comic book characters. If it ain't broke, don't fix it. And if you *are* going to wilfully ignore successful source material, you better have a damn good reason. Most of the time they didn't, and the end result suffered greatly. Hands down the most common mistake was a failure to capture the sparkling and punkish spirit of the original comics, specifically, Stan's quick wit. As a writer, he had the ability to jump from Shakespearean dialogue to snappy modern banter and anything in between. It was that sparkle that set Marvel apart. So quickly it gets overlooked.

There were attempts by Marvel Studios to influence creative direction, especially after David Maisel took the helm, but it proved tough to wade through the endless rounds of notes from studio executives. Besides, Maisel had his hands full trying to renegotiate characters back from these studios. Fortunately, he had a secret weapon: talented young producer Kevin Feige.

Feige had worked for producer Lauren Shuler Donner on 2000's *X-Men* before impressing Avi Arad with his extensive knowledge of the Marvel Universe, to the extent he hired him as a producer for Marvel Studios. There, Feige spent most of the decade delivering script notes to the studios to try and add that special Marvel flavour into the mix. In 2006, Arad quit as chairman of Marvel Studios. The following year, Maisel took his place and Feige was made president for production. It was a smart move.

Riding the wave of these varying successes, Stan Lee remained a beaming presence throughout. His cameos were fast becoming a welcome trope of all Marvel adaptations and yet another smart move in self-promotion. By the end of 2007, he was 85. Most of his colleagues from the Silver Age Marvel bullpen were gone, but there was Stan, larger than life and as enthusiastic as ever. These recent films had naturally raised his profile for a new audience, no doubt taking his mind off the various legal battles that continued to drag on. Stan proudly worked the press junkets and world premieres with the zeal of a man half his age. He was always more than happy to talk about his work with anyone who would stick a microphone in his face. An excellent BBC documentary made at this time, *In Search of Steve Ditko*, finds the elder statesman of comic books sharing some of his most candid thoughts about the Marvel creative process: 'I thought up *The Fantastic Four*, and it did well, and so we did another book called *The Hulk*, and then we did *Spider-Man* and the *X-Men*, and on and on. And of course, on the seventh day, I rested,' he said.[4] This is quintessential Stan Lee speak. In that single quote, we see the essence of the man, at once boastful and arrogant yet also acknowledging he wasn't alone. Later on in the documentary, when pushed on who ultimately created Spider-Man, Stan says, 'I really think the guy who dreams the thing up created it! You dream it up, then you give it to anybody to draw it.' This remark is clearly doing a disservice to the talent and contribution of artist Steve Ditko. Stan then immediately expressed discomfort at being asked this question, adding, 'if Steve wants to be called co-creator, I think he deserves [it].'[5] A cynic might interpret this as Stan still considering Marvel to be his vision, but also begrudgingly feeling he had to acknowledge the contribution of others.

While Stan continued to remind everyone that Marvel was his brainchild, David Maisel and Kevin Feige's crusade paid off. Marvel Studios had taken out a huge corporate loan, and used that influx of cash to successfully negotiate various key characters back under Marvel's control. While three tent-pole creations still remained with other studios – X-Men and the Fantastic Four with 20th Century Fox and Spider-Man with Sony – Marvel had gathered enough heroes back into the fold to start the ball rolling.

The following year, 2008, was the turning point, with the release of *Iron Man* and *The Incredible Hulk*. Despite being distributed through Paramount and Universal respectively, these were the first true Marvel Studios films. For the first time ever, Marvel had complete creative control. The results lit the touch paper on the most ambitious cinematic project ever attempted in Hollywood: a fully interconnected Marvel Cinematic Universe (MCU), spread out across multiple films and many years. Essentially, Marvel set about replicating what Stan and his bullpen had achieved on the page during the 1960s, now writ large on the big screen. It was a huge gamble. Were any of the individual connecting parts to fail, the whole machine would break down. But if it succeeded, it would change the way Hollywood made movies. It did. And it did.

This first stage, appropriately known as Phase One, suffered an early stumble. *The Incredible Hulk* made a profit but was not the smash they had hoped for. It's much more fun than its predecessor but it never really shines. Edward Norton does a solid job as Bruce Banner, but he lacks the intensity of Eric Bana and the easy charm of Mark Ruffalo, who replaced Norton to critical acclaim in future MCU feature films. Once again, the Hulk is entirely CGI, but seems more cartoonish than before. It's not a terrible film by any stretch, but it never sparkles.

Iron Man, however, was a triumph. Feige appointed actor-turned-director Jon Favreau at the helm. Remember him? The guy who had a small role in *Daredevil*? Anyway. Feige and Favreau knew that because Iron Man was just a suit that completely obscures the actor's face, Tony Stark had to be the star attraction. So they delivered a master stroke in casting Robert Downey Jr., back then known for being a once-promising young actor who had fallen from grace, becoming mired in drugs, arrests and jail time. Fortunately, he brought that damaged charm and weary experience to the role and gave us the perfect Tony Stark: precocious, snarky and effortlessly charming, but also intense and dangerously charismatic. It remains one of the best marriages between actor and role, something that Marvel would achieve many more times. *Iron Man* was the first film to truly capture the feisty and knowing energy that Marvel was synonymous with.

At the time, Marvel Studios had modest expectations for *Iron Man* and there wasn't a whole lot of buzz around the project. In 2008, *the* superhero film everyone was excited about was *The Dark Knight*. As we now know, Christopher Nolan's sequel to *Batman Begins* was indeed a triumph, not least because of the late Heath Ledger's phenomenal turn as the Joker. *The Dark Knight* came out in July. *Iron Man* was scheduled for an April/May release. It could hopefully slip in under the radar. It didn't have to break records, nor did it have to compete with the Bat. It just had to not fail. A board member even told Maisel, 'Don't worry. We'll be very happy if this breaks even and we can sell more toys.'[6] Made for $140 million, it grossed $585 million worldwide.

Iron Man set the template for all that would follow: find writers and a director who understand and respect the source material, nail the casting, then add that distinct Marvel sensibility that Stan and his team had pioneered back in the day. Significantly, the end of both *Iron Man* and *The Incredible Hulk* featured a hidden final scene, tacked on after the end credits, teasing that, not only were there more Marvel stories and characters to come, but that these characters all existed in the same cinematic universe. These teaser sequences, alongside the now obligatory Stan cameo, became hallmarks of Marvel films, which other non-superhero franchises began to copy. It wasn't a new idea. It's essentially a glorified version of 'James Bond will return in…' that was added to the end credits of each 007 film, but these Easter eggs grew to be so anticipated among fans, it was not unusual to see the entire cinema audience stay quietly in their seats when the credits rolled, waiting for one, maybe two or even three 'end-credit scenes' that would be subsequently dissected and analysed online the next day.

From 2008 onwards the MCU grew and grew. In 2009, David Maisel helped facilitate a deal with The Walt Disney Company to buy Marvel for an eye-watering $4 billion. What would have Martin Goodman made of that?!

Now no longer needing to rely on other studios for distribution of their films, and fully financed by Disney, all MCU films were henceforth 100 per cent the product of Marvel Studios. I'm not going to go through each and every entry in the MCU, but I will say that every single time, the casting was impeccable. Notable early examples include Chris Hemsworth, carrying the right amount of alpha swagger and sensitivity in *Thor* (2011), while Chris Evans brought a modest dignity to Second World War romp *Captain America: The First Avenger* (2011) in a role that could, in the wrong hands, easily descend into patriotic American tub-thumping. So it continued. More Marvel characters were introduced in the various sequels and Phase One climaxed triumphantly with 2012's *The Avengers,* bringing together all the superheroes it had introduced for a hugely satisfying blockbuster as effortlessly charming as it is action packed, thanks to writer/director Joss Whedon. *The Avengers* also teased in its end-credit scene the arrival of the villainous Thanos. To any comic book fan this was a golden moment. That meant Marvel were working towards one of THE event stories in Marvel history, the *Infinity Gauntlet.*

More sequels followed. Phase Two went intergalactic with the introduction in 2014 of *Guardians of the Galaxy*, arguably Marvel's biggest gamble. All the characters in this hugely entertaining sci-fi comedy were obscure and unknown to those outside of comic book conventions. The original Guardians of the Galaxy team had been created by Stan, with artist Arnold Drake, back in the late 1960s for *Marvel Super-Heroes #18* (cover date January 1969), a series of Marvel special issues. It was by no means a hit. In 2008, two Brits, writer Dan Abnett and artist Andy Lanning, rebooted the team for crossover series *Annihilation: Conquest #6* (cover date June 2008). Abnett and Lanning brought together previously unrelated characters and it was this version that more or less made its way into the movie. Again, they were unknown quantities as far as a wider audience outside Marvel was concerned. Yet, thanks once again to inspired casting, a very funny script and deft direction by James Gunn, the film was another hit. The significance of the *Guardians of the Galaxy* film is that, by this point, Marvel Studios had gained so much confidence in their storytelling powers, they knew they could sell their winning formula to anyone, regardless of whether they had heard of the characters. And they were right.

Phase Three explored the cosmic realm with the much-anticipated introduction in 2016 of *Doctor Strange*. It's an underrated gem with truly eye-popping effects that nod to Ditko's original artwork, while fan-favourite Benedict Cumberbatch offers the right amount of preening swagger as the Master of the Mystic Arts. Phase Three is also notable for two very special Marvel milestones. In 2017, Marvel and Sony finally reached an agreement to allow Spider-Man to join the continuity of MCU. Sony's Spidey films always existed in their own separate universe. After Tobey Maguire and Sam Raimi walked from the franchise,

Sony rebooted in 2012 with Andrew Garfield in the title role. The two *Amazing Spider-Man* films were an attempt by Sony to launch their own spider universe, but it failed to gain traction. Sony clearly lacked Kevin Feige's magic touch, so the two studios joined forces. *Spider-Man: Homecoming* is a truly appropriate title and young British actor Tom Holland's interpretation of the character is arguably the finest to date.

The second milestone of Phase Three was the 2018 release of *Black Panther* directed by Ryan Coogler and starring the late Chadwick Boseman. The film grossed over $1.3 billion worldwide and broke numerous box-office records. It was the highest-grossing film by a black director, the ninth-highest-grossing film of all time, the first ever superhero film to be Oscar nominated for Best Picture and the first MCU film to win an Oscar. In fact, it won three. And while this writer happens to think it is rather overrated, you cannot deny its cultural importance nor its impact. Phase Three would climax with 2019's *Avengers: Endgame*, the second of a two-part adaptation of Jim Starlin's 1991 *Infinity Gauntlet* saga. This colossal smack down featured every single major superhero that had appeared in the MCU to date, taking on the evil Thanos for control of the six infinity stones. This film was a climax to a story arc that had been building since the first *Avengers* film some seven years earlier. Clocking in at a backside-numbing three hours plus, the film was essentially a victory lap for Marvel, a nod to all it had achieved. While it's not quite as good as part one, 2018's *Avengers: Infinity War*, it's a hugely satisfying experience for all those fans who had eagerly watched every MCU film since 2008's *Iron Man. Avengers: Endgame* made $2.798 billion at the box office and is, as of writing, the highest-grossing film of all time.

At the time of writing, the Marvel Cinematic Universe has released twenty-three films, with more for Phase Four in development. Collectively, the MCU has so far made $22.5 billion, making it the most financially successful film franchise in the history of cinema.[7] Other movie franchises have tried to emulate this achievement, but none have succeeded. DC themselves tried to build their own interconnected cinematic universe but they didn't have the right pieces in place to make it work. Warner Bros thought they found their own version of Kevin Feige with director Zack Snyder overseeing proceedings. *Man of Steel* (2013) has some inspired moments, not least the great production design and spot-on casting of Henry Cavill as Superman, but they then rushed through 2016's weirdly uneven and relentlessly grim *Batman v Superman: Dawn of Justice* in an attempt to set up the Justice League. The film is a mess and, although 2017's *Wonder Woman* was great fun, the final *Justice League* film failed to deliver, mired by a family tragedy forcing Snyder to stand down as director, followed by extensive rewrites and reshoots by last-minute draft, *Avengers* writer/directer Joss Whedon. Complications aside – and even with a 'Snyder Cut' of *Justice League* being completed and set for release in 2021 – the franchise spluttered and hope of a completely interconnected DCU that they tried to set up with *Man of Steel* is pretty much dead in the water.

So what is the secret? How did Marvel get it so right when others failed so dramatically? Simple. Do what Stan and Jack and Steve and the rest of the bullpen did. Build. Play the long game and build on what went before. Truth is, only a handful of the MCU films are exceptional. Most of them are solid and a few are so-so. But none are objectively terrible. They are all prime examples of quality filmmaking. The money is on the screen. From the effects, production and design to the casting, acting and script, these films all do the one thing they are supposed to do. Build. They never drop the ball.

Marvel's single most important achievement was to establish a huge, interconnected saga with multiple characters across many different styles of filmmaking. There have been several shared universes in the history of mainstream cinema, such as the Universal Classic Monsters produced between 1931 and 1951, but compared to what Marvel Studios has achieved, no one else has ever come close. You could argue that – as Marvel's former editor-in-chief Joe Queseda observed about the comics during the early 2000s – the MCU suffered from growing increasingly impenetrable if you weren't there from the start. That, without prior knowledge of all the interconnected moments and beats, the films are unremarkable popcorn entertainment. But here's the thing. These films stand up on their own. Each one is an enjoyable piece of blockbuster entertainment that plays with different genres, from sci-fi adventure to heist caper to buddy comedy to psychedelic horror to paranoid political espionage thriller. Taken at face value, these films are great fun. Taken together, they form a truly engrossing, multi-layered universe in which to lose yourself, while at the same time reward multiple viewings. Not to say the MCU is without its share of bumps in the road. There is a lot of pressure on the next phase to deliver now that many of the original stars have bowed out. Then, of course, there was the sudden, tragic death of *Black Panther* star Chadwick Boseman in 2020.

The MCU will find it hard to make further films that remain true to the character, while also paying respect to the supremely talented Boseman whose charismatic presence will be sorely missed. Despite these challenges, the Marvel juggernaut will keep on rolling. Modern entertainment has changed, for good or ill, thanks to the phenomenal success of the MCU. That is its great power. But it also has the great responsibility to honour all it has achieved, keep evolving and keep surprising audiences across the world. And what is, perhaps, most remarkable of all, is that Stan got to see Marvel change the world in his own lifetime.

Stan Lee passed away of heart failure at Cedars-Sinai Medical Center in Los Angeles on 12 November 2018, six weeks before his ninety-sixth birthday. Two days before his death, protégé and successor Roy Thomas visited him at his home. 'I think he was ready to go,' Thomas later reflected. 'But he was still talking about doing more cameos. As long as he had the energy for it and didn't have to travel, Stan was always up to do some more cameos. He got a kick out of those more than anything else.'[8]

Stan's body was cremated and his ashes buried in an intimate private funeral. But in typical Stan style, even from beyond the grave he managed to sneak in one final cameo. In a scene from *Avengers: Endgame*, set in 1970, Stan appears as a digitally de-aged version of himself: Stan Lee in his prime, driving a fast car. By his side, a digital recreation of his beloved wife Joan, who had died in 2017, as she looked back in the day. It's a poignant moment that would have made Stan smile even more than normal.

While this final chapter has mainly been about the incredible success of the Marvel Cinematic Universe, it's worth mentioning that while this was growing, Stan himself received perhaps the three most prestigious accolades of his long life. In 2006, Marvel Comics commemorated his sixty-five years of service by publishing a series of one-shot issues in which Stan met many of his co-creations, including Spider-Man, Doctor Strange, The Thing, Silver Surfer and Doctor Doom. In 2008, President George W. Bush invited Stan to the White House and bestowed on him the National Medal of Arts. This honour is the highest given to artists and arts patrons by the US government, selecting those who 'are deserving of special recognition by reason of their outstanding contributions to the excellence, growth, support and availability of the arts in the United States'.[9] In 2011, Stan received his own star on the Hollywood Walk of Fame. While this was no doubt a genuine honour, Stan didn't really need a star. He already had an entire universe.

Epilogue

Heroes Never Die

We all know the myriad characters Stan Lee gave us. Many are household names. But, now he has left the mortal realm, what do we actually know about his own character? Stan spent at least seven decades in the public eye, yet he successfully managed to maintain a private existence. We all got to know Stan Lee, but not Stanley Martin Lieber. That was, perhaps his biggest trick. By putting himself out there so aggressively, with such a strong persona, he was able to create his own narrative. Stan was outspoken and open in the media. The press never really hounded him. He came to them. He was able to tell what ever story he liked and they would happily listen. There were never any secrets or games, so no need for a scoop. By keeping an open door, Stan was able to control who came in.

In his final years, however, that ironclad barrier broke down. When his beloved wife Joan died in 2017 aged 95, Stan lost his rock of almost seventy years. For the first time in his adult life, he was alone. The press began to intrude on his private life like never before. In January 2018, a story emerged on *Mail Online* that Stan had allegedly sexually harassed nurses who had been caring for him. These claims Lee categorically denied until the day he died.[1] Then, on 2 April 2018, an article appeared on the *TMZ* website claiming that one of his former business managers, Keya Morgan, had allegedly siphoned millions of dollars from his account, as well as some of Stan's own blood from his private nurse to sell off to fans. Thus began a rather public inquiry into how Stan was the victim of elder abuse at the hands of several parties. As just one example, Morgan had allegedly been seizing control of Stan's home, moving him to unfamiliar locations as well as isolating him from friends and family.

At the end of his life, Stan's estate was worth between $50 million and $70 million, and it was suggested in the press that even his own daughter, JC, had been manipulating her father for personal financial gain. A *Hollywood Reporter* piece dated 10 April 2018 claimed it had, in its possession, a legally binding declaration signed by Stan that allegedly painted his daughter as a rude and aggressive diva who had lived her entire life off the back of the family fortune without doing a single day's work in her life, regularly demanding vast sums of money from her father. The article then went on to mention other parties who had been manipulating both Joan and Stan to gain control of assets, property and money.[2] Several more articles emerged, the general consensus being that Stan was surrounded by vampires and leeches, all determined to swindle an old man out of his considerable fortune.

In August 2018, Stan won a protective restraining order, forbidding Keya Morgan from being less than 100 yards away from him, his daughter JC and his brother Larry, who were by then 68 and 86 respectively. The order was set for three years, although, of course, Stan passed away before 2018 came to a close.

It is, of course, important and necessary to shine a light on elder abuse, especially of someone so high profile, but the whole business was handled by the press in typically salacious fashion, delving a little too much into Stan's private life. Rumours circulated that his house was in complete disarray after his wife's death, and that he had a fundamental distrust in the banking system, instead keeping his millions littered around his house. The press has always relished a good celebrity scandal. Stan knew this better than most. For a man who lived in the public eye for so many years, he was lucky to have lasted as long as he did before becoming one of tabloids journalism's countless targets, hiding behind moral outrage to exploit lives for the sake of more sales or clicks. The stress of public exposure to such deeply personal matters, not to mention legal battles and press intrusion, on top of the fact he was still in mourning, took a toll on Stan's health. Did all this ultimately contribute to Stan's death only months later? One doesn't like to speculate, but it couldn't have helped.

These complex and troublesome events that took place in the last year of his life do not diminish Stan's singular legacy in popular culture. He wasn't just a creator. He built worlds. The only other figures from the twentieth century who reached anywhere near the scale Stan attained with Marvel Comics are Walt Disney, Jim Henson and George Lucas. Like Stan, they too expanded their original ideas into hugely influential and phenomenally successful multimedia franchises. It is perhaps the final irony that The Walt Disney Company now owns The Muppets,

Star Wars and Marvel and currently towers above all other producers of entertainment in the world. What this will mean in the long term for nurturing unique and diverse creative talent remains to be seen. Has mass entertainment become too monolithic and corporate? That's a subject for a whole other book. For better or worse, Stan's universe is now part of the Disney monopoly, and one hopes that it protects Marvel's unique voice that Stan was instrumental in creating. To paraphrase celebrated gonzo journalist Hunter S. Thompson, America in the middle 1960s was a very special time and place to be a part of, and Marvel were right in the heart of it. The plucky underdog, with vibrant panels and dynamic splash pages acting as portals into countless worlds, exciting tales of mystery and wonder, all delivered with a knowing wink and an anarchic spirit. The world is a better place if we all keep that fire going. Flame on!

But remove the public persona of Stan Lee, his achievements and accolades, victories and failures, what can we truly say about the man behind the mask? Who was Stanley Lieber? Broadly speaking, it seems that the Stan people met was entirely dependent on what mood he was in that day. He could be tough and at times his ego would get the better of him, but for most, he was always warm, friendly and enthusiastic. Of course, no one can possibly be like that all the time and, no doubt, Stan had other sides to his character. Comic historian Ned Hartley acutely observes:

> We can see various themes coming through Stan's work about alienation, pressure and anxiety, and I think some of these things give a window into Stan's soul. Many of Stan's heroes are tragic figures and have problems being part of society, I think perhaps we can see a little of the real Stan in that.

Simon Furman, co-creator of Marvel's robotic bounty hunter *Death's Head,* felt that when you met Stan, you were always getting the persona first, not the person. He says:

> I know that during the set-up of the never fully realised Excelsior Comics … he could be irascible and not easy to deal with. But he was always very nice and considerate when I was in his presence, never too busy to say 'How you doing?' … my memory of him is genial and pleasant and a man who genuinely loved the business. I kind of don't need or want to know more than that.

Writer Alan Cowsill, former Marvel UK editor and managing director of Bullpen Productions, met Stan a few times and has an especially fond memory:

> Back in the mid-1990s … Glenn Dakin (then a fellow editor) and myself learned Stan Lee was passing through London around the time of my birthday. Without my knowing, Glenn tracked down the hotel Stan was staying in and invited him to a birthday party I was having. Stan didn't make it but we got into work the following Monday to find a message from Stan awaiting me, wishing me 'Happy Birthday'. All done in the classic Stan speak.

Another time Cowsill missed an impromptu UK visit from Stan: 'He not only chatted to the bosses but made a point of going around the whole office to say hello to everyone from the post room up.'

When asked if he thought Stan was a shameless self-promoter, Cowsill is diplomatic: 'He was a creator who wanted people to read his work. I think most creators I know would have more success if they could channel even a little bit of Stan's pizzazz.' Fellow ex-Marvel UK writer John Tomlinson agrees:

> I don't necessarily see self-promotion as cause for shame – providing the self-promoter has the goods to back it up. Relentless self-promoters can come across as tiresome narcissists and show-offs, but somehow Stan never did. Like his characters, he was witty and self-deprecating, even when ballyhooing his wares to the skies. Somehow, Stan always managed to present himself as a modest egomaniac – an art in itself.

Regardless of his true nature, Stan Lee's legacy endures because he himself endured. Through every battle Marvel fought, won and lost, he endured. As the company he helped build metamorphosed under an ever-changing roster of owners, he endured. While many above him came and went, he endured. Like some omniscient celestial being, only Stan bore witness to Marvel's timely genesis, their gradual rise and dramatic fall, their ultimate resurrection and majestic exaltation. He remained their figurehead, patriarch and elder statesman throughout. To millions the world over, Stan Lee *was* Marvel and always will be.

Stan was so much more, but he was no phoney. He believed in doing the right thing and contributing to worthwhile causes. Aside from being involved in charities and foundations to help young people, he followed his gut, regardless of what people might think. Another former Marvel writer, artist and editor, Tim Quinn, was working for *The Saturday Evening Post Magazine* in Indianapolis during the 1980s when the AIDS epidemic blew up. 'People tend to forget now but there was a real fear and ignorance surrounding the disease at this time,' he says. 'Sufferers were being given a hard time across the US … . People were made outcasts.' Quinn created a book to raise awareness and help remove the stigma associated with AIDS. For its release, he hoped to get some high-profile names as endorsements, to show that they didn't mind having their name linked to AIDS. 'That sounds ridiculous now but at that time no celebrity name had come out in support of sufferers,' recalls Quinn. 'Anyway, on the same day I got letters from Stan Lee and Yoko Ono wanting to do all they could to support the project. This was huge. It meant I could go to the *LA Times* and get a front-page story thanks to dropping their names.'

An even more special and poignant memory for Quinn comes from the year Stan died. 'He had heard I was working on a literacy project comic book for the school children of Merseyside and asked if he could have a page in the mag,' he says. 'He wrote a glorious poem explaining *How To Be a Super-Hero*. It is quite beautiful in its simplicity and aim.'

Stan Lee's poem, reproduced by kind permission from the Mighty Quinn, is printed below:

You don't have to be
A super-hero
To make the world
A better place

You don't have to have
A super power
To do your bit
For the human race

Stan Lee: How Marvel Changed the World

You don't have to wear
A mask or costume
Or battle a bandit
Atop a runaway train

All you need to do
Is show compassion
Reach out your hand
To those in pain

You don't have to slay
A deadly dragon
You don't have to risk
Life or limb

You don't even have to fight
An evil villain
You didn't need to do
Anything grim

It's really not hard
To be a hero
You can do it with ease
On your own

Just give your heart
To those who are ailing
Let them know
That they're not alone!

Nuff said.

Notes

Chapter One

1. As outlined in the Proclamation of Islaz on 9 June 1848, including point 21 stating, 'the emancipation of the Israelites and political rights for compatriots of other faiths'.
2. This Romanian diaspora not only included Stan's father, but also a certain Harry Donenfeld, the man chiefly responsible for publishing the first American superhero comics. But more of him later.
3. Jones, Gerard, *Men of Tomorrow: Geeks, Gangsters and the Birth of the Comic Book*, (Basic Books, New York, 2004).
4. A view that has since been questioned by cultural historians. See the article by O'Donnell, Edward T., 'Hibernians versus Hebrews? A New Look at the 1902 Jacob Joseph Funeral Riot', *The Journal of the Gilded Age and Progressive Era* Vol. 6, No. 2, pp. 209-225, (April 2007).
5. Batchelor, Bob, *Stan Lee: The Man Behind Marvel*, (Rowman & Littlefield, Kindle Edition, 2017).
6. Lee, Stan; David, Peter; Doran, Colleen, *Amazing Fantastic Incredible*, (Simon & Schuster, 2015).
7. Lee, Stan; Mair, George, *Excelsior! The Amazing Life of Stan Lee* (Fireside, New York, 2002). It's a fun read but quite light. Onwards, brave reader, we must dig deeper!
8. Lee; Mair, p. 7.
9. Ibid, pp. 5-6.
10. Jones, Gerard, p. 296, which also references that Celia told Stan he was the most handsome, remarkable and talented boy who'd ever lived. Parents take note. If you want to raise a confident kid that'd do it just fine.

Chapter Two

1. Eastman, Irvine, E., (ed.), *The World Almanac and Book of Facts,* p. 494, (New York World Telegram, 1943). Citing both the American Jewish Committee and the Jewish Statistical Bureau of the Synagogue Council of America.
2. Lewine, Edward, 'Sketching Out His Past', *The New York Times Key Magazine,* 2007. http://www.nytimes.com/slideshow/2007/09/04/realestate/keymagazine/20070909STANLEE_3.html
3. Whatever your age, they're great romps and the classic film adaptations aren't too bad either, especially the 1954 version of *20,000 Leagues Under the Sea*. Seriously, who wouldn't want to see Kirk Douglas, James Mason and Peter Lorre hamming it up in a film together?
4. It could be argued that this type of entertainment has never really disappeared; it merely evolved into the same gaudy guff that parades in front of the bemused and disinterested gaze of a judging panel on Saturday night. Hidden among such a cavalcade of chaos, then as now, America's clearly got talent.
5. Blanc, Mel, Bashe, Philip, *That's Not All Folks*, (Warner Books, New York, 1989), p. 29.
6. It was not until the 1950s that this practice of naming a show after its sponsor began to fade away.
7. Lee; Mair, p. 10.

Chapter Three

1. Lee; Mair, p. 15.
2. There's a more detailed exploration and challenge of Stan's claim in Bob Batchelor's book. You can read that if you wish. After you finish this one of course.
3. Sci-fi fans note that this publication would feature first works by such luminaries of the genre as Isaac Asimov and Ursula K. Le Guin.
4. Howe, Sean, *Marvel Comics: The Untold Story*, (Harper Perennial, Kindle Edition, New York, 2013).
5. Tucker, Reed, *Slugfest: Inside the Epic, 50-Year Battle Between Marvel and DC*, (Little, Brown Book Group, Kindle Edition, 2017).
6. *The Funnies* (1929) and *The Funnies on Parade* (1933).
7. https://www.cnet.com/news/supermans-action-comics-no-1-sells-for-record-3-2-million-on-ebay/

Chapter Four

1. Raphael, Jordan; Spurgeon, Tom, *Stan Lee and the Rise and Fall of the American Comic Book*, p. 19, (Chicago Review Press. Kindle Edition, 2004).
2. Lee; Mair, pp. 24-25.
3. Howe.
4. Stan says this in his 2002 autobiography, and Roy mentions it in the introduction to *Marvel Visionaries: Stan Lee*, (Marvel WorldWide, New York, 2019).
5. Morrow, John, p. 10.
6. Well, he had to explain why a small boy was hanging around an army camp *somehow*, right?
7. Lee; Mair, p 26.
8. Morrow, John, *Kirby & Lee: Stuf' Said!* aka Jack Kirby Collector #75, p. 10, (TwoMorrows Publishing, North Carolina, 2018).
9. Ibid.
10. Lee; David; Doran.
11. Lee; Mair, p. 29.
12. Ibid, p. 31.

Chapter Five

1. Lee; Mair, p. 35.
2. Best Picture (Frank Capra and Harry Cohn), Best Director (Frank Capra), Best Actor (Clark Gable), Best Actress (Claudette Colbert) and Best Writing, Adaptation (Robert Riskin). The other two being *One Flew Over the Cuckoo's Nest* (director Milos Foreman, 1975) and *The Silence of the Lambs* (director Jonathan Demme, 1991).
3. Geisel, Theodor Seuss, *The Beginnings of Dr. Seuss: An informal reminiscence*, p. 18, (Dartmouth College Press, New Hampshire, 2014).
4. The director of *Hitler Lives?* was also uncredited. It was a young Don Siegel, who went on to direct *Invasion of the Body Snatchers* (1956), *Dirty Harry* (1971) and John Wayne's final film, *The Shootist* (1976). But that, True Believer, is another rabbit hole down which we do not have time to go…
5. Batchelor.
6. Lee; Mair, p. 38.

7. Ibid, p. 39.
8. https://www.familysearch.org/ark:/61903/1:1:2W55-T9B
9. Lee; David; Doran.

Chapter Six

1. Officially the baby boomer generation is said to end with those born in 1964. Despite being credited for creating the major counterculture of the twentieth century, boomers have since seen an aggressive backlash, being blamed for screwing over subsequent generations in America. They inherited a wealthy country, were blessed with golden opportunities and developed rabid consumerism that led to tax cuts at the expense of public services, inflated house prices, crowded job markets and accelerated climate change.
2. Lee; Mair, p. 90.
3. Lee; David; Doran.
4. Raphael, p. 50.
5. Ibid, p. 60.

Chapter Seven

1. Jones, p. 258.
2. Thomas, Roy, Sanderson, Peter, *The Marvel Vault,* p. 65, (Running Press, Philadelphia, 2007).
3. Lee; Mair, p 125.
4. Ibid, p. 114.
5. Told you that address was significant. You've forgotten all about it haven't you?
6. Evanier, Mark, *Kirby: King of Comics*, Anniversary Edition (Abrams ComicArts, New York, Kindle Edition, 2017).
7. Morrow, p. 18.
8. Groth, Gary, 'Jack Kirby Interview', *The Comics Journal,* 23 May 2011. http://www.tcj.com/jack-kirby-interview/6/
9. Lee; Mair, p. 115.
10. Lee; David; Doran.
11. Dated July 1961, reproduced in Thomas; Sanderson, p. 67.
12. Evanier, Mark.
13. Can you put a turkey out to pasture? I have no idea but I'd be happy to try. Answers on a postcard…

14. Bell, Blake, *Strange and Stranger: The World of Steve Ditko*, pp. 54-57, (Fantagraphics Books, Seattle, 2008).
15. Ditko, Steve, 'Jack Kirby's Spider-Man', *Robin Snyder's History of Comics* #5 (May 1990). Reprinted in Thomas, Roy, (ed.), *Alter Ego: The Comic Book Artist Collection*, p. 56, (TwoMorrows Publishing, North Carolina 2001).

Chapter Eight

1. Kane, Bob, Andrae, Tom, *Batman and Me*, p. 44, (Eclipse Books, California, 1989).
2. Thoreau's hugely influential 1854 work, *Walden; or, Life in the Woods*, explored themes of living at one with nature on a journey of spiritual discovery. His 1849 essay 'Civil Disobedience' championed the idea that it is people's moral duty to become agents of injustice and hold governments to accounts if their behavior is deemed abhorrent.
3. This vintage interview ran in *The Comics Journal* #181 (October 1995).
4. Thomas; Sanderson, p. 65.
5. Kaveney, Roz, *Superheroes! Capes and Crusaders in Comics and Films*, p. 28, (Taurus, New York, 2008).
6. Lee, Stan; Kirby, Jack, *The X-Men* #1 (cover date September 1963).
7. Lee; David; Doran.
8. Kempton, Sally, 'Super-Anti-Hero in Forest Hills', *The Village Voice*, p. 5, (1 April 1965).
9. Morrow, p. 85.
10. Kelly, Mike, 'Comicbook Legend Joe Sinott Talks About Working with Stan Lee for Almost 70 Years', therealstanlee.com, (10 May 2019). https://therealstanlee.com/entertainment/comicbook-legend-joe-sinnott-talks-about-working-with-stan-lee-for-almost-70-years/

Chapter Nine

1. Lee, Stan, interviewed in *The Baltimore Sun*, February 1968, in Morrow, p. 83.
2. Lee; Mair, p. 150.
3. 'Marvel Bullpen Bulletins', published in Marvel comics, cover date April 1966.

4. 'Marvel Bullpen Bulletins', published in Marvel comics, cover date May 1967.
5. Batchelor.
6. Lee, Mair, p 153.
7. Who are we kidding? Like anyone uses any other.
8. Morrow, p. 52.
9. Ibid, p. 54.
10. Ditko, quoted in Ibid, p. 60.
11. Lee, Ibid.
12. Lee; David; Doran.
13. Ditko, quoted in Morrow, p. 61.

Chapter Ten

1. In the US, prime time is commonly defined as 8:00-11:00 pm Eastern/Pacific time and 7:00-10:00 pm Central/Mountain time. Makes sense. You'd want to watch TV an hour earlier if you lived up a mountain because there's not much to do.
2. In 2000 they tried to make a live-action blockbuster version of this cartoon, in which Robert De Niro took great chomps out of the furniture as the villain, Fearless Leader. *Raging Bullwinkle*, if you will. It's abysmal.
3. 'Secret Love' (1953), 'Love is a Many-Splendored Thing' (1955) and 'The Shadow of Your Smile' (1965).
4. *Directions*, 11:00 am Sunday, 7 May 1967 Channel 2, TV listing, *The Billings Gazette*, referenced in Morrow, p. 78.
5. Ibid, p. 79.

Chapter Eleven

1. https://www.in2013dollars.com/
2. Lee; Mair, p. 175.
3. Lewine, Edward, *The New York Times* (9 September 2007). https://archive.nytimes.com/query.nytimes.com/gst/fullpage-9D03E3DB1E3AF93AA3575ACOA9619C8B63.html
4. Lee; Mair, p 195.
5. Buscema, John, quoted in Morrow, p. 101.
6. Thomas, Roy, Ibid, p. 101.
7. First produced in 1977, *What If..?* is a fantastic series that explores how the Marvel Universe might have unfolded differently from the mainstream continuity. With omniscient alien Uatu the Watcher

serving as narrator, there have been over 200 issues. Stories I particularly enjoyed include Spider-Man joining the Fantastic Four, Wolverine fighting Conan The Barbarian and Jane Foster finding the hammer of Thor.

8. 'Stan the Man & Roy the Boy: A Conversation Between Stan Lee and Roy Thomas', *Comic Book Artist* #2, (TwoMorrows Publishing, North Carolina, 1998). https://twomorrows.com/comicbookartist/articles/02stanroy.html
9. Ibid.
10. The drug would later be revealed in *The Amazing Spider-Man #121-122* (cover date June-July 1973) to be LSD.
11. *The Monster Maker* script was sold for $25,000, but it was never filmed.
12. Howe, Sean.
13. Lee; Mair, p. 182.
14. Ibid, p. 184.

Chapter Twelve

1. Englehart, Steve, 'Captain America II' steveenglehart.com http://www.steveenglehart.com/Comics/Captain%20America%20169-176.html
2. Thomas Roy; Johnston Rich, 'The Last Spider-Man Newspaper Strip Runs Today – Its Writer, Roy Thomas Looks Back', *Bleeding Cool*, (23 March 2019) https://www.bleedingcool.com/2019/03/23/last-spider-man-newspaper-strip-writer-roy-thomas/
3. I also recommend you hunt down the episode 'No Escape', first broadcast on 30 March 1979, for no other reason than Hulk co-creator himself, Jack Kirby, makes a cameo as a police-sketch artist. To even the score, Stan later made a cameo as a juror in *Trial of the Incredible Hulk.*
4. Lee; David; Doran.
5. Made for NBC, this 1978 animated version of *The Fantastic Four* is visually superior to its predecessor, and features many of the scripts written by Stan or Roy Thomas. However, because the rights to the Human Torch belonged to Universal Studios, NBC were not allowed to use the character. Unforgivably, the Human Torch was replaced with an annoying robot named H.E.R.B.I.E. The show only lasted thirteen episodes.
6. Lee, Stan interviewed by Ira Wolfman *Circus Magazine #186,* (20 July 1978).

Chapter Thirteen

1. OK, I may not have used the word 'damn'. I was only about 6.
2. A term coined by fan historian Richard Kyle in 1964 to describe comic book material collected or conceived as a self-contained story and presented in a single volume. As opposed to regular comics that were typically serialised story arcs published across several issues at different times.
3. Unlike the average Hollywood action hero, Swedish-born Lundgren is actually a bit of a polymath. He obtained several scholarships to study chemical engineering during the 1970s before completing a Masters at the University of Sydney, then receiving a Fulbright scholarship to the prestigious Massachusetts Institute of Technology. He also holds the rank of third dan black belt in Kyokushin karate and in 1980 was crowned European champion.

Chapter Fourteen

1. Lee; Mair, p 217.
2. Bryant, Adam, 'Pow! The Punches That Left Marvel Reeling', *The New York Times*, section 3, p. 1, (24 May 1998).
3. Stan got to know the late King of Pop a little and talks about this surreal moment in Marvel history in several film interviews, many of which are easy to find on YouTube. It's an odd one, but not unbelievable.
4. Gaiman, Neil, quoted in Bryant.
5. In my case, I was proud to have collected issues 1-100 of *Silver Surfer*, only to discover, several years later, that the complete set was worth pretty much the cover price. Not quite the nest egg I had hoped.
6. Morrow, p. 148.
7. Howe.
8. Don't go snooping around here either. Mum's the word. Nuff said.
9. Lee; Mair, p. 221.
10. Ibid, p. 222.
11. Batchelor.

Chapter Fifteen

1. Strategic Homeland Intervention, Enforcement, and Logistics Division if you must know.
2. Stan quoted in Batchelor.

Chapter Sixteen

1. Not including his cameos on TV movies. Stan did shoot a cameo for *Blade*, playing one of the cops that enters the blood-soaked night club at the start of the film, but his part was cut.
2. Factoring in ticket sales, DVDs, and global TV revenue.
3. Leonard, Devin, 'Calling all superheroes', *Fortune Magazine*, (23 May 2007).
4. Stan Lee interviewed by Jonathan Ross, *In Search of Steve Ditko*, (Hot Sauce Productions for BBC Four, original broadcast 16 September 2007).
5. Ibid.
6. Masters, Kim, 'Marvel Studios' Origin Secrets Revealed by Mysterious Founder: History Was "Rewritten"' *The Hollywood Reporter*, (5 May 2016).
7. Marvel characters continue to appear on TV, both on traditional networks as animations and live-action series, and on streaming services (special mention to the superb run of *Daredevil* and *Jessica Jones* on Netflix).
8. Couch, Aaron, 'Marvel Veteran Recalls His Final Saturday With Stan Lee', *The Hollywood Reporter,* (13 November 2018). www.arts.gov/honors/medals
9. Masters, Kim.

Epilogue

1. Parry, Ryan, 'Marvel creator Stan Lee is accused of groping nurses and demanding oral sex in the shower at his $20m Los Angeles home – but says he is victim of a "shake down"', *MailOnline*, (9 January 2018). https://www.dailymail.co.uk/news/article-5250513/Marvel-creator-Stan-Lee-95-accused-groping-nurses.html
2. Baum, Gary, 'Stan Lee Needs a Hero: Elder Abuse Claims and a Battle over the Aging Marvel Creator', *The Hollywood Reporter*, (10 April 2018). https://www.hollywoodreporter.com/features/stan-lee-needs-a-hero-elder-abuse-claims-a-battle-aging-marvel-creator-1101229

Bibliography

Batchelor, Bob, *Stan Lee: The Man Behind Marvel*, (Rowman & Littlefield Publishers, 2017), Kindle Edition

Bell, Blake, *Strange and Stranger: The World of Steve Ditko* (Fantagraphic Books, Seattle, 2008)

Blanc, Mel; Bashe, Philip, *That's Not All Folks*, (Warner Books, New York, 1989)

Evanier, Mark, *Kirby: King of Comics, Anniversary Edition* (Abrams ComicArts, New York, 2017), Kindle Edition

Howe, Sean, *Marvel Comics: The Unknown Story* (Harper Perennial, New York, 2013), Kindle Edition

Jones, Gerard, *Men of Tomorrow: Geeks, Gangsters and the Birth of the Comic Book* (Basic Books, New York, 2004)

Kane, Bob; Andrae, Tom, *Batman and Me*, (Eclipse Books, California, 1989)

Kaveney, Roz, *Superheroes! Capes and Crusaders in Comics and Films*, Taurus, New York, 2008)

Lee, Stan; Mair, George, *Excelsior! The Amazing Life of Stan Lee* (Fireside, New York, 2002)

Lee, Stan; David, Peter; Doran, Colleen, *Amazing Fantastic Incredible*, (Simon & Schuster, 2015)

Morrow, John, *Kirby & Lee: Stuf' Said!* aka Jack Kirby Collector #75, (TwoMorrows Publishing, North Carolina, 2018)

Raphael, Jordan, *Stan Lee and the Rise and Fall of the American Comic Book*, (Chicago Review Press, 2004), Kindle Edition

Thomas, Roy; Sanderson, Peter, *The Marvel Vault* (Running Press, Philadelphia, 2007)

Tucker, Reed, *Slugfest: Inside the Epic, 50-Year Battle Between Marvel and DC* (Little, Brown Book Group, 2017), Kindle Edition